Cases
in
American Politics

Cases
in
American Politics

edited by

Robert L. Peabody
The Johns Hopkins University

Praeger Publishers
New York

Published in the United States of America in 1976
by Praeger Publishers, Inc.
111 Fourth Avenue, New York, N.Y. 10003

© 1976 by Praeger Publishers, Inc.

"The Story of Revenue Sharing," by Richard P. Nathan and Susannah E. Calkins, is
adapted from Chapter 2 and Appendix C of *Monitoring Revenue Sharing*, by Richard P.
Nathan with Allen D. Manvel and Susannah E. Calkins, © 1975 by the Brookings Institution, Washington, D.C. This paper is solely the responsibility of the authors and does
not represent the views of the officers, trustees, or other staff members of the Brookings
Institution.

Library of Congress Cataloging in Publication Data
Main entry under title:

Cases in American politics.

    Bibliography: p.

    1. United States—Politics and government—1945—
—Case studies.   I. Peabody, Robert L.
JK274.C34   320.4'73   74-1723
ISBN 0-275-19970-3
ISBN 0-275-84960-0 pbk.

Printed in the United States of America

Contents

Cases
in
American Politics

Introduction

A wise, if somewhat skeptical philosopher once remarked, "Nothing is certain, except uncertainty itself." At first glance, observers of American government and politics over the past fifteen years might be forced to concur. Consider the following major political events that took place from 1963 to 1975—most of them impossible to predict and almost all of them characterized by largely unforeseeable and far-ranging consequences:

- The assassination of President John F. Kennedy in 1963.
- The passage of major civil rights legislation in 1964–65 followed by urban riots and black ghetto unrest.
- President Lyndon B. Johnson's decision not to seek re-election, and a Democratic party convention in Chicago in 1968 marked by violence and confrontation.
- Richard M. Nixon's comeback presidential election victory in 1968 (despite his famous "last press conference" statement in 1962 after losing the California gubernatorial election: "You won't have Richard Nixon to kick around any more").
- The back-to-back rejection by the Senate of two of President Nixon's initial appointments to the Supreme Court in 1969–70.
- The attempted assassination of Governor George Wallace, a presidential aspirant in 1972.
- The Watergate burglary of Democratic party headquarters in 1972.
- Vice-President Spiro T. Agnew's resignation in 1973 following a plea of *nolo contendre* (no contest) to charges of income-tax evasion.

• The impeachment proceedings in the House of Representatives leading to President Nixon's resignation in 1974.

• The overthrow of three House committee chairmen and the resignation of a fourth chairman, Wilbur Mills of Arkansas, in 1975.

• Unemployment approaching 10 percent of the labor force in 1975.

Overshadowing and dramatically affecting almost all of these political events was the prolonged tragedy of the Vietnam war. What began in the early 1960s with the entry of a small American Special Forces group to advise the South Vietnamese government, gradually expanded into heavy troop involvement, massive bombings, and the eventual loss of more than 55,000 American and possibly a million Vietnamese lives. In 1975, the war in Southeast Asia finally ended, the first war in the country's two-hundred-year history in which the United States was not on the winning side.

Many observers would agree that the Kennedy-Johnson-Nixon era was the most volatile, conflict-ridden, and chaotic period in American history since the Civil War. Some perceive in these events the seeds of revolution, while others warn against the emergence of an oppressive police state more ominous and pervasive than the one imagined in George Orwell's *1984*. Public opinion polls have indicated a steady decline in confidence in American government. The viability of our two-party system has been questioned. Voter turnout in the midterm election of 1974 was at its lowest mark—38 percent—since the midterm election of 1946. Loss of confidence in our political leaders seems to be at an all-time high.

Yet, despite the vicissitudes of American government and politics over the past several decades, a case can be made that our political system has not operated all that irresponsibly or ineffectively. More specifically, it can be argued that two hundred years after the birth of our nation, our major political institutions have responded with resiliency to the crises of the times, that our "Union," admittedly not without imperfections, continues to provide order and predictability for its citizenry.

For example, despite the assassination of Kennedy, Johnson's decision not to seek reelection, and Nixon's forced resignation, we have gone through and continue to experience a peaceful and orderly transition of executive power. In a crucial test of the Twenty-fifth Amendment to the Constitution, treating of presidential succession, a former House minority leader, Gerald Ford, and a former New York governor, Nelson Rockefeller, became the thirty-eighth president, and forty-first vice-president of the United States, respectively.

Blacks and other minorities have yet to achieve complete equality, but black political leaders have won the mayoralities of cities such as Cleveland, Los Angeles, and Washington, D.C., at the same time that the Black

Caucus has expanded its powers in Congress. The American electorate has modulated its general uneasiness about government and political parties by opting for "divided government"—one party controlling the White House, the other party maintaining majorities in the House and Senate. Abuse of presidential election campaign practices in 1972 led to a major Senate investigation, the implementation of impeachment proceedings in the House, the indictment and conviction of a number of White House aides, and, as already noted, the forced resignation of President Nixon. In 1974, the Ninety-third Congress passed the most sweeping electoral and campaign financing reform legislation in the history of the country.

Finally, after much human suffering, procrastinating, and delay, an antiwar movement with both a grass-roots and a congressional base was able to persuade a series of presidents, first to withdraw American troops and, subsequently, halt military assistance to the South Vietnamese and Cambodian regimes.

In short, while we may not be living in "the best of all possible worlds," neither are we living in the worst or most uncertain of times.

The five case studies specially prepared for this volume point up both the strengths and limitations of one or more of our major political institutions in action—Congress, the presidency, the courts, political parties, and interest groups—that pervade most governmental decision making. These studies not only examine how the institutions process important substantive issues but also focus particularly on what these issues suggest about their capacity and willingness to undertake change, whether in policy or politics.

The first study is an examination of the origins and passages of revenue-sharing legislation. First enacted into law in 1972, revenue sharing is a process by which the federal government makes periodic payments to state and local governments with few, or no, strings attached; the initial appropriations called for some 30 billion in tax dollars to be redistributed to 38,000 state and local governments over the first five years of the program. This case traces the steps in the passage of revenue sharing through Congress and evaluates the early signs of the impact of this fundamental change in federal-state fiscal relations.

The second study analyzes a presidential-congressional struggle centered on the impoundment of funds for implementing the Clean Water Act of 1972. One of the least understood but most important and controversial powers of a president, impoundment is a device by which the executive branch delays spending or refuses to spend moneys appropriated by the Congress. Policy conflicts between these two branches of the government, which cannot be resolved through compromise, the exercise of the presidential veto, or its override, are frequently decided by court litigation or further legislation. Most of these alternatives were pursued by the principal actors in this impoundment crisis as all sides were forced to test the extent of their constitutionally derived powers.

Some of the major substantive differences between the Warren and the Burger Supreme Courts are delineated in the next study through the use of historical analysis, quantitative techniques, and case-by-case descriptions. Earl Warren, former governor of California, was appointed chief justice of the Supreme Court by President Dwight D. Eisenhower in 1953. Sixteen years later, upon Warren's retirement, President Richard M. Nixon appointed Warren E. Burger of Minnesota, a former Court of Appeals judge, as the new chief justice. Comparison of the decisions rendered by the shifting membership of the Court under these two men shows rather striking differences in economic and social welfare policy preferences between the justices as related to party affiliation, region, and types of prior legal experience.

The first two studies, in particular, and the third, to a degree, demonstrate most clearly the operation of the two great structural principles upon which our governmental system rests: (1) the separation of powers, and (2) federalism. The central focus of these studies has paralleled the opening Articles of the Constitution of the United States which treat sequentially of the legislative, executive, and judicial powers. In theory, these powers are *separate;* thus:

> *Article I, Section 1.:* All legislative Powers herein granted shall be vested in a Congress of the United States, which shall consist of a Senate and House of Representatives. . . .
> *Article II, Section 1.:* The executive Power shall be vested in a President of the United States of America. . . .
> *Article III, Section 1.:* The judicial Power of the United States of America shall be vested in one supreme Court, and in such inferior Courts as the Congress may from time to time ordain and establish. . . .

In the exercise of their respective powers neither the Congress, the President, or the Courts is supposed to encroach upon those powers allocated to the other branches of government. In fact, since the Founding Fathers distrusted too much power in the hands of any one branch, all kinds of mechanisms were built into the Constitution so that each branch could serve as a "check and balance" upon the others. The portion of Article III quoted above provides a ready example. Note that it is up to Congress to decide the number and types of "inferior courts" that may be established to assist the Supreme Court in carrying out its judicial functions. (Those readers not yet familiar with the Constitution will find it a useful exercise to search out other checks and balances that each branch is charged with in relation to the others. Several of the most important, such as the president's share in the law-making power through his initiating and vetoing of legislation, have already been illustrated by the first two studies in this volume.)

The other great structural principal—federalism—may also be interpreted as a further means of limiting government powers. In abstract terms, federalism is a form of constitutional government in which two or more governmental authorities coexist in the same territory and act upon the same citizenry. Certain powers such as national defense are set aside or reserved for the national government; some may be shared, such as the raising of taxes or the construction of highways; and still others are kept explicitly or reserved for the regional units, such as state governments. As manifested in the United States of America, national powers are set forth or enumerated in the Constitution; all others not "prohibited by it to the States, are reserved to the States respectively, or to the people" (Tenth Amendment).

The Constitution remains the supreme law of the land. Its seven original articles and some 7,000 words have been supplemented by twenty-six amendments adopted and ratified over the two hundred years of the country's history. Change has also come about through judicial interpretation of key provisions of the Constitution such as the "commerce clause" (Art. I, sec. 8, clause 3), "freedom of speech" (First Amendment), and "due process of law" (Fifth Amendment). Still, much of what happens in American politics is extraconstitutional. Political parties are nowhere mentioned in the Constitution, and yet these organizations are mainly responsible for what fusion and sense of alternative choices there have been in our government. The Constitution also ignores the existence and growth of interest groups, although James Madison warned of the dangers of "factions" in his famous *Federalist* No. 10. These special interests or "lobbies" (as they are sometimes called pejoratively) have been pervasive forces in shaping public policy since the inception of the nation.

Thus, the last two studies in the book appropriately focus on political parties and interest groups. One examines the response of Chicago Mayor Richard J. Daley's party organization to the reform-oriented delegate selection procedures set forth by the national Democratic party in the late 1960s and early 1970s. Promulgated by the McGovern-Fraser Commission (the Democratic Party Commission on Party Structure and Delegate Selection), these guidelines were designed to provide for more intensive grass-roots involvement in delegate selection and broader proportional representation of women, youth, and minorities within the party. Conflicts between what the national party advocated and what the local Chicago machine would tolerate were carried all the way to the 1972 convention floor and beyond.

The last contribution consists of an exploration of the role of oil-industry groups that have long enjoyed a complex and rather special relationship with the federal government in shaping the Emergency Energy Act of 1973–74. In response to a growing energy scarcity in the sixties and seventies, magnified by the Arab oil-producing states' embargo on shipments to the United States in 1973, President Nixon and a Democratically-controlled Congress sought new and divergent solutions to the energy crisis. Congressional initiatives on appropriate energy legislation present a marked contrast to the president's relative success with the revenue-sharing legislation described in the first case study. Another intriguing contrast would seem to be the relative contributions made by state and local public-interest groups to energy legislation, as over and against the activities of the American Petroleum Institute and other oil lobbies described in the study of interest groups.

With respect to each of the five case studies the reader should ask himself or herself the following questions:

1. How was the problem defined initially, and subsequently?
2. How and why did this problem end up in the legislative, executive, and/or judicial branches?
3. To what extent did "federalism" enter into or shape the outcome?
4. What role did the political parties and/or interest groups play in bringing about a solution?
5. Who, if anybody, spoke for the "public interest"?
6. How "satisfactory" and how "permanent" has the solution been?

Uncertainty and dissonance often seem to be characteristic of American political institutions and leadership. Although the case studies in this book obviously do not cover all aspects of the American political process, they do emphasize its more central and representative aspects. Thus these cases, in terms of their individual as well as collective impact, may sometimes reinforce apprehension and discouragement about the workings of our government. They suggest that, although problems can be ameliorated, they are seldom fully resolved; that one attempt at legislative solution usually generates another, as revisions and modifications are pressed by those affected. They raise serious questions about the efficacy of national leadership; is anyone really in charge of a process whose shape and direction often seem determined more by passing power alignments of interested parties than by any larger motives of public interest?

Nonetheless, American government continues to function—if not always wisely, expeditiously, or efficiently, then with considerable resiliency, flexibility, and responsiveness. Those who would make it better—and there will always be room for sustained efforts to improve our institutions —would do well to ponder again the perennial dilemma posed in *Federalist* No. 51:

> But what is government itself, but the greatest of all reflections on human nature? If men were angels, no government would be necessary. If angels were to govern men, neither external nor internal controls on government would be necessary. In framing a government which is to be administered by men over men, the great difficulty lies in this: you must first enable the government to control the governed; and in the next place oblige it to control itself.

A final observation about the relationship between the contributors and the editor: although the editor takes responsibility for this book's framework and the recruitment of its authors, each contributor bears overall responsibility for the choice of his topic, its organization and writing, and his particular blend of institutional and policy-oriented foci. All of us would like to express our appreciation to Denise Rathbun for her invaluable editorial assistance.

Robert L. Peabody

The Story of Revenue Sharing
Richard P. Nathan and Susannah E. Calkins

Richard M. Nixon in 1969 was the first American president in the twentieth century to propose a program of revenue sharing whereby the federal government makes periodic payments to state and local governments on an essentially "no strings" basis. State and local officials, members of Congress, and academics had endorsed the idea as much as a decade earlier. Still, intense national interest in revenue sharing did not come until 1964 after the leak of a confidential report to President Lyndon B. Johnson proposing such a program.

By the time Nixon advanced his plan five years later, however, the political and economic setting for revenue sharing had shifted markedly. Instead of a potential surplus in the federal budget, which was a major argument advanced for adopting revenue sharing in the mid-sixties, the problem now was to ward off unduly large federal deficits. Under these changed conditions, many opponents of revenue sharing criticized Nixon's proposal as "an idea whose time has passed."

But the joke backfired. Although eight years had elapsed since the time revenue sharing emerged on the scene as a serious policy idea in 1964, a relatively large revenue-sharing program was enacted into law October 20, 1972. The program appropriated $30.2 billion over five years to be paid to over 38,000 state and local governments. Recounted below is the story of how this came about—the political and economic forces involved, the individuals who played prominent roles in the enactment of revenue-sharing legislation, and the principal groups which participated.

This story is important for students of American government, for although revenue sharing has some similarities to other financial aid programs of the federal government for states and localities, it was nevertheless such a substantial departure from pre-1972 as to constitute a basic shift in domestic policy. In this respect the legislative process for revenue sharing should be contrasted with the more typical, incrementally oriented process by which most domestic legislation is adopted.

THE BACKGROUND OF REVENUE SHARING

Proponents of revenue sharing portrayed this new approach to federal grants-in-aid as a way of returning power to the people and revitalizing state and local government. Despite the amorphous nature of such goals, the fact remains that a principal aim of supporters of the new law was to change relationships among levels of government, giving more emphasis to the role of states and localities at the expense of the federal government.

The relationships that existed among the various levels of government at the time revenue sharing was enacted cannot be easily summarized. The most striking characteristic of contemporary American federalism is its *diversity*. State and local governments vary substantially in the role they play, the services they finance, and the functions they carry out. In many areas special-purpose districts (for example, for education, sewers, housing, etc.) finance or administer more than half of all local spending. Altogether, there were nearly 40,000 such special-purpose governments in 1972, including 15,781 school districts.

By contrast, the nation in 1972 had 39,000 of what are referred to as "general-purpose local governments." It is these units—not special-purpose units—that were made eligible for revenue-sharing payments. The diversity among these governments is also notable. City, county, and township governments have varying powers and functions from state to state. Some states have no or very weak county governments, as in New England. Others have strong county governments, as is typical in the South. In some states, townships are very important units of local governments, having extensive powers and functions. In other states, townships as a type of local government do not exist at all; twenty-nine states had no township governments in 1972. Some citizens in urban areas are governed by as many as three layers of these general-purpose units of local government, others by only one level.

In addition to their diversity, a striking characteristic of the local governments eligible to receive shared revenue under the law passed in 1972 is their small size. One-half were under 1,000 in population, and 80 percent were under 5,000, as shown in table 1.

Table 1
County, Municipal, and Township Governments,
by Population Size, 1972

| | All types | | | Number, by type of government | | |
| | Number | Percent | Cumula-tive percent | Counties | Munici-palities | Town-ships |
1970 population						
Total	38,552	100.0	....	3,044	18,517	16,991
100,000–plus	492	1.3	100.0	312	153	27
50,000–100,000	624	1.6	98.7	326	231	67
25,000–50,000	1,204	3.1	97.1	566	453	185
10,000–25,000	2,752	7.1	94.0	997	1,134	621
5,000–10,000	2,752	7.1	86.8	538	1,398	816
2,500–5,000	3,569	9.3	79.7	204	1,911	1,454
1,000–2,500	7,225	18.7	70.4	77	3,573	3,575
Less than 1,000	19,934	51.7	51.7	24	9,664	10,246

SOURCE: U.S. Bureau of the Census, *1972 Census of Governments*, vol. 1, *Governmental Organization*, tables 7, 9, and 11.

PRECEDENTS FOR THE 1972 REVENUE SHARING PROGRAM

The State and Local Fiscal Assistance Act of 1972[1] is not totally without precedent. Several measures that provided "no strings" money to the states were adopted by the federal government during the first half of the nineteenth century. State aid to local governments also has a long history, generally taking the form of grants for specified purposes, such as education, highways, and public welfare, although numerous states also distribute general-support grants to their local governments.

Early Federal Aid Programs

The first general-assistance grant from the federal government to the states was enacted in 1803 when Congress earmarked 5 percent of the proceeds from the sale of federal lands (one of its main sources of revenues) for distribution to the states in which the land was located. These funds were expected to be used for transportation and education, but no legal strings were attached nor was any attempt made to police a state's use of the funds. Their distribution benefited mainly the developing, sparsely populated areas of the country, west of the Appalachians, where

[1] This is the official name of the act. The act itself nowhere uses the term "revenue sharing"; however, the office in the Treasury Department that administers it is called the Office of Revenue Sharing, and for most other purposes this is the designation used.

most of the land was federally owned. The more populous states of the eastern seaboard also benefited from the land sales, although only indirectly, since 95 percent of these revenues was retained in the federal treasury.

A second important source of federal revenues in this period was the tariff. Because tariff rates were the result of a delicate political compromise between the North and the South (the price of public lands was likewise the result of a political compromise between the East and West), the federal government was seriously hindered in making adjustments in either for purposes of economic policy. James A. Maxwell reports that for the twenty-one-year period 1816–1836, "the treasury had surpluses in eighteen [years], and the three deficits were of insignificant amounts." A Senate committee in 1826 referred to "the serious inconvenience of an overflowing Treasury." Funds could not be used for repayment of the federal debt; it had been completely retired.

This dilemma, which for politicians in most periods would be a happy one, came to a head in the 1830s during Andrew Jackson's administration. Acting to rid the government of its embarrassing surpluses, Congress voted in 1836 to distribute to the states all funds in the treasury as of January 1, 1837, except for $5 million.

Funds under the Surplus Distribution Act were allocated to the states in proportion to their respective number of senators and congressmen. Payments were to be made in quarterly installments. On January 1, 1837, the amount on hand to be distributed was $37.5 million. A few months later, however, because of the bank panic of 1837, an emergency session of Congress postponed the payment of the fourth installment, which was never reinstated.

In later years, discussion continued about distributing surplus federal revenues to the states, but relatively little came of it. A program was launched in 1841 to distribute land-sale proceeds, this time among all of the states on the basis of population, but only $691,000 was distributed. In the early 1880s public pressures again mounted for the distribution of surpluses, but none was made.

State Grants to Local Governments

Although the federal government did not seriously consider revenue sharing again for eighty years, many states have provided general-support grants to their local governments for a long time. Such programs accounted for roughly the same proportion of state intergovernmental spending in fiscal 1972 as they did in 1902, the first year for which data is available. (See table 2.)

The bulk of state intergovernmental spending is in the form of grants for particular functions, mainly education but also including sizable

Table 2

Amount and Percentage Distribution, by Function of State Payments
to Local Governments, Selected Fiscal Years, 1902–72

Fiscal year	Total amount (millions of dollars)	Percentage distribution				
		For general support	For specified functions			
			Education	Highways	Public welfare	All other
1972	36,759	10.2	57.7	7.2	18.9	6.1
1971	32,640	10.0	59.1	7.7	17.6	5.6
1970	28,892	10.2	59.1	8.5	17.3	4.9
1962	10,906	7.7	59.4	12.2	16.3	4.4
1952	5,044	10.9	50.0	14.4	19.3	5.3
1942	1,780	12.6	44.4	19.3	21.9	1.8
1932	801	17.5	49.7	28.6	3.5	0.7
1922	312	11.2	64.7	22.4	1.3	0.3
1913	91	5.5	90.1	4.4	0.0	0.0
1902	52	9.6	86.5	3.8	0.0	0.0

SOURCE: U.S. Bureau of the Census, *1972 Census of Governments*, vol. 6, no. 3, *State Payments to Local Governments*, table 1.

amounts for public welfare and highways; yet, in fiscal 1972, states distributed $3.8 billion of general-support aid to their local governments. This was slightly more than the first year's amount of federally shared revenue allocated to local governments under the State and Local Fiscal Assistance Act of 1972–$3.5 billion. (States, however, vary significantly in the amount of general-support grants they provided; four states had no such programs, thirteen had relatively small ones.)

While these federal precedents are interesting, and the various state programs are important background, they did not have much influence on the revenue-sharing act adopted by the federal government in 1972.

THE HELLER-PECHMAN PLAN

It was Walter W. Heller, a liberal economist from the University of Minnesota and chairman of President Johnson's Council of Economic Advisers in 1964, who introduced revenue sharing as a serious policy option in the modern period, although there had been flurries of interest in general assistance since the 1950s. Most of the occasional bills introduced in the fifties were based on the premise that the funds provided should *substitute for* existing categorical grants. For example, an early revenue sharing bill introduced by a highly placed Republican congressman from

Wisconsin, Melvin R. Laird, although it lacked explicit provisions as to how this substitution process would work, called for a reduction in existing and projected federal grants equivalent to the amount of shared revenue distributed.

In contrast to Laird's proposal, the revenue-sharing plan advocated by Heller was based on the premise that revenue sharing should be a *supplement* to existing federal grants. Heller urged revenue sharing in 1964 in the context of contemporary economic policy. He saw it as a way of distributing what he called the growing "fiscal dividends" of the federal government. Heller argued that the high elasticity (or growth responsiveness) of the federal tax system, with its heavy reliance on income taxation, ensured that revenues would rise at about $6 billion a year more than the amount needed to maintain existing federal programs. This surplus, he noted, could be used for debt retirement, tax reduction, or new federal programs. The first alternative he regarded as undesirable because of its potential deflationary impact. In 1964 a major federal tax reduction amounting to $11.5 billion a year had been enacted to stimulate private spending. Many experts in public finance (including Heller) felt that the federal government should not continue in subsequent years to use the fiscal dividend to aid the private sector in the face of large unmet needs in the public sector on the part of state and local governments.

Heller's advocacy of federal revenue sharing coincided with the heating up of the presidential campaign of 1964. During the summer of 1964, President Johnson appointed eleven task forces to draft recommendations for a new term, including one assigned to study federal-state-local fiscal relations. Most members of these task forces (as in the case of Nixon's four years later) were drawn from the academic community. The intergovernmental fiscal group was chaired by Joseph A. Pechman, director of economic studies at the Brookings Institution. The fact that it was considering a revenue-sharing proposal that closely resembled Heller's concept came to public attention a few days before the election. On October 28, President Johnson issued a campaign statement widely interpreted as his stamp of approval on the basic idea of revenue sharing, although the statement did not explicitly use that term.

> In line with the Democratic platform, this Administration is moving ahead on development of fiscal policies which would provide revenue sources to hard-pressed state and local governments to assist them with their responsibilities.
>
> At the state and local level, we see responsibilities rising faster than revenues, while at the Federal level an average annual revenue growth of some $6 billion provides a comfortable margin for Federal tax reduction, Federal programs, and more generous help to state and local units.

The National Government as a constructive partner in a creative Federal state, should help restore fiscal balance and strengthen state and local governments by making available for their use some part of our great and growing Federal tax revenues over and above existing aids.

It should also strengthen existing programs of Federal-state-local cooperation in such vital areas as public assistance, public health, urban renewal, highways, recreation and education.

Intensive study is now being given to methods of channeling Federal revenue to states and localities which will reinforce their independence while enlarging their capacity to service their citizens.

Accompanying the *New York Times* account of this presidential statement on October 28 was a page-one article by Edwin Dale, Jr., which specifically tied the president's statement to the work of the Pechman task force. According to Dale, the task force was getting ready to recommend a plan for sharing federal revenues with the states that would have the following features:

First, a fixed and constant portion of Federal income tax revenue would be set aside each year. One formula under discussion would set aside from $2 billion to $3 billion at the present tax rates and national income. The amount would gradually rise with the growth of the economy.

Second, this money would be put in a trust fund for distribution to the states at the end of the year. Thus, the payment would not be a Federal budget expenditure.

Third, the money would go to the states virtually unconditionally. That is, they could use it almost any way they wanted. The money would be in addition to the present system, under which several billion dollars in grants-in-aid go to the states annually. These are tied to specific programs such as highways, hospitals and public assistance, some of which require state matching funds.

Finally, the payment would have a mild redistributive effect, from the richer states to the poorer. The most likely formula would be distribution on a simple per capita basis.

The *Times* article added that the new proposal, which came to be known as the Heller-Pechman plan, would be recommended to go into effect no earlier than 1966. Dale said the rationale for the plan was the belief that most of the nation's unmet domestic needs were in areas of state-local responsibility. The task force was reported to believe that revenue sharing would lessen the pressure for repeated federal income tax cuts, reflecting the group's preference for federal income taxation as contrasted to less progressive state and local taxes on sales and property.

Observers of revenue sharing regard the Dale story as a major turning point. It was the only report of the eleven pre-election task forces about which any information became public. Apparently unhappy about this publicity, President Johnson ordered all drafts of the report, except those held by the members of the task force, to be returned to the White House. After the election and the formal submission of the report on November 11, the president let it be known that his administration was dropping the plan.

Although President Johnson never publicly explained his reasons for rejecting the Heller-Pechman plan, several possibilities exist. One is his unhappiness about the leak. In addition, Heller left the Council of Economic Advisers in November 1964. No one remained in the president's immediate circle to press the issue. President Johnson may have been influenced also by opposition that surfaced as soon as the recommendation for a revenue-sharing plan became public. President George Meany of the AFL-CIO expressed vigorous opposition based on the unwillingness of organized labor to trust state administrators to implement domestic reforms. Similar opposition came from the powerful education lobby, which objected to channeling federal aid funds through state governments instead of directly to state education agencies and local school districts as in the case of categorical grants for education. Educators also saw unrestricted grants as a threat to the favorable considerations of greater federal aid for education.

Inside the federal government, criticism of revenue sharing came from the administrators of existing categorical grants who saw revenue sharing as a challenge to their established programs. Secretary of Commerce Luther Hodges made his opposition known publicly; Secretary of Health, Education, and Welfare Wilbur Cohen also opposed revenue sharing. Writing about revenue sharing in *The Reporter* magazine in January 1975, Alan L. Otten and Charles B. Seib described the disclosure of the Heller task force plan as a tactic that boomeranged.

> Opponents in and out of the administration, who had been wondering just how seriously to take the plan, decided to take it very seriously and jumped into action with a variety of objections. The ensuing controversy ended when the President, at a mid-December background session for newsmen, declared that the premature disclosure of the task force recommendations had generated such opposition that he had decided to put the plan aside at least for a year.

These events of the Johnson years were an important learning experience for the interest groups which supported the idea of revenue sharing and later played a major role in its enactment. The most important groups were those of state and local government officials. For the most part they stayed in the wings during the period when the arguments about the Heller-Pechman plan were being publicly aired.

Revenue sharing did not surface again as a serious policy alternative in the Johnson years. This was in large part because of two subsequent developments which fully absorbed what there was of the "fiscal dividend" and in so doing removed one of the main arguments for revenue sharing. The two developments were, first, the increasing U.S. commitment in Vietnam and, second, the advent of Great Society programs to meet domestic needs through a wide range of categorical grants for social purposes. Federal grants to state and local government, which had amounted to $10 billion in 1964, increased to $18.6 billion in 1968. This momentum continued in the Nixon years as shown in table 3.

Table 3
Federal Grants-in-aid to State and Local Governments,
Selected Fiscal Years, 1964–72

Fiscal year	Amount (millions of dollars)	Percentage of total federal domestic outlays
1972	35,940	24.5
1970	23,954	21.9
1968	18,599	20.9
1966	12,960	19.2
1964	10,141	17.9

SOURCE: Office of Management and Budget, *Special Analysis N, Budget of the United States Government, Fiscal Year 1974.*

OTHER SUPPORT FOR REVENUE SHARING

President Johnson's rejection of revenue sharing in 1964 failed to deaden interest. In July 1965, the liberal-Republican Ripon Society and the Republican Governors' Association issued a joint research paper specifically supporting the Heller-Pechman plan and lamenting the president's decision to shelve it. During the Eighty-ninth Congress (1965–66), fifty-seven members of Congress sponsored bills providing for one or another form of revenue sharing.[2] Republican congressmen especially, many of whom saw the results of the 1966 election as indicating important reservations about the Great Society approach to domestic problems, continued in the Ninetieth Congress (1967–68) to push for revenue sharing

[2] Maureen McBreen, "Federal Tax Sharing: Historical Development and Arguments For and Against Recent Proposals" (Library of Congress, Legislative Reference Service, January 30, 1967; processed).

as an alternative to the continued expansion of categorical-grant programs. In this same period, there were further endorsements for revenue sharing—by the Governors' Conference in 1966, the Advisory Commission on Intergovernmental Relations in 1967, and President Johnson's Commission on Urban Problems, chaired by former senator Paul H. Douglas, in 1968. As a further stimulus to interest in revenue sharing, the Subcommittee on Fiscal Policy of the Joint Economic Committee of Congress held nine days of public hearings in 1967 and issued a formidable 1,500-page collection of papers on the subject.

As fiscal conditions changed, parallel shifts in rationale occurred on the part of supporters of revenue sharing. Heller's own views reflect these changes. In March 1966 he included a discussion of revenue sharing in his Godkin Lectures at Harvard University. Heller no longer tied revenue sharing to the idea of the fiscal dividend. Instead, he emphasized revenue sharing as a means of achieving two purposes—alleviating the so-called fiscal mismatch between federal resources and state-local needs, and strengthening the role of state governments in American federalism. Moreover, Heller did not advocate immediate adoption in 1966. Rather, he urged that a plan be developed and made ready to be put into effect as soon as the Vietnam war ended.

This emphasis by Heller on strengthening the federal system fit comfortably with the philosophy of Republican leaders. Many of them stepped up their efforts on behalf of revenue sharing in this period, advancing for it a federalism rationale, namely that the deficiencies of Great Society grant programs could best be remedied by having federal aid provided in the form of broad and basically unconditional grants. Politically, this marked a turning point. Key Democrats continued to endorse the idea but were not as inclined to press it. They appeared not to want to be on the wrong side of this issue, but at the same time often gave equally strong (or stronger) backing to alternatives to revenue sharing in the form of the traditional categorical grants-in-aid to states and localities.

ENTER THE NIXON ADMINISTRATION

The election of a Republican president in 1968 brightened prospects for revenue sharing. Although the concept was endorsed by both major parties in the campaign, it had been pushed harder by Republicans, whose party platform endorsed revenue sharing explicitly: "We propose the sharing of federal revenues with state governments." Candidate Nixon first spoke for a revenue-sharing plan in the New Hampshire primary campaign in February 1968. The Democratic platform was less definite but said: "To help states and cities meet their fiscal challenges, we must seek new methods for states and local governments to share in federal revenues, while retaining responsibility for establishing their own priorities and for operating their own programs."

Planning for a Nixon-administration revenue-sharing program began before election day. Ten transition task forces—like Johnson's, made up mostly of academics—were established in the fall of 1968 to formulate new policies should Mr. Nixon be elected. One of these was assigned the field of intergovernmental fiscal relations. [It was headed by Richard P. Nathan, like Pechman, also a member of the staff of the Brookings Institution, and later a budget official in Nixon's first term.] In a report submitted to the president-elect on November 29, the Nixon task force made nine proposals for the reform of federal grant programs. Most important was the recommendation that the budget for fiscal 1970 include a revenue-sharing program amounting to 0.5 percent of taxable personal income, or about $1.75 billion. The task force made the case for revenue sharing both as a fiscal tool for dealing with fundamental imbalances between the needs and resources of different levels of government and as a political instrument for decentralizing federal domestic policies and assigning greater decision-making authority to the elected chief executives of state and local governments. Revenue sharing gained the endorsement as well of a second Nixon transition planning group, the urban affairs task force, which also recommended a revenue-sharing plan along the lines of the Heller-Pechman proposal. The chairman of this group was Harvard professor of political science Edward C. Banfield.

By the time of Nixon's inauguration in January 1969, there was little doubt that a revenue-sharing plan would be forthcoming. The main questions were its size and structure. In April the president established an interagency committee on revenue sharing under the chairmanship of Arthur F. Burns, then a counselor to the president and a long-time friend and advisor of Nixon's. (Burns was chairman of the Council of Economic Advisors under Eisenhower when Nixon first met him.)

Once Burns's committee had developed what its chairman referred to as a "skeletal outline," a representative group of governors, mayors, and county officials were invited to the White House to advise on the specifications of revenue-sharing legislation. The important point about this meeting is that it drew nonacademics into the policy process. Several of the spokesmen for the interest groups represented at this session had strong ideas on how a revenue-sharing plan should be designed to make it politically most attractive. The group that met with Burns recommended the following points:

1. automatic distribution each year of a designated portion of the federal income tax base based on objective legal criteria;

2. equitable sharing of the money among state and local governments based on specific formulas to be spelled out in federal legislation;
3. no strings or restrictions on use of the money; and
4. inclusion of all general-purpose local governments, regardless of size or location.

The last recommendation, to include all general-purpose units of local governments, demonstrates the point about the political feasibility of proposed revenue-sharing legislation. It helped obtain support for the concept among officials of small jurisdictions. However, once officials of these jurisdictions and their spokesmen became aware of the possibility of inclusion in the program, it became difficult to include any kind of a minimum-size cutoff in revenue sharing, as many fiscal experts had urged. Lou Cannon and David S. Broder, in an article on revenue sharing in the *Washington Post* (June 18, 1974), quoted Vice-President Spiro T. Agnew on the political nature of this decision. (Agnew, formerly governor of Maryland and Baltimore County executive, was assigned duties in the intergovernmental area early in the Nixon administration.) Said Agnew:

> When we were developing these policies, there was a tremendous amount of disagreement about what units of local government were to participate in direct receipt of these funds. . . . Some of the compromises that resulted came about because of the political necessity of bringing enough people aboard to accomplish any kind of revenue-sharing reform. In short, obviating the distribution of money to small, inefficient local government units would have aroused enough political hostility, possibly, to defeat the program.

This concern about getting the support of small local governments resulted in the new administration at an early stage becoming locked into a revenue-sharing system involving payments to almost 40,000 governmental units, a feature that later would produce the principal administrative challenge in implementing the new program.

On August 8, 1969, President Nixon delivered a nationwide television address in which he outlined the principles of his domestic program and the part which revenue sharing would play in it:

> For a third of a century, power and responsibility have flowed toward Washington—and Washington has taken for its own the best sources of revenue.
>
> We intend to reverse this tide, and to turn back to the states a greater measure of responsibility—not as a way of avoiding problems, but as a better way of solving problems.
>
> Along with this would go a share of federal revenues.

I shall propose to the Congress next week that a set portion of the revenues from federal income taxes be remitted directly to the states —with a minimum of federal restrictions on how those dollars are to be used, and with a requirement that a percentage of them be channeled through for the use of local government.

The funds provided under this program will not be great in the first year. But the principle will have been established, and the amounts will increase as our budgetary situation improves.

This start on revenue sharing is a step toward what I call the New Federalism. It is a gesture of faith in America's state and local governments and in the principle of democratic self-government.

On August 13 Nixon followed up his television address with a message to Congress in which he proposed that revenue sharing be started in fiscal 1971. Referring to current budget stringencies, Nixon recommended that the first year's expenditures be $500 million but that there be successive annual increments to raise the figure to $5 billion in 1975. The message summarized the major elements of the administration's proposal as follows:

1. The size of the total fund to be shared with the states and local governments would be a specified percentage of personal taxable income;
2. The allocation among the states (and the District of Columbia) would be made on the basis of each state's share of national population, adjusted for the revenue effort of the state.
3. The allocation of each state's share among its general units of local government would be established by prescribed formula, with the distribution to be made by the state, and the amounts to be distributed determined by the relative roles of state and local financing in each state; states would be authorized to develop alternative distribution plans.
4. Administrative requirements would be kept to a minimum.

The message included the observation that "one can reasonably expect that education, which consistently takes more than two-fifths of all state and local general revenues, will be the major beneficiary of these new funds."

THE NINETY-FIRST CONGRESS, FIRST SESSION

With his August 13 message, Nixon formally transmitted a legislative proposal for revenue sharing to the Ninety-first Congress, then just beginning its work. Senator Howard H. Baker, Jr., a Republican from Tennessee, and thirty-two other senators introduced the administration's revenue-sharing bill on September 23, 1969. Companion bills were introduced in the House by Congressman Jackson E. Betts (R–Ohio) and seventy-five other members. Betts was the second-ranking Republican on the House Ways and Means Committee, which handled revenue-sharing legislation. The ranking Republican, John W. Byrnes of Wisconsin, opposed the plan. Betts himself was lukewarm on revenue sharing; it remained for Barber Conable, Jr., of New York, sixth-ranking Republican on Ways and Means, to take the lead for the Nixon administration in the committee.

Despite the large number of sponsors and administration endorsement, no hearings were held on revenue-sharing legislation by either the Senate Finance Committee, which has jurisdiction in the Senate, or the House Ways and Means Committee, where the legislation had to originate, during the two years of the Ninety-first Congress. There are several possible reasons for this inertia. The amount suggested for the initial years of revenue sharing may have been regarded as too small to be worth a fight on the part of proponents outside the administration. In addition, the requirement that funds for localities be distributed by the states to the eligible localities, rather than directly, may have caused mayors and other local officials to hesitate to lend their full support. The administration itself may have contributed to the lack of action in the early months, because its main efforts in domestic affairs were concentrated on welfare reform.

Actually, welfare reform was a surprise entry on Nixon's legislative agenda. It was the subject of an elaborate planning process in the early days of the administration. Harvard professor Daniel Patrick Moynihan, as executive director of Nixon's Urban Affairs Council, was responsible initially for welfare reform. The element of surprise and the early favorable comment, particularly from liberal groups, contributed to the decision to give welfare reform highest priority among domestic initiatives in 1969 and for most of 1970. Later, however, the situation changed materially.

Although neither the House Ways and Means nor the Senate Finance committee held hearings on revenue sharing in the Ninety-first Congress, the Subcommittee on Intergovernmental Relations of the Senate Committee on Government Operations, chaired by Senator Edmund S. Muskie (D–Maine), held "information hearings" in the fall of 1969. Originally, Muskie's hearings were set up to study the revenue-sharing bill developed by the staff of the Advisory Commission on Intergovernmental Relations (ACIR) and introduced at the commission's request by Muskie and Republican Senator Charles E. Goodell of New York. (The ACIR was created by federal law in 1959. It is a permanent body with twenty-six members representing the executive and legislative branches of federal, state, and local government and the general public.) During the course of the hearings, Muskie agreed to include the administration's revenue-sharing bill on the subcommittee's agenda, and much of the testimony was devoted to comparing the two measures. Nevertheless, the administration sent lower-level officials to testify, not wanting to offend the responsible legislative committees or give too much prominence to Muskie, then emerging as a possible Democratic challenger to Nixon in 1972.

Although the ACIR proposal broadly resembled the administration's, there were significant differences. In particular, the ACIR bill proposed a far larger initial distribution of revenue-sharing funds, estimated at $2.8 billion for the first year. There were other important differences. The ACIR bill sought to encourage states to make greater use of personal-income taxation by including as a major provision a federal tax credit for state income taxes. This provision was estimated to cost $2.6 billion per year in reduced federal revenue. The ACIR bill also limited the direct local distribution of shared revenue to cities and counties of at least 50,000 population (some 800 governments) rather than providing payments to all general-purpose local governments (over 38,000) as in the administration plan. In addition, the ACIR bill, unlike the administration's, provided for a "pass-through" distribution by state governments of a formula-based amount to local school districts.

NINETY-FIRST CONGRESS, SECOND SESSION

By January 1970, when the second session of the Ninety-first Congress convened, the Nixon administration had become very concerned about the lack of progress on revenue sharing. Members of the White House congressional relations staff (notably Richard K. Cook, in charge of liaison with the House and himself strongly interested in revenue-sharing legislation) initiated a major effort to mobilize congressional support. State and local officials were urged by their national organizations (which Cook enlisted for this effort) to contact their congressmen on behalf of revenue sharing. Four organizations of state and local officials wrote on April 14, 1970, to Congressman Wilbur D. Mills, chairman of the House Ways and Means Committee, and Senator Russell B. Long, chairman of the Senate Finance Committee, requesting them to hold hearings on revenue sharing. The four organizations were the National Governors' Conference, the U.S. Conference of Mayors, the National League of Cities, and the National Association of Counties. Two days later, this group, joined by the National Legislative Council representing state legislators, held a press conference to announce "agreement on the basic form and principle of revenue sharing and our determination to see its immediate legislative enactment."

Meanwhile, the administration stepped up its own efforts. Secretary of the Treasury David M. Kennedy held a press conference to "welcome this announcement of unified support." The president enlisted active support from senior administration officials in a memorandum that described revenue sharing as "the financial heart of the New Federalism." Cabinet and subcabinet officials, led by Assistant Secretary of the Treasury Murray L. Weidenbaum, made numerous public appearances on behalf of revenue sharing in this period. But despite these various efforts, congressional leaders did not appear to be impressed.

In reply to the letter of April 14 from the interest groups of state and local officials, Mills said he was busy with other important matters and did not have time to consider revenue sharing in 1970. Senator Long never replied.

It was in this period, the waning days of the Ninety-first Congress, that the Treasury Department adopted a new technique for encouraging interest in revenue sharing. At a press conference on July 31, 1970, Assistant Secretary Weidenbaum, an economist from Washington University (St. Louis) with a long interest in revenue sharing, released a comprehensive statistical report on how much each individual jurisdiction might expect to receive under the administration's revenue-sharing plan. The press coverage of Weidenbaum's release was far more extensive than were earlier stories about revenue-sharing legislation. Armed with specific figures of how much their communities would receive, a large number of newspapers ran stories with local commentary on the potential impact of the president's plan.

Toward the end of 1970, with prospects for legislation dimming in the Ninety-first Congress despite the efforts to spark interest, the emphasis of supporters shifted to strategy for the Ninety-second Congress. Important lessons had been learned by the participants, which influenced their plans for the next Congress to convene in 1971. By now the public interest groups of state and local governments were formed into a coalition which they called the "Big Six." It included the National League of Cities, the U.S. Conference of Mayors, the National Association of Counties, the International City Management Association, the National Governors' Conference, and the Council of State Governments. (The Big Six were joined at times by the National Legislative Conference, as well as other groups, and attempts were later made to change the name of the umbrella organization to the "Big Seven" and at one point the "Big Eight"; but the "Big Six" remained the name most commonly used.) This coalition, again with White House advice and encouragement, sent letters in September

1970 to all candidates for seats in the new Congress, pressing them to support revenue-sharing legislation in the Ninety-second Congress. The object was to nail down commitments at the most opportune moment. Moreover, the fact that the petitioners were state and local politicians, who could easily be opposing candidates in future elections, was bound to make it harder than it might otherwise be to defer responding, much less to oppose the purposes of the claimant groups. The prospect of having one's opponent blame him or her for a tax increase or the failure to make tax cuts or necessary program improvements (because of the absence of shared revenue) is not a happy one for a politician.

By the end of October, nearly 400 incumbents and challengers for seats in the Ninety-second Congress had responded. Of these, 93 percent were reported to be in favor of revenue sharing. In addition, citizens' committees for revenue sharing were organized in forty-four states, with a central office in Washington under the direction of Sumner Whittier, a former lieutenant governor of Massachusetts. Whittier's group sponsored newspaper ads, wrote letters on behalf of revenue sharing, and mobilized governors and other state and local officials to write to their congressmen. This effort, too, was a product of White House planning and was closely tied to Richard Cook's liaison activities.

Just as this push for enactment in the Ninety-second Congress was being mounted, an important disagreement arose within the Big Six. Although the reasons for this controversy are complicated, they are of considerable interest. Local officials claimed that at the initial White House meeting, in the fall of 1969, with Dr. Arthur Burns, Assistant Secretary Weidenbaum, and others the administration had committed itself to a 50–50 split of revenue-sharing funds between the states and local governments. (What administration officials claimed they actually said was that the revenue-sharing bill would reflect the fact that state governments raise about 50 percent of all state and local revenue.) In developing the legislation, however, it was decided to limit revenue sharing to *general-purpose* local governments. Of the 50 percent of total state-local revenues raised by local governments, about three-fifths is raised by general-purpose local governments; the remainder is raised by special-purpose jurisdictions, notably by school districts. Thus, limiting revenue sharing to general-purpose governments produced an average state-local split of 27 percent local and 73 percent state. This division was unacceptable to organizations representing local governments. Although refraining from public criticism, privately they raised strong objections and threatened to withhold their support from revenue-sharing legislation in the Ninety-second Congress. To deal with these objections, the administration had to revise its basic formula and return to the original 50–50 ratio. It was in this way possible to hold together the sometimes tenuous—but in the final analysis, lasting—coalition of state and local organizations in support of revenue-sharing legislation.

THE NINETY-SECOND CONGRESS: FIRST SESSION

It was the Ninety-second Congress, composed of 254 Democrats and 179 Republicans in the House and 54 Democrats and 44 Republicans in the Senate, that enacted revenue sharing. The process involved the entire two-year period of the Ninety-second Congress commencing in January 1971. It began with the president's recommendations on revenue sharing in his State of the Union message on January 22, 1971, and ended with Senate approval of the conference committee report on October 13, 1972, just five days before final adjournment. The president signed the bill on October 20, 1972.

Nixon's State of the Union message in 1971 was devoted entirely to domestic issues. It was organized around "six great goals" for governmental reform. Welfare reform, the first goal, was identified as the most important. The fifth goal was "strengthening and renewing state and local governments." A new revenue-sharing program, which the president described as "historic in scope and bold in concept," was advanced for this purpose.

This new revenue-sharing program represented more than just a resubmission of the legislation that had failed to attract support in the preceding Congress. It provided for the distribution annually of $16 billion. Of this amount, $5 billion was in the form of unrestricted funds, that is, general revenue sharing in essentially the form that had been proposed to the Ninety-first Congress, but at a start-up level ten times as high. The other $11 billion was to be provided by allocating $1 billion of new funds and converting $10 billion of existing categorical grants into so-called "special revenue-sharing programs" for six broad functional areas. The six areas were urban development, rural development, education, transportation, job training, and law enforcement.

Inclusion of these new special revenue sharing proposals in Nixon's program had an important impact on legislature tactics. Many advocates of what was now called general revenue sharing were not happy with this strategy, fearing that the new classification system would weaken their position because special revenue sharing would engender opposition that would spill over to general revenue sharing. This may have been true in some instances, but there were also cases in which the existence of the special revenue sharing proposals had the opposite effect. In the education field, for example, various interest groups that had argued against revenue sharing in the past now felt obliged to devote their main energy to opposing special revenue sharing for education. While it was not intended to distract possible opponents of general revenue sharing in this way (in fact, this effect was not perceived in the planning process), the addition of special revenue sharing in cases such as this ended up as a net plus in terms of the chances for enactment of general revenue sharing.

Even before President Nixon formally transmitted his new revenue-sharing bills to the Congress, congressional leaders put up storm signals. On January 26, Chairman Mills of the House Ways and Means Committee delivered a lengthy speech criticizing general revenue sharing. He later told reporters he would indeed hold hearings on revenue sharing, but they would be "not for the purpose of promoting it, but for the purpose of killing it." Senate majority leader Mike Mansfield, characteristically more mild, described the administration's 1971 revenue-sharing proposals as "possibly a dangerous procedure to follow." The AFL-CIO joined congressional critics urging "complete rejection" of revenue sharing. The U.S. Chamber of Commerce followed suit, endorsing a recommendation by its Committee on Taxation to oppose revenue sharing.

In this not exactly friendly setting, the administration's revenue-sharing bill was introduced by Congressmen Jackson E. Betts, Barber B. Conable, Jr., Harold R. Collier (all Republican members of the Ways and Means Committee), and 138 other members. The bill was referred to Ways and Means.[3] A companion bill was introduced in the Senate by Howard H. Baker, Jr., of Tennessee and thirty-eight of his Senate colleagues. These numbers represented an increase of sixty-nine sponsors over the previous Congress.

The most significant change in the administration's proposal for general revenue sharing was the increase in the amount. The new bill proposed the automatic distribution of 1.3 percent of taxable personal income—$5 billion in the first full year of operation. As taxable income rose with economic growth, it was estimated that this amount would expand—to $10 billion by 1980. This exceeded the amounts of shared revenue proposed in any comparable legislation. The Humphrey-Reuss bill called for expenditures of $3 billion during the first year. The ACIR plan proposed $2.8 billion. On the other hand, Governor Nelson A. Rockefeller of New York, a strong advocate of revenue sharing, proposed in January 1971 (although not in legislative form) an immediate $10 billion in shared revenue. Other enthusiasts among governors and mayors had similarly ambitious plans.

The second major difference from the earlier administration proposal

[3] Under the congressional reforms of the Ninety-fourth Congress in 1975, jurisdiction over revenue sharing was shifted to the House Government Operations Committee.

was the greater proportion of funds to be allocated to local governments. To meet the objections raised by local-government groups, the new legislation provided that in the aggregate, one-half of the shared funds should go to local governments, rather than the 27 percent they would have received under the 1969 version. States were given the authority to work out their own intrastate allocation plans. For states failing to adopt such plans, the legislation provided an automatic formula that assigned funds to state governments and their component local units in proportion to the amounts of revenue raised by each level.

Again, the legislative reaction was quiescent. As the months went by and no action was taken on revenue sharing, the mayors, governors, and other officials who were now devoting major effort to this legislation became increasingly restive. (These groups significantly expanded their Washington offices, notably the legislative liaison staffs, for this purpose.) A particular lack of enthusiasm was shown by Democratic members of Congress, and as a result Democrats among the mayors and governors launched a special lobbying effort to win their support. State legislatures also began to exert pressure by enacting resolutions calling for a constitutional convention to establish a revenue-sharing program. By June 1971, eleven states had passed such resolutions. (Two-thirds of the state legislatures are required to act in order to call a convention to amend the constitution; amendments must then be ratified by three-fourths of the state legislatures.)

Finally, on June 2, the House Ways and Means Committee began hearings on revenue sharing. In his opening remarks, Chairman Mills repeated his earlier statement that the purpose of the hearings would be to expose the weaknesses of the concept and kill it. Midway through the hearings, however, a crucial turning point was reached. Mills did an about-face. After a series of meetings with state and local officials, he indicated on June 10 that he would favor legislation giving aid to cities and urban areas; but such a program, he stressed, should not be called revenue sharing.[4] Mills's conversion, while sudden, was by no means out of character. For a long time his power in the House had been achieved and solidified through skillful tactics whereby he took command of troops *on the way to* successful battles. His record reflected an uncanny ability to select winning causes. Another likely element in Mills's plans in this period

[4] *New York Times,* June 11, 1971. The Mills approach differed from most other revenue-sharing plans in several respects. Two of the most important differences were its provision of aid to local governments only—no funds for states were contemplated—and its use of a fixed dollar appropriation rather than a percentage of federal tax base or yields. It is interesting how the position of the states appeared to deteriorate in this period, no doubt a reflection of the relatively stronger fiscal position of most state governments. Few had deficits; many had surpluses in the offing.

was the fact that he then was mounting an effort to win the Democratic nomination for president in 1972.

On July 9 the Ways and Means Committee went into executive session. The administration bill was set aside and work was begun to draw up new legislation acceptable to Mills. The chairman reiterated that the new bill would be directed primarily at meeting the needs of local governments for emergency aid. He stated that local expenditures out of these funds should be limited to defined areas of priority need.

During the executive sessions, representatives of the Big Six met often with staff members of both the House Ways and Means Committee and the Joint Committee on Internal Revenue Taxation (a continuing body made up of members of the House Ways and Means and Senate Finance committees, which was given the major responsibility for drafting revenue-sharing legislation). Most of the discussion revolved around the nature of the formula for allocating shared revenue and the extent to which states should exercise control over the funds assigned to local governments. Mills by now had conceded that states should receive some shared revenue.

Just when the momentum was picking up, an important hitch arose during this drafting process. President Nixon's announcement on August 15, 1971, of his "New Economic Policy" included, along with price and wage control and related economic measures, a proposal to delay the beginning of revenue sharing and welfare reform in order to alleviate their potentially inflationary impact. The proposal caused dismay among supporters of revenue sharing and led to strong protests to the White House. Nixon, in response, attempted to soften the blow in an address on his new economic plans to a joint session of Congress on September 9, 1971. He stated that the postponement of revenue sharing was only for three months (until January 1, 1972) and should be regarded as a realistic reappraisal of the legislative prospects. The president said to the joint session:

> Because the Congress has not yet enacted two of my principal legislative proposals—welfare reform and revenue sharing—I have recommended that their effective dates be postponed, three months for revenue sharing, one year for welfare reform. This adjustment recognized that there is no longer sufficient time to get the administrative machinery in place by the previously scheduled dates.

By the beginning of September 1971, a bill acceptable to Mills had been drafted by Laurence N. Woodworth, chief of the staff of the Joint Committee on Internal Revenue Taxation, and his aides. The next task was to secure endorsement of the public interest groups. Most members of the Big Six, realizing that their inability to reach agreement would de-

lay introduction of a committee bill, managed fairly quickly to compromise points at issue. In mid-October, a letter to Mills from each of
the five local-government organizations urged him to introduce the bill.
The National Governors' Conference, however, was reluctant to add its
endorsement, but finally joined the rest and sent its endorsement to Mills
on November 9.[5] On November 30, Mills and nine cosponsors, all Democrats—Hugh L. Carey (N.Y.), Dan Rostenkowski (Ill.), Al Ullman
(Oreg.), James A. Burke (Mass.), Charles A. Vanik (Ohio), Richard
Fulton (Tenn.), James C. Corman (Calif.), William J. Green (Pa.), and
Joseph E. Karth (Minn.)—introduced the Intergovernmental Fiscal Co-
ordination Act of 1971, to provide $5.3 billion a year for five years to
states and local governments, with two-thirds of this amount going to local governments and one-third to the states. This bill, like its predeces-
sors, was referred to the Ways and Means Committee.

At this juncture, with revenue sharing still in committee in the House,
the first session of the Ninety-second Congress adjourned on December
17, 1971. But there was now cause for optimism. A new bill was in the
hopper, endorsed by the Big Six and drawn up under the supervision of
Chairman Mills. A major uncertainty still remained—namely, the degree
to which the administration would be willing to support the Mills version.

NINETY-SECOND CONGRESS: SECOND SESSION

President Nixon's State of the Union message, delivered on January 20,
1972, at the opening of the second session of the Ninety-second Congress,
cleared the air as to the administration's position. Welfare reform was
identified as the first item of business; the president expressed his strong
hope that it would be enacted in 1972. Next came revenue sharing:

> At the same time that I introduced my welfare proposals two and a
> half years ago, I also presented a program for sharing Federal reve-
> nues with state and local governments. Last year I greatly expanded
> on this concept. Yet, despite undisputed evidence of compelling
> needs, despite overwhelming public support, despite the endorse-
> ment of both major political parties and most of the Nation's Gov-
> ernors and Mayors, and despite the fact that most other nations with
> federal systems of government already have such a program, reve-
> nue sharing still remains on the list of unfinished business.

The president made a specific reference to the House Ways and Means
Committee, publicly signaling an administration decision to work with

[5] Richard E. Thompson, *Revenue Sharing: A New Era in Federalism* (Revenue Sharing Advisory Service, Washington 1973), p. 82.

Mills: "I am pleased that the House Ways and Means Committee has made revenue sharing its first order of business in the new session."

House Committee Action

Despite this steadily improving situation, consideration of the Mills bill by the full Ways and Means Committee did not proceed rapidly. The committee was delayed at the beginning of the second session, first by a back injury to the chairman, which kept him away from Washington, and then by the necessity of acting on an increase in the debt ceiling, a measure bound to remind members of Congress that the federal government did not have a fiscal dividend in 1972 to finance an ambitious new revenue-sharing program.

In this period, just as when the administration's bill was presented and initially publicized, there was a lively interest in the amounts of shared revenue to be received by individual jurisdictions. Precise figures however were not available. The bill had been drafted without the use of a computer, and no attempt had been made to draw up full tables showing the amounts to be received by all eligible governments. Nevertheless, the provisions of the bill had now been made public, and various individuals and groups could make their own estimates of its allocations. These estimates produced so much confusion and dissatisfaction with the formula, particularly on the part of the cities, that the president of the Conference of Mayors wrote a letter of protest to Chairman Mills, stating that it was "clearly apparent that the formula does not allocate the federal funds to the local governments that need them most."[6] The National Governors' Conference also asked for changes.

At this stage, Deputy Secretary of the Treasury Charls E. Walker, an experienced legislative tactician, having formerly been the chief lobbyist for the American Bankers Association, joined the Ways and Means proceedings. Walker, aided by James E. Smith, special assistant to the secretary for congressional relations, and Treasury Department attorney Otto G. Stoltz, also made available the services of a technical staff and computer facilities under the supervision of Dr. Robert P. Strauss. During this period the committee met in executive session almost daily to work on modifications of the formula. Each day's new version was computer-tested the same evening so that on the following day committee members could study its impact. The printouts, however, were limited to showing how various changes affected governments in the districts of the members of the Ways and Means Committee, plus a handful of other major governmental units. This iteration process went on until March 23, when a formula acceptable to a majority of the committee was devised, and the committee was then ready to put the bill into final form. Throughout this last

[6] Ibid., p. 87.

phase of the committee's decision process, the Treasury computer was a formidable tool in the political decision process.

On April 17 the committee draft was approved by a vote of 18 to 7, and on April 26 the committee reported a "clean" bill. Although the vote was more than 2-to-1 in favor, one member of the committee, James C. Corman (D–Calif.) said in frustration that the final compromise was "reached as a result of exhaustion and despair, rather than the feeling that the committee had finally stumbled on a workable formula."

Mills in this period was deeply involved in the legislative process on revenue sharing. One week before the committee vote, he sent a letter to each of his colleagues in the House urging them to support the new bill. Richard E. Thompson, in his history of efforts to enact revenue sharing, notes that this was the first such "Dear Colleague" letter Mills had sent to all House members. Now full data on the impact of the committee plan was brought to bear. Thompson notes:

> Enclosed with the letter was the estimated amount that communities within each congressman's district would receive under H.R. 14370 and a sample press release to assist congressmen in disseminating the allocation information to their districts. Apparently Mills' strategy was to let individual congressmen reap the political benefits involved in announcing such a boon to their district and thereby encourage each representative's support of H.R. 14370 when it came before the entire House.[7]

The Reported Bill: House Version

The Ways and Means Committee report, in line with Mills's thinking, stressed that "many localities face a most severe financial crisis." The report added that state fiscal problems are less severe, and put emphasis on helping states make more extensive use of their own resources. It acknowledged that a federal deficit was forecast, but said the postponement of revenue sharing to cut the federal deficit in effect would assign a lower priority to state and local financial problems than to other needs. A seven-member minority filed dissenting views, characterizing the legislation as "the biggest giveaway program ever enacted."

The principal differences from the administration's plan, other than changes in the formula, were (1) the change in the method of determining the total amount, from a percentage of the income tax base to a specific dollar appropriation, amounting to $5.3 billion for the first year; (2) the allocation of one-third of the total amount, rather than one-half, to the states; (3) the change from the administration's suggestion of a permanent appropriation to that of predetermined annual appropriations limited to a five-year period; (4) provisions to stimulate increased state

[7] Ibid., p. 94.

use of personal income taxation; and (5) a prohibition against the use of revenue-sharing funds to match other federal grant funds. The committee also inserted a list of "priority-expenditure categories" for the use of shared revenue. They applied to local governments, not states. (The categories contained in the committee bill covered operational and maintenance expenses for public safety, environmental protection, and public transportation, as well as capital expenses for sewage collection and treatment, refuse-disposal systems, and public transportation.) The effect of the six priority-expenditure categories was reduced later when the provision requiring local maintenance of effort was deleted before the Ways and Means bill was reported.[8] Expenditures for welfare were not included as a priority area; according to the report, welfare reform (which the Ways and Means Committee had acted upon previously) would provide substantial assistance for that purpose. The committee also stated that education expenditures were not included as a priority-expenditure category because the federal government was already providing substantial federal grants for this purpose. A further reason for this exclusion was the assumption, not made explicit, that the Congress would act soon—which it did not do—on federal aid for education.

A separate title of the Ways and Means revenue-sharing bill gave authority to the states to have the federal government collect state individual income taxes where the state tax provisions generally conform to the federal. (This provision was retained in the final act. As of mid-1974, no state had entered into agreement with the Internal Revenue Service for this purpose.)

Negotiation and Passage

By gaining Ways and Means approval, the revenue-sharing measure had now advanced an extremely important step. But problems arose in getting the bill through the House. Representative Mills, following his usual custom with tax legislation, said he would not be willing to bring

[8] The first versions of the committee bill required that in order to receive revenue-sharing funds, local governments must spend as much for the various priority-expenditure categories as they did on the average in the two preceding years. Mayor Stephen May of Rochester, New York, in a letter of April 6, 1972, to Congressman Barber Conable, Jr. (Rochester is in his congressional district), pointed out that the city had been forced to lay off employees precisely because they could no longer spend in the future what they had in the past. Mayor May argued therefore that a maintenance-of-effort requirement under revenue sharing would result in a constraint on city budgeting. He also claimed that such a requirement would discourage improved efficiency in local operations. Mayor May apparently persuaded the committee on these points. The provision requiring local maintenance of effort was deleted near the end of the committee's deliberations.

the revenue-sharing measure before the House unless he could obtain a closed rule, under which no amendments may be proposed during debate on the floor, as well as a waiver of any points of order. Such procedural arrangements required approval first of the House Rules Committee and then a vote by the entire House membership on the rule authorized by this body.

Mills's insistence on a closed rule and a waiver of points of order was intended to avoid two potentially serious obstacles to passage of the legislation. The waiver was felt to be necessary because the bill was vulnerable to a point of order that it should be referred to the House Appropriations Committee since it provided for the expenditure of $30.2 billion over five years. Proponents of revenue sharing were convinced that referral to the Appropriations Committee would be fatal to their hopes for passage; it was unlikely that the measure could be reported from the committee in time to be voted upon in the second session of the Ninety-second Congress. Supporters also feared that the Appropriations Committee would remove the provision for permanent five-year funding and subject revenue sharing to the annual appropriations process. They feared that such annual scrutiny would destroy the concept of revenue-sharing funds as money on which the state and local governments could count on a regular basis. The closed rule was also felt to be necessary, to protect the formula to which the Ways and Means Committee had devoted so many hours of hard work and analysis.

Mills's first attempt to obtain a rule met with resistance. Chairman William H. Colmer (D–Miss.) twice postponed the date for Rules Committee consideration of his request. Supporters of revenue sharing held their breath in this period, hoping that the Rules Committee would not successfully assert its customary conservative role of bottling up spending measures.

To move the Rules Committee, advocates of revenue sharing mounted an intensive lobbying campaign. The administration pressed Republican members of the committee and influential members of the House, pointing out that the measure was of top priority. The Big Six at this stage was joined by the American Federation of State, County, and Municipal Employees, which decided to support the bill despite opposition by its parent organization, the AFL-CIO. Governor Rockefeller of New York lent a member of his staff, James Cannon, for these lobbying efforts; the State of New York was particularly interested in prompt passage, because revenue sharing funds were counted on to help balance the state's budget for fiscal year 1973.

In this crucial period for revenue-sharing legislation, liberal opposition also intensified. Liberal congressmen fought against a closed rule for revenue sharing. Four members who had previously been in the revenue-sharing camp—Donald M. Fraser (Minn.), Charles A. Vanik (Ohio), David R. Obey (Wis.), and Henry S. Reuss (Wis.)—announced their intention to oppose the closed rule in order to propose a "fiscal responsibility amendment" which would raise funds for revenue sharing by plugging major tax loopholes. Since these congressmen were influential in the liberal Democratic Study Group, their opposition to the closed rule was potentially serious. The staff of the Congressional Black Caucus also urged opposition to the measure on the grounds that the bill did not meet the needs of the black community.

Perhaps most serious of all of the various obstacles presented in the spring of 1972, Chairman George Mahon (D–Tex.) of the Appropriations Committee sent a letter to all members of the House on May 22, urging that revenue sharing be referred to the Appropriations Committee because it constituted an appropriation bill. In this particular case, fiscal concerns may have been important, but considerations of turf also played a role.

On May 23 the Rules Committee voted 8 to 7 to grant the closed rule. The ten Democratic members of the committee split evenly. The five Republican members voted 3 in favor and 2 against.

Despite Rules Committee approval, the rules battle was still not over. It was now necessary to obtain sufficient votes in the House to uphold the committee's ruling. In the month that followed, there was intensive lobbying by both sides. Although the vote in the House on the rule was scheduled for June 13, supporters of revenue sharing obtained a postponement since they were not certain they had sufficient votes. Finally, on June 21, the House voted 223 to 185 to uphold the Rules Committee. The next day the revenue-sharing bill (H.R. 14370) was passed without amendment, 275–122. Republicans supported the bill by a 2-to-1 margin. Northern Democrats, undoubtedly reflecting pressures from their mayors, favored the bill by a 4-to-1 margin. Their more conservative Southern colleagues, however, voted against it, 48–29. The pattern was an unusual one—a coalition of Republicans and Northern Democrats.

Action in the Senate

Revenue-sharing legislation had taken eighteen months to pass the House. It was now late June; little time was left in the Ninety-second Congress for Senate consideration. Moreover, because it was a presidential election year, Congress would have to recess for the Democratic and Republican conventions. Members would be anxious to get home as soon as possible thereafter. Prospects were slim for a resumption of the session after the election.

To add to these time pressures, the revenue-sharing bill in the Senate came under the jurisdiction of the Finance Committee, which had not yet reported out the administration's welfare-reform bill, although the measure had been under consideration by that committee since it had passed the House on June 22, 1971. Supporters of revenue sharing saw the necessity for speed and a spirit of compromise.

A first obstacle was removed when the Senate Finance Committee decided to put aside consideration of welfare reform, thereby probably killing any chances that remained for its passage. Senator Russell B. Long of Louisiana, chairman of the Finance Committee and a vigorous opponent of the Nixon administration's Family Assistance Plan for welfare reform, scheduled hearings on revenue sharing to begin June 29. Testimony by Treasury Secretary George P. Shultz made it clear that the administration considered it more important to pass revenue sharing than to be doctrinaire about particular features. Shultz, an architect and main spokesman for the administration on domestic and economic issues, stated that "the House [revenue-sharing] formula represents a series of constructive compromises on the difficult matter of within-state allocation." He added that if Finance Committee members wished to re-examine the formula in the House bill, the administration would be happy to work with them to improve it. Specifically, Shultz agreed to accept the five-year trial period in the House bill rather than the original open-ended approach. He indicated also that the administration would prefer dropping the incentive provision relating to state income taxes in distributing funds among state governments; that it also would favor dropping the designation of local "priority-expenditure categories"; and that the use of urbanized area population as a factor in the distribution among the states discriminated rather severely against three states, Alaska, Vermont, and Wyoming. His testimony concluded by endorsing in general the bill passed by the House, expressing the hope that the administration could work with the Finance Committee to improve it, and urging "all deliberate speed" in reporting a measure to the Senate.

As it turned out, one of the most time-consuming issues for the consideration of revenue sharing by the Finance Committee was the special bonus amount of shared revenue tied to state income taxes that had been included late in the Ways and Means Committee deliberation. The composition of the Senate Finance Committee was not favorable for the retention of such a provision: of the sixteen committee members, ten were from states having no income taxes or ones with a low rate. Senator Baker of Tennessee (one of the sponsors of the original legislation, although not a member of the Finance Committee) pointed out in testimony that his state did not have an income tax, and furthermore that it had a constitutional prohibition which probably would make adoption of an income tax impossible during the five-year period of the proposed legislation. Examination of the amounts that would have been paid to states under the income-tax incentive feature showed that almost one-third of the payments attributable to this factor would have gone to New York and California. Neither state had a senator on the Finance Committee.

Senate Finance Committee hearings recessed on July 27 for the Democratic National Convention. Executive sessions on revenue sharing began shortly after Congress reassembled August 1. When the Finance Committee was ready to report a bill, a familiar problem arose. Senator John McClellan (D–Ark.), who had just assumed chairmanship of the Senate Appropriations Committee, stated that the revenue-sharing bill was an appropriations measure and should be referred to his committee for review before going to the floor. This was the first such assertion by McClellan, who only a few days before had acceded to the chairmanship on the death of Senator Allen J. Ellender. The outcome in this instance may have been influenced by the new chairman's lack of experience in his new role. In short, McClellan was outmaneuvered. To avoid referral to the Appropriations Committee, Senator Long removed from the revenue-sharing bill all language that referred to appropriations. The final version as reported by the Senate Finance Committee provided instead for automatic financing by requiring the secretary of the treasury to transfer annually 7 percent of income-tax receipts to the revenue-sharing trust fund.

The Reported Bill: Senate Version

On August 16, the Finance Committee approved revenue sharing by a vote of 12 to 4. The measure allocated $5.3 billion for the first year, but substituted a split of one-third to states and two-thirds to localities in place of the fixed dollar amounts (involving approximately the same proportions) specified in the House version. In addition, annual growth was to be shared by the states and localities, rather than limited to the states as in the House bill.

Most important of all, the committee version revised the allocation formula to favor low-income states with predominantly rural populations, not surprisingly, considering the composition of the Senate membership compared with that of the House. The revised formula omitted the controversial state-income tax factor, which Shultz had opposed, on the grounds that the federal government should not dictate to the states on the structure of their tax laws. The committee also removed the priority-expenditure categories for localities and added a requirement that recipient governments report to the Treasury and in the press on their "planned" and "actual" uses of revenue-sharing funds.

Senate Debate and Passage

On August 18 debate began in the Senate, which almost immediately thereafter recessed for the Republican convention. The debate resumed three weeks later on September 5 when the Senate reconvened. Thirty amendments were offered in the course of the debate; eleven were accepted. The most important vote was the defeat by 49 to 34 of a McClellan motion that would have subjected revenue sharing to the annual appropriations process after the first eighteen months. The principal amendments accepted contained provisions (1) applying the prevailing-wage requirements of the Davis-Bacon Act to construction projects where 25 percent or more of the cost is financed by revenue-sharing funds; (2) making Indian tribes and Alaskan native villages eligible for payments; and (3) allocating supplemental funds to the noncontiguous states of Alaska and Hawaii because of their relatively high cost of living.

On September 12 the Senate voted 64 to 20 to enact revenue sharing. The bill was sent immediately to joint House-Senate conference. In the Senate, Republicans overwhelmingly backed revenue sharing, voting for it by a 6-to-1 margin. Again, the Republicans, as in the House, were joined by Northern Democrats, in this instance by a margin of 21 to 8. However, unlike the House, Southern Democrats in the Senate supported revenue sharing, although by a much smaller margin (9 to 6) than their Northern colleagues.

House-Senate Compromise and Final Enactment

The next step was the establishment of a conference committee to iron out differences between the House and Senate. Its twelve members were senior members of the Senate Finance Committee and the House Ways and Means Committee. Their most serious challenge was the divergent nature of the two formulas for the state-by-state distribution of the funds. The House version gave more funds to highly populated and industrialized states; the Senate version favored low-income states with heavily rural populations. For example, New York State would have received $643 million for calendar 1972 under the House version and $501 million under the Senate version. Alabama, on the other hand, stood to receive $73 million under the House version and $99 million under the Senate version.

Although representatives of the state and local governments had exercised considerable restraint while the bill was under consideration—a reflection of their conviction that it would be easy for opponents to defeat the entire measure if there was squabbling among its supporters—it appeared almost impossible to produce a generally acceptable compromise formula in the time remaining. Fortunately for revenue sharing, the conference committee resolved its dilemma with a Solomon-like compromise. Each state would have its entitlement determined under both the House and Senate formula; it would then receive its allocation under whichever formula would give it the higher amount. Because this approach would allocate more than the full amount of the sum available nationwide, the allocations for all states were then to be proportionally reduced by enough to conform to the available appropriation.[9] Once the formula for state-by-state allocations had been determined, the conference bill followed the Senate version in allocating funds among local governments.

The conference committee made another important decision, this one concerning the limitations on the expenditures of shared revenues by local governments to "priority-expenditure categories." The House version of the bill contained three categories for maintenance and operating expenditures and three for capital expenditures; the Senate version eliminated the priority categories altogether. As a way out of this impasse, the conference committee expanded the House list substantially and also permitted all types of capital expenditures. The net result was a plus for the Senate, significantly diluting the effect of the priority categories as contained in the House bill.

The conference committee retained the requirement for planned-use and actual-use reports, which later was to become an important factor in program administration. It subjected states as well as local governments to the accounting, antidiscrimination, antimatching, and Davis-Bacon requirements.

The final version provided for a five-year program to be financed out of appropriations to a trust fund from federal funds "attributable to the collections of federal income taxes not otherwise appropriated." In reflection of the lengthy period required to enact the legislation, the act provided that the first two entitlement periods would be for calendar 1972. This meant that at the outset of the program, recipients received "windfall" or bunched payments covering fifteen months' worth of shared revenue in the four-month period from December 1972 to April 1973. The third entitlement period covered from January 1 to June 30, 1973; the fourth, fifth, and sixth covered successive one-year periods beginning on July 1, 1973. The seventh and final entitlement period was for six months, July 1 to December 31, 1976.

The conference report (Senate Report 92–1229) was submitted September 26. The House accepted the report on October 12 by a vote of 265 to 110, the Senate on October 13 by a vote of 59 to 19. The second session of the Ninety-second Congress ended the following day.

The State and Local Fiscal Assistance Act became law on October 20, 1972, when President Nixon signed H.R. 14370 in a ceremony at Independence Hall, Philadelphia, in the presence of a large group of state and local officials. He expressed the hope that revenue sharing would renew the American federal system created in Philadelphia two centuries earlier.

[9] This produced a reduction of 8.4 percent for the first year.

Revenue sharing marks a quite fundamental change in direction in the domestic policy of the federal government. It is a break with the past, more than an incremental change. It reflects many different ideas and purposes. In this respect it is consistent with Charles E. Linblom's comment that to have major legislation adopted by a legislative body, one should be vague about his purposes. Big city mayors supported revenue sharing as a way of meeting urban needs. Decentralists regarded it as a major advance. Some fiscal conservatives wanted revenue sharing in order to relieve state and local tax burdens, particularly local property taxes. Other more liberal supporters saw it as a way to equalize conditions among rich and poor states and localities. The individuals and groups participating in the story of revenue sharing reflect both this diversity of goals and the fact that in some respects they involved contradictory objectives.

The main actors in this decision process were—the president, powerful and well-placed members of Congress, a coalition of interest groups, and academics, both in government and outside. Which actors were most important? What events were crucial? The material presented here provides a basis for making such assessments.

As of the time of this writing, the legislative process for the extension of revenue sharing has reached its critical phase. The outcome as yet is not clear, but all signs point to an extension.

BIBLIOGRAPHY

Advisory Commission on Intergovernmental Relations. *General Revenue Sharing: an ACIR Re-evaluation.* Washington, D.C., 1974 (A-48).

Caputo, David A., and Cole, Richard L. *Urban Politics and Decentralization: The Case of General Revenue Sharing.* Lexington, Mass.: Heath Lexington, 1974.

Dommel, Paul R. *The Politics of Revenue Sharing.* Bloomington: Indiana University Press, 1974.

Nathan, Richard P.; Manvel, Allen D.; and Calkins, Susannah E. *Monitoring Revenue Sharing.* Washington, D.C.: Brookings Institution, 1975. (This is the first in a series of reports from the Brookings Institution on the distributional, fiscal, and political effects of revenue sharing, based in part on data for a sample of 65 governmental recipients of revenue-sharing funds.)

National Clearinghouse on Revenue Sharing. *General Revenue Sharing in American Cities: First Impressions.* Washington, D.C., 1974.

Reuss, Henry J. *Revenue Sharing. Crutch or Catalyst for State and Local Governments.* New York: Praeger, 1970.

Stolz, Otto G. *Revenue Sharing: Legal and Policy Analysis.* New York: Praeger, 1974.

U.S. Comptroller General. "Revenue Sharing: Its Use by and Impact on Local Governments." Washington, D.C., August 1974.

U.S. Comptroller General. "Revenue Sharing: Its Use by and Impact on State Governments." Washington, D.C., August 1973.

U.S. Congress, Joint Committee on Internal Revenue Taxation. *General Explanation of the State and Local Fiscal Assistance Act of 1972.* February 12, 1973.

See also the U.S. Census of Governments of 1972 for basic data on state and local government; *Revenue Sharing Bulletin* (published by the Revenue Sharing Advisory Service, Washington, D.C.); the congressional hearings on the 1972 act; and publications of the Office of Revenue Sharing, U.S. Department of the Treasury.

Impoundment of Clean-Water Funds

The Limits of Discretion

Louis Fisher

In recent decades Congress has acquired the reputation of being an unequal partner in the legislative process, losing much of the initiative to the president. Any number of cases could be assembled, however, to show that such a view is oversimplified. Often we give credit to the president when the impetus, innovation, and leadership lay with legislative forces. Often it is the president who behaves in a negative fashion, trying to restrain an active and assertive Congress. Such was the situation in 1972–73 when President Nixon refused to spend $9 billion that Congress had provided for water pollution control.

A few weeks before the presidential election of 1972, amid recriminations between the executive and legislative branches regarding prerogatives and balance of power, President Nixon vetoed the Clean Water Bill. Although both houses quickly and decisively overrode the veto, President Nixon proceeded to impound exactly half of the $18 billion that Congress had provided for waste treatment plants. The impoundment crisis became a bitter element in the confrontation between the two branches, eventually giving rise to dozens of cases in the federal courts, a U.S. Supreme Court decision, and passage of the Impoundment Control Act of 1974.

LEGISLATION ENCOUNTERS A VETO

The purpose of the Clean Water Act (the Federal Water Pollution Control Act Amendments of 1972) was "to restore and maintain the chemical, physical, and biological integrity of the Nation's waters." To that end the act provided $18 billion in federal assistance to construct publicly owned waste treatment works. Deadlines were established to eliminate the discharge of pollutants into navigable waters and to provide for the protection and propagation of fish, shell-life, and wildlife. Major research efforts were required to develop the necessary technology.

The responsibility for administering this complex act, which runs to almost a hundred pages, fell to the Environmental Protection Agency (EPA). In addition to protecting the responsibilities and rights of the states to eliminate pollution, the act encouraged public participation in the development, revision, and enforcement of regulations established by EPA and the states.

The Clean Water Act was more than two years in the making. The Senate Subcommittee on Air and Water Pollution, part of the Committee on Public Works, held hearings during the spring of 1970. Because of action on the Clean Air Act of 1970 and the Resource Recovery Act of 1970, the subcommittee did not report legislation for water pollution control that year. But hearings were held the following year, at the start of the Ninety-second Congress, and on October 28, 1971, the Senate Public Works Committee reported a Clean Water Bill, S. 2770.

The committee found that the national effort to control water pollution "has been inadequate in every vital aspect." Rivers, lakes, and streams were being used as a waste treatment system to dispose of man's wastes, rather than to support life and health. The committee proposed a major change in the federal enforcement mechanism. Instead of relying on water quality standards (purity levels), the committee wanted pollutants controlled at their source (effluent limitations for "point sources"). After a day's debate, the bill was adopted unanimously on November 2, 1971, by a Senate vote of 86 to 0.

The House Public Works Committee conducted its own set of hearings over a seven-month period and reported legislation on March 11, 1972. Three days of debate ended with a vote of 380 to 14 in favor of the bill.

At that point the House and Senate bills went to conference committee to resolve the many differences between the two bills. After thirty-nine different meetings, many of them starting early in the morning and running late into the evening, the bill emerged from conference on September 28, 1972. Senator Edmund Muskie, floor manager of the bill, told his colleagues that during his thirteen years in the Senate he had never participated in a conference "which has consumed so many hours, been so arduous in its deliberations, or demanded so much attention to detail from the members." On October 4 the Senate agreed to the conference report by the unanimous vote of 74 to 0. On the very same day the House of Representatives adopted the conference report, 366–11.

Despite the top-heavy majorities by which the two houses had passed the bill, it was vetoed on October 17. President Nixon told Congress that the attack on water pollution could not ignore "other very real threats to the quality of life, such as spiraling prices and increasingly onerous taxes." The "laudable intent" of the legislation, he said, was outweighed by its "unconscionable" cost. The price tag seemed to him so high that it literally "broke the budget." He maintained that the highest national priority was the need to protect workers against tax increases and renewed inflation. The presidential rhetoric increased in tempo as Nixon declared his intention to veto any bill which would lead to higher prices and higher taxes: "I have nailed my colors to the mast on this issue; the political winds can blow where they may."

And indeed the political winds were blowing. The veto was handed down on the eve of the presidential election, just a few short weeks away. For a number of months President Nixon had berated Congress for excessive and irresponsible spending. On July 26 he claimed that the budget crisis of deficits and inflation was the result of "hoary and traditional" congressional procedures. A nationwide radio address on October 7 warned that excessive spending by Congress might cause a "congressional tax increase" in 1973.

The issue reached fever pitch when President Nixon asked Congress to establish a spending ceiling of $250 billion for fiscal year 1973. Whenever outlays threatened to go above the statutory ceiling, Nixon wanted complete discretion to decide which programs to curtail or eliminate. To delegate such authority to the president was offensive to many members, and yet they were under heavy pressure to support the president's stance on economy. Wilbur Mills, a ranking Democrat and chairman of the House Ways and Means Committee, warned his colleagues that a vote against the spending ceiling would put an end to their political careers.

It was in the midst of this intense "Battle of the Budget" that Nixon vetoed the Clean Water Bill. Conscious though they were of the economy motif and the risk to their own careers, the Congress voted overwhelmingly to override the veto. Republicans deserted the president in droves. The final tally in the Senate was 52–12, far in excess of the two-thirds needed. The override vote in the House was even more lopsided: 247–23.

$9 BILLION IMPOUNDED

In vetoing the bill, President Nixon had called attention to the existence of of a certain amount of discretionary spending authority. Some of the provisions, he said, "confer a measure of spending discretion and flexibility upon the president, and if forced to administer this legislation I mean to use those provisions to put the brakes on budget-wrecking expenditures as much as possible."

A month later, on November 22, President Nixon instructed EPA administrator William Ruckelshaus to withhold from the states more than half of the waste treatment allotments. Instead of the statutory schedule of $5 billion for fiscal 1973 and $6 billion for fiscal 1974, $3 billion was held back from each year. Later President Nixon released only $4 billion of the $7 billion scheduled for fiscal 1975. In short, exactly half of the $18 billion provided for the three years was impounded.

The response from Congress was swift and critical. Senator Muskie, in a joint statement with the chairman of the House Public Works Committee, John Blatnik, denounced the president for acting in "flagrant disregard" of the intent of Congress. In a separate address, on December 12, Muskie said that the president had apparently "defied constitutional limitations of his powers in an area where the public and the Congress have left no doubt as to their desires and their determinations to pay the costs of restoring water quality." Anti-impoundment legislation was introduced in both houses. States and private parties filed suit in federal courts to have the clean-water funds released. To comprehend the issue, and its final settlement in the courts, the reader must grasp the essential language of the statute and its legislative history.

Statutory Language

In most cases, when Congress funds a program, it passes an appropriation act. Agencies then obligate and spend the money. The Clean Water Act relied on a different financing method called "contract authority," which allows agencies to enter into obligations in advance of appropriations. To pay for those obligations ("liquidate" the contract authority), Congress must appropriate funds at some later date. In other words, contract authority reverses the usual chain of events. Instead of first appropriating funds, followed by obligations and expenditures, obligations *precede* appropriations.

The act directed the EPA administrator to allot contract authority to the states on the basis of ratios established by Congress. The states would then submit to the administrator, for his approval, proposed projects for the construction of waste treatment works. His approval would represent a contractual obligation of the United States to pay 75 percent of the cost. The states would pay the remaining amount (a 75–25 matching grant program).

If the administration wanted to limit the level of spending for waste treatment plants, there were two potential means of control: withholding the initial allotments of contract authority from the states, or withholding the obligation and expenditure of funds at a later date. Whether discretion existed at either stage requires a close reading of the statute.

On its face, the Clean Water Act appeared to make the allotment step mandatory. Section 205 directed that sums authorized to be appropriated "shall" be allotted by the EPA administrator not later than the January 1 immediately preceding the beginning of the fiscal year for which they were authorized, except that the allotment for fiscal year 1973 was to be made not later than thirty days after the act (which became law October 18, 1972). The amounts authorized to be appropriated were governed by Section 207, which provided $5 billion for fiscal 1973, $6 billion for fiscal 1974, and $7 billion for fiscal 1975—a total of $18 billion.

However, the mandatory nature of Section 205 was weakened by two changes made in the bill while in conference. The original language of the House bill had directed that "all sums" shall be allotted. The word "all" was eliminated by the conferees. Moreover, the conferees appeared to enhance administrative flexibility by inserting the phrase "not to exceed" before the dollar amounts authorized in Section 207. That made it appear that the amounts were mere ceilings rather than mandatory levels.

Statements abound throughout the legislative history, demonstrating without question that the president was granted a measure of spending flexibility. Crucial issues were left hanging. First, did the president enjoy any flexibility at the *allotment* stage, or was he required to allot the full amount to the states? And second, if he had discretion at the obligation and expenditure stages, what was the *extent* of that discretion? On neither point was the legislative history unambiguous. Normally we could turn to the conference report for guidance as to legislative intent; but the report was silent. It merely indicated that the word "all" had been deleted from Section 205 and that the phrase "not to exceed" had been added to Section 207. There is nothing in it to explain the purpose or motivation behind those two changes.

The next place to look are the floor debates that took place when the House and Senate acted on the conference report. Edmund Muskie, leading Senate sponsor of the bill, explained that the two changes had been made in conference to reduce the possibility of a veto. Clearly a concession had been made by Congress, since President Nixon had "gone public" on the need to control spending. But what was the concession? What had Congress given away? Muskie explained that all of the sums authorized "need not be committed, though they must be allocated [i.e., allotted]." The two provisions had been added to give the administration "some flexibility concerning the obligation of construction grant funds."

According to Muskie, then, the allotment step was mandatory, while some flexibility existed for obligations and expenditures. The scope of the latter discretion appeared to be modest. Muskie stressed that the two changes made in conference were not to be used "as an excuse in not making the commitments necessary to achieve the goals set forth in the act." Only in cases where the obligation of funds might be contrary to other congressional policies (such as expressed in the National Environmental Policy Act) would the EPA administrator be expected to refuse to enter into contracts for construction.

When the House took up the conference report, additional qualifications were added. William Harsha of Ohio, ranking Republican on the conference committee, said that elimination of the word "all" and insertion of the phrase "not to exceed" were intended to "emphasize the president's flexibility to control the rate of spending." What was meant by "flexibility" and "rate"? Could the president dictate the *scope* of the program? What was the relationship between "rate of spending" and the specific statutory step of allotting contract authority to the states? Some legislative history was developed by a dialogue between Harsha, Robert Jones (D–Ala., and chairman of the House conferees), and minority leader Gerald Ford:

> *Mr. Ford:* Mr. Speaker, the gentleman from Ohio [Harsha] has made a very excellent presentation and as I listened I thought he answered the major question that I have in my mind. I am for the conference report, but I think it is vitally important that the intent and purpose of Section 207 is spelled out in the legislative history here in the discussion on this conference report.
>
> As I understand the comments of the gentleman from Ohio, the inclusion of the words in Section 207 in three instances of "not to exceed" indicates that is a limitation. More importantly that it is not a mandatory requirement that in 1 year ending June 30, 1973, there would be $5 billion and the next year ending June 30, 1974, $6 billion and a third year ending June 30, 1975, $7 billion obligation or expenditure?
>
> *Mr. Harsha:* I do not see how reasonable minds could come to any other conclusion than that the language means we can obligate or expend up to that sum—anything up to that sum but not to exceed that amount. Surely, if the Executive can impound moneys under the contract authority provision in the highway trust fund, which does not have the flexible language in this bill, they could obviously do it in this instance.

Ford then asked Jones whether he agreed with the statement by Harsha.

> *Mr. Jones:* Mr. Speaker, if the gentleman will yield. My answer is "yes." Not only do I agree with him but the gentleman from Ohio

offered this amendment which we have now under discussion in the committee of conference, so there is no doubt in anybody's mind of the intent of the language. It is reflected in the language just explained by the gentleman from Ohio (Mr. Harsha).

Mr. Ford: Mr. Speaker, this clarifies and certainly ought to wipe away any doubts anyone has. The language is not a mandatory requirement for full obligation and expenditure up to the authorization figure in each of the 3 fiscal years. Therefore, without any reservations Mr. Speaker, I support the conference report.

Of course that did not resolve all of the doubts about the bill's intent. The only point acknowledged was that there was some discretion at the obligation and expenditure stages, which Muskie himself had conceded. The extent of that discretion was still in the air. Nor was it clear whether the president had any discretion over allotments. Neither issue was clarified when the two houses overrode the veto. Muskie continued to say that the president had some flexibility concerning obligation. Harsha spoke of the president's flexibility to control the "rate of spending" and the "rate of expenditures."

Harsha's reference to highway impoundments did not do much to advance the administration's cause. On August 7, 1972, a U.S. district court had decided that the secretary of transportation could not withhold obligational authority from Missouri. Chief Judge Becker described the attempt to impound highway funds—part of the administration's anti-inflation policy—as "unauthorized by law, illegal in excess of lawful discretion and in violation of the Federal-Aid Highway Act." His decision was upheld the following April by the U.S. Court of Appeals for the Eighth Circuit. Subsequently the administration lost seven more highway impoundment cases, the decisions being handed down in Iowa, South Carolina, Montana, California, and Nebraska (all in 1974), and in Alabama, Kansas, and the District of Columbia (in 1975). The latter was a class action suit involving twelve states: Louisiana, Nevada, Oklahoma, Pennsylvania, Texas, Washington, Alaska, Idaho, Wisconsin, Arizona, Utah, and Michigan.

Commitment and Timetable

The issue of presidential spending discretion in the Clean Water Act cannot be decided simply by examining the language and legislative history of Sections 205 and 207. They must be read in concert with another central feature of the act: the commitment on the part of Congress to combat water pollution within a scheduled period of time. Section 101, which set forth the declaration of goals and policy, established a national goal of eliminating the discharge of pollutants into navigable waters by

1985. It was also a national goal that, wherever attainable, an interim goal of water quality—providing for the protection and propagation of fish, shell-life, and wildlife, and providing for recreation in and on the water—be achieved by July 1, 1983. Section 301 defined additional goals for effluent limitations.

The nature of the commitment was the subject of conflicting interpretations. During action on the conference report, Muskie admitted that $18 billion was "a great deal of money," but insisted it would cost that much to "begin to achieve the requirements set forth in the legislation." That was the "minimum amount needed to finance the construction of waste treatment facilities which will meet the standards imposed by this legislation." But Robert Jones, manager of the bill on the House side, characterized the 1985 target date as a "goal, not a national policy." While he hoped that the date could be met, he said that the conference report recognized that "too many imponderables exist, some still beyond our horizons, to prescribe this goal today as a legal requirement." The chairman of the full House Committee on Public Works, John Blatnik, offered this answer to those who called the bill too costly: "We must act now, and must be willing to pay the bill now—or face the task of paying later when, perhaps, no amount of money will be enough." Harsha, while agreeing that the committee had accurately assessed the need for a large sum of money, argued that spending flexibility had been added because of the many competing national priorities.

Those statements were made in the hope of averting a veto. But after Nixon's disapproval the congressional tone switched more firmly to the concept of a commitment. Jones was now to say that everyone knew the program was a costly undertaking, but "we know also that the people who are the greatest Nation on earth are prepared to pay the price of this undertaking." Harsha added that Congress had "an overriding environmental commitment to the people of this Nation. We must keep it." Would overturning the veto, Harsha asked, mean a vote for higher taxes? He gave this counsel: "So be it, the public is prepared to pay for it. To say we can't afford this sum of money is to say we can't afford to support life on earth."

On the Senate side, during the vote to override the veto, Muskie stressed that the "whole intent of this bill is to make a national commitment." The legislation imposed requirements on industry, on the states, and on local governments. The commitment on those sectors required a commitment by the federal government. As Muskie concluded, "What we were asking of the Congress was a commitment that these people in other levels of government and the private sector could rely upon. Of course there is a commitment."

Spokesmen for President Nixon claimed that it was administratively impossible to use the full amount of contract authority provided by Congress. John Ehrlichman, as director of the Domestic Council, said that there are "only so many contractors who can build sewer plants. There is only a certain amount of sewer equipment that can be purchased. It becomes obvious that there is no point in going out and tacking dollar bills to the trees. That isn't going to get the water clean."

Why did the administration assume that the environmental industry lacked the ability to respond and to increase its capacity? A more realistic assumption would have been to expect industry to gear up to meet the clean-water commitment—provided that the government committed itself financially to the goal and expressed a determination to adhere to the target dates. When President Eisenhower and Congress joined in a commitment to build 41,000 miles of interstate highways, or when President Kennedy announced the goal of putting a man on the moon by the end of the 1960s, no one argued that those commitments could not be met because of a lack of contractor capability. The commitment came first; the capability followed.

After the president's veto, EPA administrator Ruckelshaus appeared before Senator Ervin's hearings on impoundment to argue that it was economically unwise to allot the full amounts authorized by Congress: "The fastest way to increase inflation is to pour more money into the community than the construction industry can absorb." Not only did that argument rest on the idea of an industry fixed in size, it contradicted what Ruckelshaus had written to Office of Management and Budget director Caspar Weinberger *prior* to the veto. At that time Ruckelshaus strongly recommended that the president sign the bill. With regard to near-term construction costs, he said that they would correspond closely to what would have been initiated under the administration bill. Thus, the "potential inflationary impact upon the entire construction sector would be minimized."

As to the total costs resulting from the $18-billion figure, Ruckelshaus pointed out that the additional spending authority provided by Congress was "largely the result of the Congress adopting a later EPA needs survey than the one that provided the basis for the administration's request." Moreover, the EPA estimate did not allow for inflation, nor did it include funds for combined, storm, and collection sewers, or for recycled water supplies. Those were some of the responsibilities under the bill that passed Congress. During Senate debate on the override, Muskie offered several other reasons to justify the $18-billion figure. The EPA estimate was based on existing standards and requirements. The clean-water act, in making those standards more stringent, would make it more expensive to meet them. Also, the older estimates did not take into account the statutory deadlines, which accelerated the construction timetables and required spending more money in less time.

During the 1973 Government Operations hearings on impoundment, under the chairmanship of Senator Ervin (D–N.C.), Senator Muskie and EPA administrator Ruckelshaus jostled on the question of whether Congress had voted an unreasonable and impractical sum of money to combat water pollution. After Ruckelshaus had defended the record of the administration, pointing out how much had been spent in the past few years, this exchange occurred:

> *Senator Muskie:* Have you heard Senator [Eugene] McCarthy's definition of a liberal Republican? He is a fellow who would throw a rope ten feet long to a fellow drowning twenty feet offshore. If you are spending $10 million and it is only 20 percent as much as the need, you are not doing enough.
>
> *Mr. Ruckelshaus:* You don't need to throw him a forty-foot rope either when he is twenty feet offshore.
>
> *Senator Muskie:* You look at your letter to Weinberger at the time of the first veto in which you don't describe this as a forty-foot rope, you describe the dollars in this as based upon your own statements of what is needed. So don't give me the forty-foot rope business.

SEARCH FOR JUDICIAL REMEDIES

How could the conflicting concepts of spending flexibility and goal commitment be reconciled? If a commitment existed, why would Congress give the president unbridled discretion in releasing the funds? Did the administration use its discretion to undermine the commitment? These were some of the complex issues injected into the federal courts.

The first decision handed down was by Judge Oliver Gasch of the U.S. District Court for the District of Columbia. He concluded that the discretion implied by "not to exceed" and the deletion of "all" referred to the obligation and expenditure stages, not to allotment. He held that the Clean Water Act required the administration to allot the full sums authorized to be appropriated by Section 207. Note that the court was not called upon to determine whether the EPA administrator should *spend* any given amount of money for sewage treatment works. Allotment, in the words of Judge Gasch, was not "tantamount to *expenditure* or even commitment of the funds."

His decision was affirmed by the U.S. Court of Appeals for the District of Columbia, which found in the legislative history an intent by Congress to specifically commit federal funds: "It did so in recognition of the necessity of assuring the states that federal aid would be available." The

goal by Congress guided the court in interpreting the funding mechanism, "for if discretion in allotment would make the achievement of this
goal more difficult, it must be assumed that Congress intended no such
authorization." With regard to Harsha's statement that the president had
discretion to "control the rate of spending," the court restricted that control to the obligation and expenditure stages.

A number of other district courts agreed that full allotment was mandatory. Judge Lord of the U.S. District Court in Minnesota emphasized
the commitment given by Congress to environmental protection:

> Any such exercise of discretion must be consistent with the policy
> and provisions included in the Act itself. Congress has clearly given
> the highest priority to the cleaning up of the nation's waters. Noth-
> ing in the Act grants the Administrator the authority to substitute
> his sense of national priorities for that of the Congress.

Similar decisions were handed down by district courts in Florida and
Texas. In each case the courts determined that the act required full allotment (though not necessarily full obligation and expenditure). The
purpose of Congress in adopting the contract authority and allotment
approach was to permit long-range planning against water pollution. It
was a method of ensuring an unequivocal financial commitment by the
federal government, enabling state and local governments to enter into
long-term contracts and to finance long-term bonds. It would be illogical,
said Judge Roberts of Texas, to think that Congress would inject uncertainty back into the funding system by giving the administration discretion to choose how much to allot. Evaluation of the act as a whole evinced
"an unmistakable congressional intent to marshal the requisite federal
funds to achieve the water quality goals set forth in the Act." In the
Florida decision, Judge Middlebrooks also stressed Congress' concern
with the ability of states to effect long-range plans in combating inflation:
"Indeed the planning problem was the reason for the implementation of
the allotment procedure rather than the normal appropriation procedure
in the Act."

District courts in Illinois, Ohio, and Maine also decided against the
administration. Although newspaper accounts typically reported that
federal courts had directed the administration to "spend" the clean-water
funds, the courts were careful to limit its holding to the allotment stage,
not to obligation and expenditure.

In a Los Angeles decision—the nearest the administration came to a
"victory" on these lower court decisions—Judge Hauk dismissed the case
for reasons of standing. He said that the plaintiffs had failed to show that
they had been injured or impaired by EPA's refusal to allot the full
amount. They had not produced affidavits indicating that proposals had

been rejected by EPA because of impoundment. But having disposed of the case on procedural grounds, he later maintained in dicta that even if the case did proceed to the merits, the plaintiffs could not compel the EPA administrator to allot the funds. The legislative history of the act demonstrated to Judge Hauk that the statute did not require full allotment. The two changes in conference, as proposed by Congressman Harsha, pointed to a desire to limit funds, not maximize them: "The passage 'sums authorized to be appropriated . . . shall be allotted' hardly means that the entire amount must be disgorged, and the phrase 'not to exceed' connotes limitation, not disbursement." Furthermore:

> No one has convinced us that when a legislature removes the word "all" from the phrase "All sums authorized to be appropriated shall be allotted," they mean that every penny must be spent. Nor has anybody argued successfully that adding the phrase "not to exceed" before a sum means anything more than that an upper limit must be imposed.

Of course the issue before Judge Hauk was not whether "every penny must be spent" but whether the entire sum had to be allotted. He attempted to buttress his argument by quoting a long passage from President Franklin D. Roosevelt, who wrote to Senator Richard Russell in 1942: "While our statutory system of fund apportionment is not a substitute for item or blanket veto power, and should not be used to set aside or nullify the expressed will of Congress, I cannot believe that you or Congress as a whole would take exception to either of these purposes which are common to sound business management everywhere." But when we turn to the full text of Roosevelt's letter, we find that it does not reinforce the argument of Judge Hauk. Quite the opposite, in fact. What did Roosevelt mean by "either of these purposes"? He was referring to two types of routine withholding actions: setting aside budgetary reserves either to prevent deficiencies or to effect savings. In contrast, the clean-water funds were impounded for policy reasons. The administration believed that Congress had appropriated too much, that it had paid insufficient regard to combating inflation. Moreover, the impoundment of clean-water funds *was* a substitute for "item or blanket veto power." As to whether impoundment was used to "set aside or nullify the expressed will of Congress," that was the precise issue before the courts.

A wholly different type of interpretation was handed down by Judge Robert Merhige of the U.S. District Court for the Eastern District of Virginia. Although he ruled that the impoundment of 55 percent ($6 billion out of $11 billion for the first two years) constituted a violation of the Clean Water Act, he concluded that Congress *did* intend for the executive branch to exercise some discretion with respect to allotment.

Judge Merhige found the deletion of "all" in Section 205 to be "highly significant." Even the plaintiffs, Campaign Clean Water, conceded some discretion at the allotment stage.

Nevertheless, the withholding of $6 billion conflicted with Congress' commitment to environmental protection and its willingness to incur "vast expenses in achieving that commitment." While Congress had purposefully incorporated provisions in the act to give the president some discretion, motivated in part by a desire to avoid a veto, the large margins by which Congress overrode the veto reaffirmed the "massive national commitment to environmental protection." Judge Merhige was satisfied that the impoundment of 55 percent of the funds was a "violation of the spirit, intent and letter of the Act and a flagrant abuse of executive discretion." Instead of issuing an injunction against the administration, to compel the release of funds, he simply declared that the impoundment policy was null and void.

This opinion was not sustained at the circuit court level. The U.S. Court of Appeals for the Fourth Circuit returned the decision to Merhige for further proceedings. It wanted to know whether the exercise of discretion at the allotment could be reviewed by the courts and, if so, what standards or criteria should be used to assess the validity of its exercise. The circuit court questioned the right of a district court to find an executive action arbitrary, on its face, without any other evidentiary support. The administration had made a number of claims. The EPA administrator denied that he was evading any responsibilities given him under the act. The withholding of allotments was justified on the ground that greater amounts could not be spent in a "wise or expeditious manner" in achieving the goals of the act. Moreover, it was argued that there was insufficient technical capacity to carry out a more extensive program. The administrator also asserted that a more rapid rate of spending would inflate the cost of the program without appreciably accelerating the program.

The court of appeals concluded that there was "no way for us at this juncture to venture an opinion whether the administrator had been 'dragging his feet' in approving projects or whether these figures indicate that the allotments made represented reasonable goals for the two fiscal years in controversy." The issue could not be resolved by a per se rule. It required an inquiry into the basis for the administrator's action. The district court had to develop a record which would support its decision. Why was the withholding of 55 percent a "flagrant abuse"? What if the administrator had withheld 40 percent? Thirty percent? At what point would withholding no longer conflict with the policy and provisions of the Clean Water Act?

Enter the Supreme Court

The State of Georgia tried to resolve such questions by taking the issue directly to the U.S. Supreme Court. On May 10, 1973, Georgia brought action against the Nixon administration for withholding funds from three federal programs: Federal-Aid Highways, National Defense Education Act, and the Clean Water Act. The action requested the Court to exercise its original jurisdiction, granted under Article III of the Constitution, and thereby dispense with the initial review by lower courts. In view of the controversy and acrimony swirling around the impoundment dispute, Georgia felt it would be in the national interest to put to rest, at the earliest possible time, the constitutional question of who was entitled to terminate or curtail a federal program.

The administration urged the Court to accept the case and refer it to a "special master" who would conduct a full evidentiary hearing and make an initial determination of the legal issues. The brief by the government, contending that the matter lay within the Court's original jurisdiction, claimed that the controversy constituted "one of those extraordinary and important cases which ought to be taken directly by this Court." Unless there was a final determination by the highest court, Congress could not know the full effect of its legislative efforts. The brief also argued that the state of uncertainty made it difficult for the president to know whether to veto an appropriation bill he regarded as inflationary. Could he sign the measure and withhold the excess funds? If not, veto might be his sole recourse.

Ten states filed a brief asking the Court to deny Georgia's petition. Each of the states—Connecticut, Louisiana, Massachusetts, Missouri, Minnesota, Oklahoma, Pennsylvania, Texas, Vermont, and Washington— was a party in one or more impoundment cases pending in the lower courts. A number of private organizations joined the ten states in the brief, pointing out that the exercise of original jurisdiction would probably retard the progress of impoundment cases through the lower courts "since those courts would be reluctant to rule on issues pending before this Court." And whereas the government took the position that only at the Supreme Court level (with the assistance of a special master) could impoundment issues be decided on a fully developed record, the brief for the ten states contended that the Court would be better able to decide the issues after they had first been considered and resolved by lower courts.

The brief also expressed doubt that the exercise of original jurisdiction would have any appreciable effect in expediting the Court's ultimate resolution. The investigation contemplated by the government "would surely require months of discovery, let alone trial, as dozens of depositions

would have to be taken, documents requested and produced, interroga-
tories filed and answered, and, of course, objections raised and ruled on."
The brief, noting that any delay would serve the interests of the government, added that there was an understandable desire by the government
to "rush headlong into this Court with an impoundment case before they
and other federal officials receive any further judicial rebuffs at the hands
of the district courts and, especially, the courts of appeal."

In a separate brief, the City of New York also opposed the granting of
the Georgia petition. The brief said that the Supreme Court should not
permit its original jurisdiction to be used as a litigating tactic to circum-
vent lower-court decisions "with which the Government is unhappy." Furthermore, unless the Court decided that presidential discretion to withhold funds was unreviewable by the courts, a decision by the Court
would not put an end to litigation. There would always be questions of
statutory construction and interpretation, unique to each law, giving rise
to new action in the courts. On October 9, 1973, the Supreme Court declined to hear the Georgia case.

Meanwhile, as the clean-water cases progressed through the federal
courts, the Supreme Court was faced with a new demand—not of original
jurisdiction but of appellate jurisdiction. After decisions had been handed
down at the circuit court level on the District of Columbia and Virginia
clean-water cases, the Court agreed, on April 29, 1974, to hear the two
cases.

In its brief before the Supreme Court, the government maintained
that the case was not one in which the president asserted a power to control the rate of spending in opposition to the wishes of Congress. Rather,
it was a case "in which courts have improperly cut into and endangered a
discretion Congress intended the president to have." It was the president's job to estimate the level and timing of spending that would ensue
from a commitment; the income resources likely to be available to the
government; the nature of competing program needs and demands; the
state of the economy; and the impact of spending on the economy. "The
very nature of those judgments," said the government, "makes it inap-
propriate for the courts to attempt to review the Administrator's judgment."

Oral argument was held on the afternoon of November 12, 1974. The
exchange between the justices and the attorneys lasted slightly more
than an hour. Robert Bork, solicitor general for the government, told
the Court that the full amount of $18 billion would be allotted to the
states at some time. According to Bork, the issue was therefore solely one
of timing, not of scope. To many in the room, including the author, this
marked the first time that the administration had promised full allotment.
Chief Justice Burger asked the attorney for Campaign Clean Water,

W. Thomas Jacks, if this announcement by the government did not weaken the plaintiff's case. Jacks replied that it gave him no comfort to hear that the government would release all of the funds "at some time." The Clean Water Act had established specific deadlines for the achievement of various standards of water purity.

One could also add that the distinction between "timing" and "scope" was imaginary. To the extent that the government could dictate timing, stretching out the program for a number of years, the scope of the program would be very much affected. Each year of delay meant that inflation was consuming the potential value of the $18 billion that Congress had provided. The cost of constructing waste treatment plants was increasing by hundreds of millions of dollars each year.

The Court handed down its decision on February 18, 1975. It was unanimous, all nine justices deciding against the administration. The thirteen-page opinion, delivered by Justice White, was rather brief considering the complexity of the case. Most of the opinion consisted of a review of the legislative history, the administration's action, and lower court decisions. Justice White rejected the argument that the addition of "not to exceed" in conference implied administrative discretion to allot less than the full amounts. The language merely reflected the possibility that approved applications for grants might not total the maximum amount authorized to be appropriated. As for striking the word "all" from Section 205, White said that the word "sums" had no different meaning in the context of that section than the words "all sums." In either case the action was mandatory upon the government to allot the full amount. Here the concept of a legislative commitment came into play:

> We cannot accept the addition of the few words to §207 and the deletion of the one word from §205 as altering the entire complexion and thrust of the Act. As conceived and passed in both Houses, the legislation was intended to provide a firm commitment of substantial sums within a relatively limited period of time in the effort to achieve an early solution of what was deemed an urgent problem. We cannot believe that Congress at the last minute scuttled the entire effort by providing the Executive with the seemingly limitless power to withhold funds from allotment and obligation.

The decision was a convenient one for the Court. Not much was at stake, in the sense of having the administration defy the Court's order. Two weeks before the decision was handed down, the administration's budget for fiscal 1976 had announced the release of $4 billion in clean-water funds. That left $5 billion impounded. The solicitor general had promised full allotment in his oral argument. Thus, release of the funds had already been settled before the Court reached its decision.

To read the legislative history differently, as surely was possible, would have placed the Court in an awkward position. If it adopted the argument of Judge Merhige, and maintained that the EPA administrator possessed some discretion at the allotment stage but not as much as actually exercised, where would the Court draw the line? At 20 percent withholding? Ten percent? To justify a given percentage would require a needs survey by the Court of the environmental problems facing the nation's water supply, a task for which the Court was ill equipped. The simplest thing was to come down on the side of full allotment.

As for the administration, one could say that it lost the battle but won the war. Despite numerous setbacks in the lower courts, and a resounding defeat at the hands of a unanimous Supreme Court, it had succeeded in delaying the program for several years. From the time of President Nixon's directive to EPA administrator Ruckelshaus on November 22, 1972, to the decision by the Supreme Court, almost twenty-seven months had elapsed. It was now impossible for the administration, even with full allotment, to meet the deadlines established by Congress. When EPA administrator Russell Train appeared before the Senate Public Works Committee on March 1, 1974, Senator Muskie asked whether because of underfunding by the administration "we have abandoned any hopes that we can meet the deadlines established in the act, the performance deadlines established in the act, 1977–78 and 1983." Train replied that the reduction in the levels of funding "certainly are resulting in slowing down the program and deferring the accomplishments of these targets."

Besides the slowing down of the program because of impoundment, progress was also delayed because of administrative difficulties in using even the funds that had been allotted. Here we enter the world of "quasi-impoundments."

QUASI-IMPOUNDMENTS

As one court after another delivered blows to the administration, some members of Congress began to conclude that the impoundment dispute might be resolved once and for all by the courts. Let the litigation continue, they reasoned—a convenient proposition, since it eliminated the need for congressional action.

This strategy assumed that a single decision, announced from on high by the Supreme Court, would dispose of all the problems. But in case after case the courts avoided the larger constitutional questions, preferring to treat each dispute as one of statutory construction. Typically the central question was: Did the statute confer the discretionary authority claimed by the executive branch? Disposition of one case, therefore, had little bearing on other impoundments arising from different statutes. It was highly unlikely that the Supreme Court could (or would want to) devise a general remedy for the whole area, issuing a sweeping declaration either for or against that kind of executive power. In the absence of a general remedy, there would always be new statutory language, new questions of construction and congressional intent, and thus fresh opportunities for continued litigation.

Moreover, the courts were not in a position to administer the government. Federal judges cannot be expected to sit within the confines of an agency to supervise its operations. At some point, after Congress has passed its laws and the courts have handed down their judgments, a program needs implementation. That requires thousands of agency officials to draw up regulations, promulgate them, receive and process applications, and disburse funds to qualified recipients. In cases where the courts have ordered agencies to process applications and implement a program, judges necessarily relied on good-faith administrative efforts to carry out the program in accordance with statutory criteria and judicial directives.

The manner in which the Nixon administration impounded funds allowed courts to play a large role. Funds were withheld in an overt and public manner, with presidential documents at hand and administration justifications finely honed. But "quasi-impoundments" are more difficult to detect and to litigate. Programs can be delayed because of slow processing of applications, frequent change of agency regulations, rejection of applications for minor technical deficiencies, and many other administrative actions (or inactions). How does one know whether the resulting delays are inherent in the legislation, a deliberate effort by the administration to sabotage a program it did not want, or merely the by-product of normal bureaucratic problems? It is difficult for plaintiffs to contest actions that are so deeply imbedded in the administrative process.

The framers of the Clean Water Act had anticipated some of this problem. Section 101(f) of the legislation set the national policy that to the "maximum extent possible the procedures utilized for implementing this Act shall encourage the drastic minimization of paperwork and . . . prevent needless duplication and unnecessary delays at all levels of government." Still, the complexity of the legislation and its subsequent implementation by EPA produced the very paperwork and delay that the act had sought to avoid.

The procedures of the act necessitated a considerable amount of paperwork. For the purpose of encouraging the development of area-wide waste treatment management plans, the EPA administrator was required to publish guidelines in order to identify areas that had substantial water quality control problems. Those guidelines were to be published within

ninety days after enactment of the Clean Water Bill. After publication
of the guidelines, the governors of each state would have sixty days to
identify problem areas. Within another 120 days the governors were to
designate the boundaries of each area and the organization capable of
developing effective waste treatment management plans. In the case of
areas that involved more than one state, governors would have 180 days
to designate the boundaries and select the organization.

Not later than one year after their designation, the organizations were
to have in operation a planning process. Among other features, the plans
would identify the treatment works needed to meet the requirements
of the area over a twenty-year period, updating the list each year. The
initial plan was to be certified by the governor (or governors where
interstate areas were involved) and forwarded to EPA within two years
from the time the planning process was in operation.

Administrative complications began to surface during the early months
of 1973. Members of Congress, waiting for EPA to write regulations and
begin the process of approving applications, became concerned that the
clean-water program was being truncated not only by presidential impoundment but by agency delays. A subcommittee of the House Public
Works Committee held a hearing on June 14, 1973, to determine the
extent of the bureaucratic problem and what could be done to relieve it.
James Cleveland, Republican of New Hampshire and ranking minority
member on the subcommittee, protested that the president's impoundment had been augmented by "another little wrinkle in the program now
which for all intents and purposes has brought this thing to a screeching
halt."

Among those invited to testify at the hearing was Clarence Metcalf,
director of municipal services for the New Hampshire Water Supply and
Pollution Control Commission. He vigorously rejected the claim of the
administration that there was a shortage of contractor capability in the
country to carry out the clean-water legislation, even at the reduced pace
contemplated by the administration. He anticipated no shortage of qualified construction services. On a recent small project, about three-quarters
of a million dollars, sixteen contractors picked up bid documents. In the
past two years New Hampshire had never had a job where there were
fewer than five to six contractors bidding on a project. Metcalf predicted
that if the clean-water program were fully funded, at the $18-billion level
established by Congress, there would be sufficient contractual services in
the building field in his state to take care of any additional work.

Another member of the subcommittee, Kenneth Gray (D–Ill.), said
that many communities found themselves "between a rock and a hard
place." The EPA would issue a cease-and-desist order to force a community to stop polluting the waters, but when local officials applied to

EPA for money to construct waste treatment plants they were told that federal funds were not available.

The same House Public Works subcommittee held hearings in 1974, meeting on ten separate days between February 5 and July 16. Jim Wright of Texas, the chairman, announced that the subcommittee staff had informed him that "a proliferating array of galloping guidelines and changing directives from EPA has badly impeded the flow of even those funds which the president has released." One city had to rewrite its application nine times over a period of two years.

One official from Pennsylvania noted that under the 1965 water pollution control act, there were ten federal guidelines; under the 1972 legislation the number of guidelines and regulations leaped to 132. Another state official, from New York, told the subcommittee that he had planned to bring the rules and regulations to the hearings in a wheelbarrow, "but I just lost my courage when I saw them. I have a back problem, and after I lift so much, it throws it out." An official from the New England area computed that EPA had produced regulations, guidelines, and support reference material at a rate of approximately two pages per minute, or about double the average person's reading speed. EPA was churning out material faster than it could be read.

Congress relied on its watchdog agency, the General Accounting Office, but even there the results were uneven. Dr. Robert Sansom, an environmental consultant, told the Senate Public Works Committee on February 28, 1975: "The problem now is that the intervention of the Congress in the process has been largely by sending the GAO out to second-guess some bureaucrat who has made a decision about a grant, and to ask him why he did it that way, and most of these kinds of investigations have had the effect of scaring the people more than . . . of getting them to commit themselves to getting more money out." Senator Muskie added that Congress had tried to "prod every way we can, but words don't always seem to move bureaucracy."

IMPOUNDMENT CONTROL ACT OF 1974

Impoundment has been an executive practice from the earliest administrations. There is no difficulty in discovering early precedents. However, in an effort to lend respectability to its own actions, the Nixon administration misapplied those precedents. For example, officials in the administration took great delight in pointing out that President Jefferson had impounded $50,000 for gunboats. But that was a routine impoundment, not in the least bit threatening to the prerogatives of Congress. Jefferson explained that the "favorable and peaceable turn of affairs on the Mississippi rendered an immediate execution of that law unnecessary." Since the emergency contemplated by Congress failed to materialize, because of the Louisiana Purchase, Jefferson saw no reason to spend the money. Nor did any member of Congress. A year later, having taken the time to study the most recent models of gunboats, Jefferson informed Congress that he was proceeding with the program.

In what possible way does this episode relate to the Nixon impoundments? Jefferson's action was temporary, in contrast to decisions by President Nixon to terminate such programs as the Rural Environmental Assistance Program (REAP) and subsidized housing. Jefferson did not damage or curtail a program; Nixon used impoundment to cut in half the Clean Water Act. The routine action by Jefferson did not challenge the right of Congress to make policy and decide priorities; Nixon's behavior was a distinct threat. And lastly, Jefferson acted in response to a genuine change in events, a change which made unnecessary the immediate release of funds. The critical issues facing the country during the Nixon years—such as housing shortages and polluted water—did not disappear.

Faced with the unprecedented scope of impoundment under President Nixon, Congress enacted an impoundment reporting bill on October 27, 1972. The bill directed the president to report the following: the amount of funds impounded, the date the funds were ordered to be impounded, the date the funds were actually impounded, the departments involved, the period of time during which the funds were to be impounded, the reasons for impoundment, and the estimated fiscal, economic, and budgetary effects of impoundment.

The first report in response to this act announced $8.7 billion in "budgetary reserves." The report managed to leave out approximately $9 billion in other funds that had been impounded: $6 billion in clean-water funds (for fiscal 1973 and 1974), $441 million held back because of the housing moratorium, $382 million in proposed rescissions (requests to cancel budget authority), $1.9 billion withheld from the departments of Labor and Health, Education and Welfare, and $300 million for the farm disaster loan program.

How could the administration impound $6 billion in clean-water funds and not include that action in the impoundment report? The answer lies in the definition of contract authority, for in the context of the Clean Water Act it is "budget authority" that allows states to enter into obligations. But the states could not enter into obligations until the EPA administrator allotted the authority. From the standpoint of the Office of Management and Budget (OMB), the unallotted portion of $6 billion did not satisfy the technical definition either of contract authority or budget authority. By that reasoning, nothing existed to impound or place in reserve. The problem with this kind of reasoning is that Congress called for reports on *impoundment*, not "budgetary reserves," and no amount of technical distinctions could obscure the fact that clean-water funds had been impounded. To believe otherwise would be to assume that the courts were entertaining themselves with imaginary issues.

The coequal status of Congress as a branch of government was severely tested by the Nixon impoundments. In response, legislation was introduced in both houses to curb the president's power to withhold funds. On June 25, 1973, the House of Representatives passed legislation which allowed either house of Congress to disapprove an impoundment within sixty days. This was one of many examples of recent decades in which Congress turned the constitutional tables, allowing the president to initiate a policy but subjecting it to a "legislative veto."

The Senate adopted a different tack. It felt strongly that once Congress had passed an appropriation, and perhaps had to act again to override a veto, it should not have to act a third time to disapprove an impoundment. The Senate bill therefore required the funds to be released unless both houses supported the impoundment within sixty days. Thus, where the House of Representatives placed upon either the House or the Senate the responsibility for overturning an impoundment action, the Senate put the burden on the administration to enlist the support of both houses. In other words, the presumption of the House bill was in favor of impoundment, unless disapproved by one house. The presumption of the Senate bill was *against* impoundment, unless supported by both houses within a specified number of days. The conceptual and philosophical differences between the two bills were so substantial, with neither house willing to make concessions, that the legislation remained in a dormant state in conference committee.

During this suspended state of affairs Congress made progress with budget reform legislation. At the height of the furor over the $250 billion ceiling proposal, in the fall of 1972, Congress established a Joint Study Committee on Budget Control. The committee was directed to propose procedures for "improving congressional control over budgetary outlay and receipt totals" and to assure full coordination of an "overall view of each year's budgetary outlays" with an "overall view of the anticipated revenues for that year." An interim report of February 7, 1973, promised recommendations on impoundment, but the final report of April 18, 1973, was silent on that subject.

The general idea of congressional budget reform was to establish budget committees in each house and make them responsible for reporting a budget resolution in the spring. The resolution would establish tentative targets for outlays, budget authority, and revenues, including an appropriate surplus or deficit in light of economic conditions. The spring resolution would also divide the budget totals into large functional categories, such as National Defense, Commerce and Transportation, and Income Security. The purpose was to permit Congress to establish control not only over budget totals but also over budget priorities.

After passage of the initial budget resolution, Congress would proceed to act on individual appropriation bills and other legislation that affected budget authority and revenues. In the final month prior to the start of the new fiscal year (now changed to begin October 1, rather than July 1, to give Congress additional time), members would pass a second budget resolution, this time fixing binding totals. If a discrepancy existed between the second budget resolution and action on other bills involving appropriations and revenues, Congress would complete a reconciliation process.

At the heart of this process was a desire by members of Congress to reassert legislative control over budget priorities. Members from both houses began to realize that what had been done at budget resolution time could be undone later by impoundment. To preserve the shape of the budget, as passed by Congress, an impoundment title would have to be added to the budget reform legislation. But how could the House and Senate approaches, seemingly incompatible, be reconciled?

The impasse was broken by devising two types of impoundment: "deferral" (to be governed by the one-house veto) and "rescission" (requiring the support of both houses within forty-five days). A deferral was meant to be a temporary kind of impoundment; the administration intended to spend the money but not now. Rescission was a step which canceled budget authority; it was thus a permanent action.

The comptroller general of the General Accounting Office received major new responsibilities. As the auditing and investigative body of Congress, GAO was directed to monitor the impoundment actions of the president. If the comptroller general found that the president, the OMB director, or any other executive official impounded funds and failed to report the matter to Congress, the comptroller general would notify Congress. The report of the comptroller general would be received just as though it had come from the president. Thus, Congress would be free to disapprove it (in the case of a deferral) or let the forty-five-day period run out (in the case of a proposed rescission). Another responsibility of the comptroller general was to examine impoundment reports to see that they are correctly classified. If he determined that the president submitted an impoundment as a deferral, which was actually a proposed rescission, or vice versa, he could reclassify the action. Furthermore, if the administration failed to release funds in accordance with the procedures of the act, the comptroller general was authorized to bring suit in the U.S. District Court for the District of Columbia. Those were the main provisions of the Impoundment Control Act of 1974 (P.L. 93-344).

President Ford presented the first packet of proposed rescissions and deferrals, transmitting the messages to Congress on September 20, 1974. He notified the lawmakers that, in the opinion of the attorney general, the Impoundment Control Act applied "only to determinations to withhold budget authority which have been made since the law was approved" (July 12, 1974). Some of the impounded items were listed merely for the information of Congress, not for congressional ratification or disapproval. Those items, marked with an asterisk, included the deferral of $9 billion in clear-water funds—$3 billion withheld from each of the fiscal years 1973, 1974, and 1975.

This raised an issue that Congress had not anticipated. Did the Impoundment Control Act apply only to new impoundments, or was it retroactive? In an October 15 letter to Congress, Comptroller General Elmer B. Staats disagreed with the attorney general's interpretation. Staats maintained that the act *did* apply to deferrals made prior to the statute's enactment. He based his conclusion on two factors: a disclaimer in the act (nothing in the act was to be construed as ratifying or approving any prior impoundment) and the definition of deferral (which included executive action or inaction). The decision not to release the clean-water funds after July 12, 1974, represented an inaction by the administration.

But now that the issue was joined, who would resolve it? Administration officials said they would follow the interpretation of the attorney general. Congress, of course, sided with the comptroller general. But it is in the nature of coequal branches that the comptroller general could not force his decision upon the executive branch when the attorney general held to a different interpretation. The matter was ripe for the courts.

A number of legislators treated the deferral of clean-water funds as an action subject to congressional disapproval. Resolutions were introduced to disapprove the impoundment, but none was ever acted on. In fact, the administration received a measure of support from the GAO and the House Appropriations Committee. On October 15, 1974, the comptroller general advised Congress that the "inability to expend the [clean-water] funds effectively is a possibility." This was a practical judgment regarding the effect of releasing $9 billion, raising doubts as to the capability of EPA and the states to use the money, but it duplicated the misconception of Judge Hauk in the Los Angeles case. Expenditure (or even obligation) was not at issue. What was at stake was the *allotment* of contract authority so that states could enter into long-range planning and be confident of federal assistance.

The House Appropriations Committee also acted in a way to support the administration's deferral of clean-water funds. During hearings on November 21, 1974, Congressman Jamie Whitten, chairman of the appropriations subcommittee on Agriculture-Environmental and Consumer

Protection, criticized the Clean Water Act as "probably the prime example of how far and wide of the mark an authorizing committee will go and what the Appropriations Committee is willing to match in dollars and cents." His protest was directed at the back-door method (contract authority) by which Congress had circumvented the Appropriations Committee. When funds had to be appropriated later to liquidate the obligations, the committee's role was perfunctory. It was denied an opportunity to control the level of the program. Whitten said that the authorization committees (in this case the Public Works Committees) "had no doggoned relationship to what we could appropriate with the resources available."

The House Appropriations Committee reported a rescission bill on November 26, 1974, accepting some of the proposed rescissions by President Ford but rejecting the major items. The report also chose to comment on deferrals, even though no impoundment resolution—the vehicle for disapproving deferrals—was before the House of Representatives. The comments could be described as a form of legislative dicta in the sense that they were not necessary for the rescission bill.

Nevertheless, the report listed eight deferrals "accepted" by the committee, including $9 billion in clean-water funds. A footnote to the table explained: "Committee has been assured of *immediate* release of such funds as can be effectively utilized to increase employment and protect the environment and accepts the deferral only because of such assurances." The Clean Water Act was now characterized as a type of anti-recession measure, with funds released to stimulate the economy. That was never part of the original intent. Moreover, the language in the report overlooked the need for full allotment of clean-water funds as a necessary step for long-range planning by states. The issue of full allotment, at least, was laid to rest by the Supreme Court's decision of February 18, 1975.

CONCLUSION

A large factor at stake in the impoundment controversy was the ability of Congress to delegate power. If Congress can delegate broad grants of discretionary authority, without having the discretion abused, administrators are able to adapt to changing circumstances and carry out the purposes of legislation more effectively. But when flexibility in a statute is used to frustrate congressional policy, the lesson for members of Congress is to confine executive action, to restrict administrators to narrow statutory details.

That point was brought home forcefully in 1973 when EPA administrator Ruckelshaus appeared before the Ervin impoundment hearings.
Senator Muskie complained that Congress had given EPA some flexibility in carrying out a difficult piece of legislation, only to have that flexibility used to cut in half a legislative commitment. The administration's
action, Muskie warned, was "just a temptation to Congress to be more
inflexible, not more flexible in the future." Then he added:

> Having in mind the devious motives that you pursued to undercut
> the purposes of the Congress, I could now write better language and
> believe me, I will. Believe me, I will.
>
> The clear language and debate was what we were giving you, is
> what we understood to be legitimate administrative discretion to
> spend the money, not defeat the purposes. Then to have you twist
> it as you have, is a temptation to this Senator to really handcuff you
> the next time.

The extraordinary and unprecedented use of impoundment by the
Nixon administration left Congress with the choice of fighting back or
having its power over the purse impaired, perhaps permanently. Congress could not allow the president to justify impoundment on the grounds
of combating inflation and higher taxes. Those policy objectives, attractive though they may be, do not stand alone. Constitutional government
depends on more than the pursuit of desirable goals. More fundamental
than goals are the means employed. Who sets the goals? What standards
and procedures shall be devised to ensure that public policy is built
upon the law rather than administrative convenience? The response to
those questions was the Impoundment Control Act of 1974.

For all its trappings of conservatism and "strict constructionism," the
Nixon administration never demonstrated an understanding of what lies
at the heart of the political system: a respect for procedure, a sense of
comity and trust between the branches, an appreciation of limits and
boundaries. Used with restraint and circumspection, impoundment was
a viable instrument, capable of being used on occasion without precipitating a crisis. But restraint was replaced by abandon, precedent stretched
past the breaking point, and statutory authority pushed beyond legislative
intent.

Without good-faith efforts and integrity on the part of executive officials, the custom of delegation, discretion, and nonstatutory controls must
be abandoned. The consequences for public policy, implementation, and
program effectiveness are profound. Long after the impeachment proceedings and the resignation of Richard Nixon, the practical need for good-faith
efforts on the part of administrative officials was being felt.

BIBLIOGRAPHY

Fisher, Louis. *Presidential Spending Power*. Princeton, N.J.: Princeton University Press, 1975. Covers the growth of presidential budgeting and the various types of discretionary spending powers available to executive officials. In both cloth and paperback editions.

Schick, Allen. "Budget Reform Legislation: Reorganizing Congressional Centers of Fiscal Power," *Harvard Journal on Legislation* (February 1974): 303–50. Analysis of the executive-legislative conflicts that led to enactment of the Congressional Budget and Impoundment Control Act of 1974.

U.S. Congress. *Impoundment of Appropriated Funds by the President,* Joint Hearings before the Senate Committees on Government Operations and on the Judiciary, 93d Cong., 1st sess. (1973). Provides essential background material and documents from executive agencies.

———. *A Legislative History of the Water Pollution Control Act Amendments of 1972,* a committee print prepared for the use of the Senate Committee on Public Works, 93d Cong., 1st sess. (1973). A two-volume collection of committee reports, floor debate, and other parts of the legislative history.

———. *Court Challenges to Executive Branch Impoundments of Appropriated Funds,* cumulative to March 15, 1974. Special report of the Joint Committee on Congressional Operations, 93d Cong. 2d sess. (1974). Reprints forty-five court decisions involving impoundment of agriculture, education, health, water pollution control, and other funds.

———. *Analysis of Executive Impoundment Reports,* a committee print prepared by the Senate Committee on the Budget, 94th Cong., 1st sess. (1975). Includes the impoundment proposals of President Ford and a committee critique.

Wildavsky, Aaron. *The Politics of the Budgetary Process,* 2d ed. Boston: Little, Brown, 1975. Standard study on the strategies employed by agencies as they seek funds from Congress. In paperback.

Supreme Court Voting Behavior
A Comparison of the Warren and Burger Courts
Richard E. Johnston

During the 1968 presidential campaign Richard Nixon expressed dissatisfaction with the United States Supreme Court, blaming its decisions, in part, for the increase in "law and order" problems faced by the nation. What the Court needed, Nixon believed, was justices who would not inject their own social and economic beliefs into decisions, but who would narrowly construe the law in terms of the Constitution. Throughout his presidency Nixon went to great lengths to nominate and obtain Senate confirmation of such "strict constructionists" to vacated seats on the Court. After the Senate's stinging rejection of the nominations of Harold Carswell and Clement Haynesworth, two Southern Republicans who had supported Senator Barry Goldwater in the 1964 presidential race, Nixon did secure the appointments of Harry Blackmun as associate justice and Warren Burger as chief justice, both Minnesotans and Republicans. During their first months on the bench in the latter part of 1970 and most of 1971, the voting behavior of Blackmun and Burger was so consistent that they became known as the "Minnesota Twins." But, more importantly, their votes, when added to those of fellow Republicans John Marshall Harlan and Potter Stewart (occasionally joined by Democrat Byron White), produced marked changes in the direction of the Court's decisions, particularly in contrast with the period immediately preceding their appointment. Nixon's strategy appeared to be succeeding.

This success in altering the direction of the Court can be demonstrated by some examples. In *Dutton* v. *Evans*, 91 S. Ct. 210 (1970), Burger, Blackmun, Stewart, and Harlan (all Republicans) were joined by Justice

Byron White in a decision which ruled that the Georgia co-conspirator
hearsay exception did not violate the confrontation of witnesses clause
of the Sixth Amendment (as applied to the states by the due process
clause of the Fourteenth Amendment), even though it did not coincide
with the federal rule, and would not be permitted in federal prosecutions.
Four Democrats, William O. Douglas, William J. Brennan, Thurgood
Marshall, and Hugo L. Black, in dissent pointed out that this judicial retreat was in direct contradiction to two 1965 decisions of the Court.

The best example of the emerging negative majority occurred in *United
States* v. *Arizona*, 91 S. Ct. 260 (1970). Congress, in 1970, had legislated
to reduce the legal minimum voting age for both national and state
elections to eighteen. The legislation raised some interesting constitutional questions. The Constitution says nothing at all about state elections,
although the Fifteenth Amendment prohibits racial discrimination in such
elections, and the Nineteenth Amendment prohibits sex discrimination.
The only other possible constitutional basis on which Congress could
legislate age requirements for state elections would be the Fourteenth
Amendment prohibitions against states denying "persons" due process of
law or equal protection of the law. Since due process seems to be a kind
of shorthand statement of "fundamental fairness," could one logically
argue that it was fundamentally unfair not to let eighteen-year-old persons vote? If so, why not seventeen-year-olds? And since "equal protection" has been interpreted as meaning "no arbitrary classification" of
persons, is a classification of eighteen, nineteen, or twenty-year-olds any
less arbitrary than a classification of twenty-one-year-olds?

The Constitution does, however, give Congress the power to set the
"Time, Place, and Manner" of holding federal elections, and the Congress
has, beginning in 1842, legislated broadly and often in respect to federal
elections. Among the topics of such legislation were acts related to false
registration, bribery, voting without legal right, making false returns of
votes cast, interference with voting rights, appointment of federal regis-
trars and judges, and election of representatives by districts. The courts
had never invalidated such legislation, although in 1876 the Supreme
Court had declared such legislation aimed at municipal elections to be
beyond the power of the Reconstruction Congress.

Faced with this Constitution, and this history, the four Republicans on
the Court said that Congress had no power to set age requirements in
any election, whether national or state, while four Democrats (Douglas,
Brennan, Marshall, and White) argued that Congress had full authority to
set age requirements whether the elections concerned were national or
state ones. One Democrat, Hugo Black, became the swing man by voting
that Congress did have authority over federal elections, but that it had no
such authority over state elections. Thus, by a vote of 5 to 4, eighteen-

year-olds received the right to vote in national elections, and by an identical vote of 5 to 4, they were refused that right in state elections. As a consequence of this interesting result, constitutional scholars were quick to point out that perhaps Black had become confused by actually reading the Constitution!

More seriously, perhaps nowhere else in the world would a court have come up with such a decision as the American Supreme Court did in this case. The primary reason is that no other supreme court has sufficient independent political stature to actually (and successfully) oppose social, economic, and particularly political policies of the executive and legislative branches of its government. Even in those nations where the highest court has great power, such as Canada and Australia, judicial policy autonomy (as pointed out by Glendon Schubert) has been negative rather than positive, and selective and episodic rather than general and continual. In contrast, the American Supreme Court's intervention in the political system has been, at least for the past fifty years, positive, general, and continual. If one examines such national policy issues as racial equality, due process of law for criminal defendants, religious tolerance, right to privacy, legislative reapportionment, the rights of women and of the poor, free speech and press, and even civic equality, it becomes all too apparent that it is the Supreme Court, not the Congress or the presidency, which has been the foremost proponent and active catalyst of change.

The Constitution says that the judicial power of the United States "shall be vested in one supreme Court, and in such inferior Courts as the Congress may from time to time ordain and establish." The result of the constitutional command and the subsequent actions of Congress in establishing "inferior" courts is a national judiciary with a three-tiered pyramidal structure. At the bottom of the pyramid are the ninety-four federal district courts, each staffed by from one to twenty-seven judges. The district courts are the actual trial courts (with juries deciding questions of "fact") in the federal judicial system and almost all federal cases originate in these courts.

A disappointed claimant in the district court usually has the right to have a decision reviewed by one of the United States circuit courts of appeal, which are the intermediate courts in the pyramid. There are eleven such courts, each staffed by from three to fifteen judges. There are no trials and no juries at the circuit court level. Most decisions are on questions of the meaning of law, rather than on the truth of disputed facts. The great majority of cases are decided by three-judge panels, although on occasion the entire group will be empaneled. In addition to hearing appeals from the district courts, the circuits also review actions of several federal administrative agencies for errors of law.

At the apex of the judicial pyramid is the Supreme Court. Early ex-periments with the number of justices (as few as five and as many as ten) were made by Congress, but since the 1860s there have always been nine, except for temporary reductions in staff due to death or resignation. The importance of the Supreme Court is that it is the final arbiter of the mean-ing of law and of the Constitution. While the Congress can straighten out the Court's rulings as to the meaning of congressional legislation, decisions on the meaning of the Constitution can only be altered by the Court's changing its decision at a later date, or by the constitutional amending process. For this reason American presidents have been quite concerned (as was Mr. Nixon) with using the appointive process to at-tempt to fix or alter policy as enunciated by the Court.

Justices at all three levels go through the same "formal" method of appointment. The president presents nominations to the Senate, and if the Senate confirms by a majority vote, the candidate may be appointed. Time and tradition have added some nonconstitutional steps of interest. At the district court level the senator (or senators) of the president's own political party suggest candidates (usually three) for a vacancy in his state. The practice of "senatorial courtesy" virtually assures the defeat of a nominee by the Senate if the president should submit a name other than one on the nominating senator's list. In the absence of senators from the president's own party, the president may ask for suggestions from the representative from the district where the vacancy occurred, but ac-tually has much more freedom to choose a nominee independently.

The practice from this point on is the same for nominations to each of the three levels. The American Bar Association makes its recommenda-tions based on an assessment of "legal competency," and the FBI exam-ines the private life of the nominee. The attorney general's office usually finds itself with the responsibility of assessing the "political" inclinations of the candidate. All the information is passed on to the president, who then (if he has not changed his mind) submits the name of the nominee to the Senate. The Senate Judiciary Committee then holds hearings on the fitness of the nominee, at which witnesses testify for or against him. The hearings may be completely routine, taking a few moments (as is the case for most district court judges), or may involve long debate. In the case of the first John Marshall Harlan, for example, a bitter but unsuccess-ful effort to block his nomination resulted in forty-one days of acrimonious debate on his fitness (read: political opinions on the issues of the day). The importance of the appointments cannot be overstated, for at all three levels, they are for "good behavior," which means for life, subject only to the impeachment process. No Supreme Court or circuit judge has ever been impeached and convicted, and only three district judges have been removed from office by that process. There are some special courts in the federal system, such as the court of claims, the customs court, the court of customs and patent appeals, the tax court, and the court of military appeals, but they are of lesser importance. In the three-tiered system under discussion there are presently more than 650 justices, including some 100 in the circuit courts, more than 450 in the district courts, and the nine members of the Supreme Court. The political nature of the presidential appointments to this highest-level court is obvious from table 1, which shows that of the twenty-one members who served on the Warren and Burger Courts, seventeen (or 81 percent) were appointed from the president's own political party.

Supreme Court justices sometimes do resign, but most serve very long terms. Of the Court's 100 members since 1789, 20 percent have served twenty years or more, and more than 10 percent have served more than thirty years. Justice Oliver Wendell Holmes sat through his ninetieth year, and Associate Justice William O. Douglas reluctantly retired because of ill health in his thirty-sixth year as a Supreme Court justice. In our entire history there have not yet been three times as many Supreme Court judges as there have been presidents, despite the number of judges serving at the same time (never less than five, and nine for more than 100 years). This tenure, coupled with the fact that the number of judges is high enough that the addition of a single judge can seldom have great impact on decisions rendered, gives the Court the possibility of a policy continuity that neither the president nor Congress can match. Because of this, more effort has been made to examine the policy making of the American Supreme Court than that of any other high national court.

Much material is available for those who wish to study the decisions of the Court. Most of the cases which the Court examines arise either from appeals from any of the more than ninety U.S. district courts, or from the very large number of suits which begin in any of the state judicial systems and which, because they involve either federal questions or suits between citizens of diverse judicial jurisdictions, may be successfully appealed to the Supreme Court. Of the hundreds of thousands of such cases which begin at these lower levels, some four thousand a year currently are presented to the Supreme Court, and from this number the Court chooses some two or three hundred cases in which it will hear arguments and make decisions. This may in some respect limit the Court's political activity to the demands of the actual litigation which arises (because the course of its business lies beyond its immediate control), but the limit is more illusory than real. No people of any nation press so many questions of law and the Constitution before their courts. Many scholars have noted the excess legalism of any federal system, and this has been compounded by rapidly changing conditions and altered political, economic, and social requirements demanding continuous adjustments in the

Table 1
Members of the Warren and Burger Supreme Courts

Justice	Party affiliation	State	Term appointed	Appointed by	Presidential party affiliation	Member Warren Court	Member Burger Court
Hugo Black	D	Ala.	1937	Roosevelt	D	Yes	Yes
Stanley Reed	D	Ky.	1938	Roosevelt	D	Yes	No
Felix Frankfurter	I	Ind.	1939	Roosevelt	D	Yes	No
William O. Douglas	D	Conn.	1939	Roosevelt	D	Yes	Yes
Robert Jackson	D	N.Y.	1941	Roosevelt	D	Yes	No
Harold Burton	R	Ohio	1945	Truman	D	Yes	No
Tom Clark	D	Tex.	1949	Truman	D	Yes	No
Sherman Minton	D	Ind.	1949	Truman	D	Yes	No
Earl Warren	R	Calif.	1953	Eisenhower	R	Yes	No
John M. Harlan	R	N.Y.	1955	Eisenhower	R	Yes	Yes
William Brennan	D	N.J.	1956	Eisenhower	R	Yes	Yes
Charles Whittaker	R	Mo.	1957	Eisenhower	R	Yes	No
Potter Stewart	R	Ohio	1958	Eisenhower	R	Yes	Yes
Arthur Goldberg	D	Ill.	1962	Kennedy	D	Yes	No
Byron White	D	Colo.	1962	Kennedy	D	Yes	Yes
Abe Fortas	D	Tenn.	1965	Johnson	D	Yes	No
Thurgood Marshall	D	N.Y.	1967	Johnson	D	Yes	Yes
Warren Burger	R	Minn.	1969	Nixon	R	No	Yes
Harry Blackmun	R	Minn.	1970	Nixon	R	No	Yes
Lewis Powell	D	Va.	1972	Nixon	R	No	Yes
William Rehnquist	R	Ariz.	1972	Nixon	R	No	Yes

formal use of power. The ever more centralized control demanded by modern-day requirements necessitates a concentration of power that runs counter to the accepted requisites of pluralistic and community-oriented policy making, and the industrialization and urbanization of America have created threats to traditional civil liberties in the effort to ensure safety to all. At all stages of the policy struggles which have been precipitated, the Court has been the final arbiter.

But when twentieth-century social scientists began to examine the judicial process and attempt to understand and explain it, they found themselves faced with some formidable obstacles. From the beginning, members of the legal profession, and particularly members of the Supreme Court itself, had surrounded the entire judicial process with a number of fallacious beliefs. Perhaps the oldest and most pernicious was that judges do not make law. Even John Marshall, who perhaps as much as any judge in the Court's history made the Constitution what he wanted it to be, never admitted that he was doing so. He insisted that "Courts are the mere instruments of the law, and can will nothing. . . . Judicial power is never exercised for the purpose of giving effect to the will of the Judge; always for the purpose of giving effect to the will of the Legislature." A century or so of such rhetoric was responsible for the development of this myth of mechanical jurisprudence, which in its clearest sense simply means that judges are automatons (or worse yet, clerks or mechanics) who have no discretion but merely apply "law" and find answers to political questions. Justice Roberts perhaps expressed it best in *United States* v. *Butler*, 297 U.S. 62 (1936), when he said:

> When an act of Congress is appropriately challenged in the courts as not conforming to the constitutional mandate, the judicial branch of the Government has only one duty—to lay the article of the Constitution which is invoked beside the statute which is challenged to decide whether the latter squares with the former.

The only way to accept this myth is to believe, first, that judges really have no discretion, and second, that they are neutral. While it is generally true that judges have no particular partiality as to which litigant wins a particular law suit, it is quite unrealistic to believe that judges do not have feelings with respect to the major competing principles of law, or that they do not have perceptions of what constitutes a better political or social order, or as to which particular economic order best fits their own or the nation's needs.

A second belief which developed (probably as an attempt to cover up the fact that the first belief was a myth) was that the Constitution actually gives clear and precise answers to all legal questions that arise. Oliver Wendell Holmes, in an effort to dispel this myth, once stated that the

Supreme Court never got any questions that the Constitution really answered, because such questions were so easily disposed of at the lower court levels. He insisted that the Supreme Court only got "hard" cases in which experience, not law, provided the answers. To any student of the Constitution, it is obvious that this second belief is also fallacious. The Fourth Amendment prevents "unreasonable" searches and seizures, but what exactly is the definition of "unreasonable"? The First Amendment prohibits infringements on freedom of speech and press, but does it protect symbolic speech, electronic speech, obscene speech, or motion pictures? What is a "Republican form of Government"? Government can take your life, liberty, or property only with "due process of law," but not even the Court has ever been in agreement as to what that means. No state may deny any person "equal protection of the law," but abnormals, criminals, and children are surely persons, and did the Constitution intend to grant them such rights as voting, marriage, and holding public office? The fact is that the Supreme Court is really in "continuous constitutional convention" in respect to the important policy questions which are regularly presented to it. And because their decisions do vitally affect not only the litigants involved but also the general conditions under which public policies operate, it is important to understand what the judges of the Supreme Court do and, if possible, to determine why they do what they do.

Thus, if social scientists were actually to examine and understand the judicial process, newer tools of analysis had to be developed. The early twentieth century saw the development of "legal realism," which gradually began to replace the abstract analysis and superficial description that had characterized legal study previously. Legal realists such as Edward S. Corwin, Robert E. Cushman, and Thomas Reed Powell refused to accept the postulate that judges were simply technicians who "discovered" the law, and instead asserted that they were really value-laden and policy-oriented participants in the ongoing political process. They insisted that litigation, particularly that which came before the Supreme Court, was but a part of the total political struggle between competing economic, social, or political opponents, and that the results often were the by-product of the personal values of the members of the Court. From that time to this, there has been an ever-accelerating effort to identify those personal values and to determine what factors were important in socializing particular judges into the value patterns they held.

Since Charles Grove Haines, in the early 1920s outlined a set of factors which he believed likely to affect judicial voting behavior, there has been some agreement that judicial background affects judicial decision making. But it was forty years before anyone began a really systematic effort to determine the effect of social background factors on judicial voting behavior. In the early 1960s John Schmidhauser published a number of articles, mostly in law reviews, which shed some light in the area. He was able to demonstrate that sectional and party identifications were related to voting behavior, at least as it concerned sectionally devisive issues. An additional study showed some relationship between individual tendencies to dissent on the one hand, and a willingness to change, to reverse, or to abandon *stare decisis* (past decisions) on the other, and certain social background factors.

Also in the sixties, Stuart Nagel published several articles (later collected and reprinted in his book *The Legal Process from a Behavioral Perspective*) which demonstrated relationships between voting behavior and background characteristics, using as his sample a large number of American appellate court judges. He discovered clear relationships between behavior and such characteristics as party affiliation, religious preference, ethnic derivation, and even membership in the American Bar Association. An interesting point was the relationship he was able to establish between former occupation as a prosecutor and voting negatively in criminal procedure cases. Even earlier than this, Glendon Schubert and Sidney Ulmer had shown the role of party affiliation to be an important variable in voting behavior on the Michigan Supreme Court. Kenneth Vines also explored the party affiliation variable in his 1964 article entitled "Federal District Judges and Race Relations Cases in the South."

Other attempts were generally less successful. Sheldon Goldman's study of the United States courts of appeals showed a relationship between party affiliation and voting in cases involving economics, but in other areas the relationship was so vague that Goldman downgraded his own findings. Goldman also tested a number of demographic variables, but without success. When Kenneth Dolbeare attempted to replicate Nagel's findings, using a number of New York courts, he failed to find any significant relationships between ethnic derivation or party affiliation and voting behavior in any but very narrow partisan issues. John Sprague then examined the voting behavior of American Supreme Court judges over the seventy-year period from 1889 to 1959. Using "federalism" as the issue, he examined blocks of judges, but was unable to find any background variable that helped discriminate between such blocks. In 1969 David Adamany examined the voting behavior of the Wisconsin Supreme Court justices. The study showed that political party affiliation, taken alone, did not even divide the judges on the same kinds of issues that Ulmer had found divided the judges on the Michigan Supreme Court. And when E. Lindstrom, using a different methodology but the same data base as Sprague, found that there were positive correlations between Su-

preme Court justices' backgrounds and their voting behavior, where
Sprague had been unable to find any such correlations, it became evident
that methodology might be the cause of some of the conflicting results.

The problem seemed to be that even those studies which found relationships did not demonstrate the worth or value of such variables as
predictors of judicial voting behavior. Finally Don Bowen, replicating
Nagel's study of appellate court judges, asked not only whether there
were significant variables, but also to what extent those variables actually
accounted for or explained the variance in voting behavior. Bowen chose
as his method partial and multiple regression. These are statistical techniques which allow one to determine the direction and the extent of predictability between a dependent variable and two or more independent
variables, even though the independent variables themselves may be in-
terrelated. The result is that correlations between variables can be expressed in percentage figures, and Bowen was able to show that six social
background variables were able to account from some 20 to 33 percent of
the variance in voting behavior he found. If Karl Deutsch was correct in
stating that "anyone who suggests a variable explaining an additional 10
percent of the variance has made a contribution to political theory," then
Bowen's work was worthwhile.

Sidney Ulmer then reconsidered some of Schmidhauser's work on dissent behavior and was able to find four background factors, which as
variables were capable of correctly predicting almost 70 percent of the
Supreme Court justices' voting on the single issue of "reputation as a dis-
senter/no reputation as a dissenter." In the late 1960s and early 1970s an
increasing number of political scientists turned their attention to the
judges in other national courts in an effort to determine whether methods
used or relationships discovered in this nation were valid elsewhere.
David Danelski, James Dator, and Takeyoshi Kawashima studied the
Japanese supreme court, while George Gadbois worked with the supreme
court of India. Fred Morrison examined the Swiss federal court, while
Glendon Schubert and Richard Johnston studied the Australian high
court. Abelardo Samonte and C. Neal Tate did social background studies
of members of the Philippine courts.

Perhaps because of the conflicting nature of the results from so many
of the studies, both in the United States and abroad, many students of
judicial behavior came to agree with Glendon Schubert, who had finally
concluded that the voting behavior of judges, particularly those on the
American Supreme Court, could only be explained by "individual ideology," not by an examination of social, economic, or educational background factors. To many, however, this seemed the easy way out, for
almost anything could be hidden by, or subsumed under, the heading
"ideology." In fact, what all these scholars had been attempting to do

all those years was to examine factors in order to determine which of them were paramount in socializing particular judges into individual "ideological" molds.

My own study of the Court's voting behavior began as an effort to determine whether all the proper factors had really been examined. My first decision was to re-examine the Schmidhauser variables because they were the most exhaustive list available. Another decision was to use the individual case or decision as the unit of analysis, and to take advantage of the work of Glendon Schubert and his graduate students, who had actually read and coded on IBM cards and tape all the nonunanimous decisions of the Warren Court for its entire sixteen-year period. This material was available from the Inter-University Consortium for Political Research. The cards indicated the case itself, with one card for each decision, the subject matter of the case, the disposition (negative or affirmative) of the case, the justices who participated in the decision, and how each individual justice voted, again, negatively or affirmatively. The use of nonunanimous decisions only does not mean that unanimous decisions are unimportant; in fact, almost the first decision of the Warren Court (*Brown* v. *Topeka,* 347 U.S. 483 [1954]—the original school desegregation case) and the last decision of the current Burger Court (*United States* v. *Nixon,* 94 S. Ct. 3090 [1974]—the presidential tapes case) were unanimous decisions, and no one could question their importance. What it does mean is that cases were chosen where justices could and *did* choose differently from competing policy alternatives. If one wishes to examine the *differences* in voting behavior, there is little point in using cases where everyone is in agreement. One is still left with a significant number of cases, for during many of the Warren years as many as two-thirds of the decisions of the Court were nonunanimously decided.

An additional decision was made to limit the study to cases concerned with "civil rights" and with "economic" practices, two areas which comprise the bulk of the Court's work, in terms of both the numbers of cases and the national importance of the issues raised. Schubert had described the civil rights area as that category which includes any case where the claimant posed as the major question the issue of personal freedom, which included not only claims to freedom as a substantive value, but also claims concerning the procedures used relative to the substantive claims. The category included First Amendment claims relating to free speech, press, religion, assembly, and association, Fourth-through-Eighth-Amendment claims relating to searches and seizures and fair trial procedures, and racial equality claims relating to the Fourteenth and Fifteenth Amendments. Of course state cases relating to the Fourteenth Amendment due process and equal protection clauses make up the bulk of the cases. No effort was made to substantively or subjectively arrive at the merit of a claim, whatever the area. If a claim was made that a civil right had been violated, a yes vote was an affirmative vote for civil rights, and a no vote was a negative vote in the area. By the same token, if the Court majority favored the claim that a right had been violated, the case itself was scored as an affirmative vote for civil rights. The specific categories of civil rights used by Schubert included fair procedure, voting equality, political freedom, religious freedom, racial equality, right to privacy, and civil equality.

The "economic" practices area is primarily concerned with legal conflicts between the "haves" and the "have-nots." Included are disputes between unions and management, workers against employers, and small business people against major corporations. The two specific categories used by Schubert are "pro-union," and "pro-economic underdog." Exactly as in the civil rights area, a vote in favor of the claim of the union or the economic underdog is scored as an affirmative vote, while a vote against the claim is scored as negative. Schubert used an additional category called "liberal" to describe the votes of justices which favored both the civil rights and economic underdog claims, and one called "conservative" to describe the votes against such claims. The words "liberal" and "conservative" have come to have such pejorative connotations of late that their use is not continued in this study. Decisions, votes, and justices are merely stated to be "affirmative" or "negative" in their relationship to the claims.

The fifteen original background factors used by Schmidhauser, which were to be used as the independent or "predictor" variables, could not be used in their original form. For example, Schmidhauser's religious variables was subdivided into all the various religious affiliations of all members of the Court, and included Catholic, Jewish, Baptist, Unitarian, and so on. In regression analysis, it is necessary to convert such variables into categories which clearly indicate the presence of some property as opposed to its absence. Thus the religious variable must be "dichotomized," which produces such variables as "Protestant/non-Protestant" or "Catholic/non-Catholic." The original variables included ethnic origin, political occupation, judicial experience, religious affiliation, region of birth, occupation, type of lawyer, humble or other origin, legal education, parents' occupation and education, parents' political party, nonlegal education, size of town from, and others. Dichotomizing these variables produced such results as "Anglo-Saxon/non–Anglo-Saxon," "Ivy League law school/non–Ivy League law school," "father in politics/father not in politics," "corporation lawyer/other type lawyer." One of the variables, "political occupation," had originally been subdivided into such categories as federal executive career, federal legislative career, and federal judicial career. Examination proved that the most usual federal executive career of members of the Supreme Court had been as United States attorney general or assistant attorney general, or United States solicitor general. Dichotomizing the variable produced "prior service as federal attorney general, assistant attorney general, or solicitor general/no such prior service." Federal judicial career became "prior service as federal judge/no prior service as federal judge." Party affiliation became "Democrat/non-Democrat," which provided nicely for Justice Felix Frankfurter, who insisted throughout his long life that he was neither Democrat nor Republican, but a political Independent.

Once all the variables were dichotomized, and the votes dichotomized in the same manner (yes/no), the Schubert cases were all subjected to the Bowen methodology (multiple linear regression), and a finding resulted that was most interesting when compared with patterns of past investigation. Only three background factors accounted for 67.81 percent of the variation in Supreme Court voting behavior for the entire sixteen-year period. The correlation between these factors and variance in voting behavior was thus remarkably high, considering the broad range of issues covered by the study. The three factors were *"Democrat/non-Democrat," "prior service as federal judge/no prior service,"* and *"prior service as high federal prosecutor/no prior service."* Subsequent experimentation proved that virtually identical results were produced if the two occupational variables were combined into the single variable *"prior service as federal judge or high federal prosecutor/no prior service."*

Several questions were raised by the findings. First, if Supreme Court justices who had previously been lower-court federal judges voted differently from those without this background, why—and in what way—did their votes differ? Schmidhauser had recognized that this factor could be important and had discussed in some detail the views of President Eisenhower, Senator Smathers, and others that requiring Supreme Court judges to have prior high-level judicial experience was desirable. Schmidhauser had postulated that individuals possessing such experience would be more likely to develop attitudes of restraint and would possibly make decisions based more upon "law and precedent" than upon their perceptions of the political, social, and economic needs of the moment. He had pointed out that almost 25 percent of Supreme Court justices had had extensive judicial service prior to appointment, and that they had almost uniformly been strong ideological partisans. Senator Talmadge (whose Senate record proved him to be strongly negative in his response to the kinds of issues this study is examining) had even introduced Senate bill 1184 into the Eighty-fifth Congress, and that Bill would have provided that

no person shall be appointed after the date of enactment of this
paragraph to the office of Chief Justice of the United States or to
the office of Associate Justice of the Supreme Court unless, at the
time of his appointment, he has had at least five years of judicial
service . . . as an Associate Justice of the Supreme Court, a judge
of a court of appeals or district court of the United States, or judge
of the highest court of a State.

Perhaps Senator Talmadge would have partially failed had the bill become law, for the variable "prior service as high *state* judge/no prior
service" had produced no statistically significant relationship with voting
behavior. A possible explanation might be not only that a federal lower-
court judge with strongly developed partisan attitudes could act upon
those attitudes because of his life-tenured position, but that he would
have no reason to change those attitudes in his voting on the Supreme
Court, which is also a life-tenured job. Evan Evans, in his "Political In-
fluences in the Selection of Federal Judges," had pointed out as early as
1948 that appointment to an inferior federal court had generally been in
the nature of political rewards for obvious and sometimes notorious partisan aspirants who could not remain aloof from party or ideological issues. On the other hand, most state judges are elected, and must consistently and consciously please an electorate. Doing so may be a cover
for real feelings and attitudes which, if expressed, might result in defeat.
Such persons, after moving to a nonelective and life-tenured position on
the Supreme Court, might very well let their real attitudes and feelings
be reflected in changed judicial voting patterns.

The voting behavior of those whose prior occupation had been in the
prosecutorial field seems even more obviously related to the nature of
that occupation. Nagel had found a significant relationship between that
occupation and negative voting in criminal justice cases. It does not seem
unreasonable that those who daily deal with persons accused of criminal
behavior should view the claims of those facing criminal prosecution
with a less sympathetic attitude than those who have never directly or
personally dealt with lawbreakers. Many members of the Supreme Court
have simply no experience in criminal law matters before coming to the
Court, where what experience they gain is as appellate judges, never personally facing either defendants or witnesses. It was Justice Frankfurter
who once remarked that, however unfortunate it was, most persons accused of crime were guilty and not really very nice people. Schubert had
even pointed out that Justice Jackson had become measurably more conservative toward civil liberties claims after his experience as prosecutor
at Nuremberg.

The party identification variable had not proven very useful in most of
the studies previously made when the issue was a civil liberties one; how-

ever, there was some reason to believe that if it really accounted for much of the variation in voting on the Supreme Court, it would follow much the same lines that party identification had followed in recent years in voting in the Congress. The supposition was that Democrats on the Court would favor civil rights claims, just as non-Southern Democrats in the House and Senate supported (for the most part) legislation favoring or extending civil rights. Similarly, the assumption that non-Democrats would generally be less sympathetic to civil rights claims reflected the voting of non-Democrats in Congress.

In regard to economic matters, various scholars, such as Sheldon Goldman, had discovered some relationship between party affiliation and voting, with Democrats generally exhibiting sympathy for the claims of labor against management, and of the economic underdog's claims against big business. Congressional voting seemed to have followed much the same pattern. Using these kinds of findings, certain hypotheses were set up before the study proceeded further. If there was a difference in voting behavior based upon the two variables, certain things should be predictable. Hypothesis 1 stated that in the field of civil rights, Democrats on the Court would demonstrate marked partiality toward the claims that a civil right had been violated, and conversely, that non-Democrats would favor the claims of government rather than the individual. Hypothesis 2 stated that those with no prior service as federal judge or high federal prosecutor would vote affirmatively in civil rights cases, and conversely, that judges who had previously served as federal judges or high-level federal prosecutors would vote negatively in those cases. Hypothesis 3 stated that the effect of the two variables would be additive or cumulative, that is, that the most affirmative voters would be Democrats without prior service, while the most negative voters would be non-Democrats with such prior service. This would also be reflected in Democrats with such service being more negative than Democrats without such service, and non-Democrats without such service being more affirmative than non-Democrats with such service. Hypothesis 4 stated that in economic matters, Democrats would favor the claims of unions, workers, and the economic underdog, while non-Democrats would favor the claims of management and big business. Hypothesis 5 stated that prior occupation of federal judge or prosecutor would have no effect on voting behavior in the economic area. The assumption was that negative attitudes toward the little man in his civil rights claims would not carry over into negative attitudes toward the little man in economics.

For the purposes of this study, and to reduce the number of tables to a manageable proportion, an experiment was done to determine if it was possible to reduce the number of categories (nine in the civil rights field) which had been coded. Schubert, in his book *The Judicial Mind,* had demonstrated through use of "cumulative scaling" that reduction did not affect results. He surmised that all civil rights cases appeared to raise only one kind of legal, constitutional, or policy issue in the minds of the individual judges, and that consciously or unconsciously each justice was simply "for" or "against" claimants in civil rights cases, whatever the substantive issue. He found the same thing in the economic area. Those justices who favored labor over management also favored the corner-drugstore operator in his dispute with Dow Chemical. It immediately became clear that Schubert was correct. Any judge who voted affirmatively in one area did so in all. Democratic Justice Douglas, for instance, voted at the full 100-percent level affirmatively in several areas (voting equality, political freedom, religious freedom, and racial equality), but his least affirmative voting (in fair procedure) was still at the 94-percent level. Republican Justice Harlan, on the other hand, voted negatively in all civil rights areas, with his most affirmative voting (in right to privacy) only 44 percent in favor of the claims. An additional question was whether one could really cross-compare justices who served at different times on the Court and who did not vote on the same cases, nor even on precisely the same issues. Examination showed that even those justices who served for long periods on the Court, and with many different colleagues, still voted the same way, whatever the time period. The only significant exception was Hugo Black, a former Democratic senator from Alabama, who did vote more negatively in civil rights claims in the latter part of his Court service, although he continued his high level of affirmative voting in economic underdog cases. For all the rest of the justices, a civil rights claim in 1953 seemed to provoke the same response as a civil rights claim in 1960 or 1968, whatever the specific claim.

The two economic issues proved to be subject to the same kind of combination. The result was that only two issues, or categories, were produced. The first was simply called "civil rights," and the second "economic issues." The dichotomies were "pro–civil rights/con–civil rights" and "pro–economic underdog and labor union/con–economic underdog and labor union." These two issues were then used to test the five hypotheses, with the membership of the Court divided into nine groups (see table 2) for purposes of the test.

The next step was the examination of the cases. In the field of civil rights there was a total of 762 cases examined. In each instance, the vote of the judge was compared to the outcome of the case and then listed as a "yes" vote (a vote that favored the claim being made, whether the litigant won or lost) or a "no" vote (one that did not favor the claim). The total number of votes cast by each judge was counted, and the percentage of affirmative votes was calculated. A table was then constructed (table 3) which showed the performance of each individual justice of the Court.

Table 2 *(Warren Court)*
Groups Produced by the Two Variables

Group 1. All Democrats: William O. Douglas, Hugo Black, William J. Brennan, Arthur Goldberg, Thurgood Marshall, Abe Fortas, Byron White, Tom Clark, Sherman Minton, Robert Jackson, Stanley Reed.

Group 2. All Democrats with *no* prior service as federal judge or high-level federal prosecutor: Douglas, Black, Brennan, Goldberg, Fortas.

Group 3. All Democrats *with* prior service as federal judge or high-level federal prosecutor: Marshall, White, Clark, Minton, Jackson, Reed.

Group 4. All non-Democrats: Earl Warren, Harold Burton, Charles Whittaker, Potter Stewart, John M. Harlan, Felix Frankfurter.

Group 5. All non-Democrats with *no* prior service as federal judge or high-level federal prosecutor: Warren, Burton, Frankfurter.

Group 6. All non-Democrats *with* prior service as federal judge or high-level federal prosecutor: Whittaker, Stewart, Harlan.

Group 7. All Court members, regardless of party affiliation, with *no* prior service as federal judge or high-level federal prosecutor: Douglas, Black, Brennan, Goldberg, Fortas, Warren, Burton, Frankfurter.

Group 8. All Court members, regardless of party affiliation, *with* prior service as federal judge or high-level federal prosecutor: Marshall, White, Clark, Minton, Jackson, Reed, Whittaker, Stewart, Harlan.

Group 9. All Court members who served during the sixteen-year period: Douglas, Black, Brennan, Goldberg, Marshall, Fortas, White, Clark, Minton, Jackson, Reed, Warren, Burton, Whittaker, Stewart, Harlan, Frankfurter.

The judges are listed with the most affirmative voter at the top of the table, with the descending order being based on lesser levels of affirmative voting. The Court average was included at its proper place based on the total Court percentage of affirmative voting. The lower half of table 3 does precisely the same thing with the nine groups created by the two variables, and at the bottom of the table the total number of affirmative cases and the percentage of such cases is listed. On each part of the table the party affiliation and prior occupation variables are listed. In the Party column, D means Democrat, while non-D means non-Democrat. In the Prior Service column, "No" means that the person never served as a federal judge or as attorney general, assistant attorney general, or solicitor general of the United States before coming to the Court. "Yes" in that column indicates that he did so serve. "All" in the Previous Service column indicates "All Democrats," or "All non-Democrats" regardless of whether

Table 3 (*Warren Court*)

CIVIL RIGHTS—INDIVIDUAL VOTING RECORD

Name of judge	Party	Prior service	Yes votes	No votes	Percent yes
Douglas	D	No	738	22	97
Goldberg	D	No	149	18	89
Fortas	D	No	206	40	84
Marshall	D	Yes	104	22	83
Brennan	D	No	544	140	80
Warren	Non-D	No	586	151	80
Black	D	No	553	200	73
Court average					59
White	D	Yes	215	217	50
Stewart	Non-D	Yes	271	317	46
Frankfurter	Non-D	No	209	177	38
Jackson	D	Yes	8	13	38
Clark	D	Yes	151	444	25
Whittaker	Non-D	Yes	50	144	25
Harlan	Non-D	Yes	162	548	23
Burton	Non-D	No	28	133	17
Minton	D	Yes	11	55	17
Reed	D	Yes	5	69	07

CIVIL RIGHTS—GROUP VOTING RECORD

Party	Prior service	Yes votes	No votes	Percent yes
Democrat	No	2,200	420	84
All Parties	No	2,923	881	77
Democrat	All	2,694	1,239	68
Non-Democrat	No	723	461	61
Whole Court		3,900	2,709	59
Non-Democrat	All	1,206	1,470	45
Democrat	Yes	494	819	38
All Parties	Yes	977	1,828	35
Non-Democrat	Yes	483	1,009	32

CASES DECIDED

Number of total cases	Yes cases	No cases	Percent of yes cases
762	496	266	65

they had Previous Service as federal judges or prosecutors, and corresponds to Groups 1 and 4 on Table 2.

Table 3 shows the record of the Warren Court judges on all nonunanimous civil rights cases over the sixteen-year period. The table fully substantiates hypothesis 1, which stated that Democrats would vote favorably to the claims of civil rights litigants, while non-Democrats would not. The five most affirmative justices are all Democrats, and seven of the eight most affirmative voters belonged to that party. Only one non-Democrat, Chief Justice Earl Warren, former governor of California, voted above the 50-percent level or above the Court average. As a group, Democrats voted to favor the civil rights claim 68 percent of the time, while non-Democrats favored those claims only 45 percent of the time. It is interesting to speculate what the results might have been without Warren, for he personally cast more than 48 percent of the affirmative votes registered by non-Democrats during the entire period.

Hypothesis 2 stated that persons with *no prior service* would vote more affirmatively in civil rights than persons *with prior service*. The hypothesis is proven. Six of the seven most affirmative justices had *no prior service*, while eight of the ten most negative voters were justices *with prior service*. This factor is perhaps even more important than party affiliation in accounting for variations in voting in civil rights cases, for as groups, those with *no prior service* voted at the 77-percent affirmative level, while those *with prior service* voted at only the 32-percent level. This 45 percentage point spread is almost double the 23 percentage point spread based on party affiliation alone.

Hypothesis 3 stated that the effect of the two variables would be additive, or cumulative, and that the most affirmative voters would be Democrats with *no prior service*, while the most negative voters would be non-Democrats *with prior service*. The Group Voting section of the table shows that Democrats with *no prior service* voted 84 percent of the time to favor the claims in civil rights. In contrast, non-Democrats *with prior service* voted to favor those claims only 32 percent of the time. This 52 percentage point spread is greater than the spread for party affiliation or *prior service* taken separately. An interesting point is the interrelationship between the two variables. Democrats *with prior service* voted at only the 38-percent level to favor civil rights claims, which was 46 percentage points lower than Democrats with *no prior service*, and non-Democrats with *no prior service* not only voted 29 percentage points higher than non-Democrats *with prior service*, but actually voted 23 percentage points higher than even Democrats who had been federal judges or high-level federal prosecutors before appointment to the Supreme Court. The hypothesis is fully proven.

Table 4 shows the record of the Warren Court judges on economic issues. Hypothesis 4 stated that Democrats would be more favorable to the claims of labor unions and the economic underdog, while non-Democrats would favor management and big business. Were it not for Earl Warren, the individual voting section of the table would perfectly substantiate

Table 4 (Warren Court)

ECONOMIC ISSUES—INDIVIDUAL VOTING RECORD

Name of judge	Party	Prior service	Yes votes	No votes	Percent yes
Black	D	No	388	78	83
Warren	Non-D	No	386	83	82
Douglas	D	No	383	85	82
Brennan	D	No	311	100	76
Clark	D	Yes	276	123	69
Marshall	D	Yes	22	10	69
Fortas	D	No	63	31	67
Goldberg	D	No	65	33	66
White	D	Yes	140	76	65
Court average					60
Minton	D	Yes	32	40	44
Reed	D	Yes	29	40	42
Burton	Non-D	No	48	89	35
Stewart	Non-D	Yes	113	214	35
Harlan	Non-D	Yes	99	329	23
Frankfurter	Non-D	No	44	163	21
Whittaker	Non-D	Yes	23	132	16

ECONOMIC ISSUES—GROUP VOTING RECORD

Party	Prior service	Yes votes	No votes	Percent yes
Democrat	No	1,210	327	79
Democrat	All	1,709	604	73
All Parties	No	1,688	662	71
Democrat	Yes	499	277	63
Whole Court		2,424	1,614	60
Non-Democrat	No	478	335	59
All Parties	Yes	738	965	43
Non-Democrat	All	715	1,010	41
Non-Democrat	Yes	237	675	36

CASES DECIDED

Number of total cases	Yes cases	No cases	Percent of yes cases
512	339	273	66

this. The section shows that the ten Democrats voted more affirmatively than the non-Democrats, with the exception of Warren. In fact, only two Democrats voted below the 65-percent level affirmatively, and only one non-Democrat (Warren) voted above the 35-percent level. Warren cast an amazing 54 percent of all votes cast affirmatively by non-Democrats. The group section of the table shows that Democrats favored the claims 73 percent of the time, while non-Democrats did so only 41 percent of the time. Hypothesis 4 is fully substantiated, and seems to prove that the variable of party affiliation is somewhat more important in economics than in civil rights—at least the fit is more perfect on the tables.

Hypothesis 5 is completely false. It stated that there would be no significant relationship between *prior service* and voting in economic matters. While there is some confusion on the individual scale of the table, with three persons *with prior service* voting above the Court average, a look at the group section of the table shows that a relationship exists. All justices with *no prior service* vote to favor the economic claims of the little man 71 percent of the time, while all those *with prior service* vote for such claims only 43 percent of the time. This spread of 28 percentage points is not significantly less than the 32 point spread based on party affiliation, and indicates that a lack of sympathy for the little man in his civil rights disputes with government carries over into a lack of sympathy for the little man in his disputes with management and big business. There was no hypothesis 6 to correspond to hypothesis 3 because it was not believed that prior service was important in economic issues. There should have been, however, for the two variables have an additive effect in economic matters also. The most affirmative voters were Democrats with *no prior service* (79 percent), while the most negative justices were non-Democrats *with prior service* (36 percent). This 43 point spread is not so great as the cumulative spread of 52 points in civil rights, but it is still a very great difference. It should be noted that in economics, the group record shows that any kind of Democrat votes more affirmatively than any kind of non-Democrat.

The analysis of the tables shows what one of the problems had been in past examinations of Supreme Court voting behavior. The key to the significance of the variables is their interrelationship. It is difficult to see any voting similarity between, for example, either Douglas or Brennan on the one hand, and Clark or White on the other, although all are Democrats. But when one adds the negative effects of the variable of *prior service*, the difference becomes quite clear. For while Clark and White are far more negative in their voting behavior than Douglas or Brennan, who have not had that same occupational background, they are still far less negative than non-Democrats who have had that background. Of the judges examined, those with significant numbers of votes in both areas seem to fit the pattern quite well, even as individuals. Earl Warren is the major aberration, for he is far more affirmative in both civil rights and economics than a non-Democrat ought to be (according to the hypotheses). The fact that he had only one of the negative variables in his background somewhat ameliorates this. Thurgood Marshall, on the other hand, is perhaps too affirmative in his voting for one who has been both a high-level prosecutor (solicitor general) and a federal judge before coming to the Court. The fact that he is the first black judge on the Court, when coupled with the knowledge that he was specifically appointed as solicitor general to prosecute violations of civil rights (rather than to uphold government against the claims of civil rights litigants), helps to explain his voting record. Again, he only had one of the negative factors in his background, having been a lifelong member of the Democratic Party.

At this point in the study, two questions arose. The first was, Were the variables which had been used successfully for the Warren Court era equally valid for a different period in the Court's history? And the second was, If so, would they help explain some of the observed differences already noted in the voting behavior of the Warren Court and that of the Burger Court? That there were differences in terms of substantive issues had become abundantly clear, and while it is not the purpose of this study to examine the issues themselves, some comparison of the manner in which the Warren and Burger Courts have handled substantive issues might prove useful.

There are several specific issue areas in which innovations by the Warren Court had provoked controversy. They include the First Amendment areas of free speech (both political and other), press, association, and assembly; Fourth Amendment searches and seizures problems; Fifth and Sixth Amendment problems relating to the entire criminal procedure area; and last but certainly not least, the whole panoply of voting equality questions, from poll tax and registration to malapportioned legislatures. Perhaps no other single decision of the Warren Court provoked as much public debate as well as official and unofficial noncompliance (continuing even into 1975 in Boston and other cities) as *Brown* v. *Topeka*. Although decisions of the Supreme Court between 1938 and 1953 regarding segregation practices at the law school, graduate school, and university level should have prepared the nation for a decision declaring segregation unlawful in public elementary and secondary schools, the unanimous decision which did so apparently came as a surprise and a shock to much of the country. The fact that the decision was based on largely sociological (rather than constitutional) grounds was obvious, not only from the opinion of the Court with its references to such studies as Gunnar Myrdal's *An American Dilemma: The Negro Problem and Modern Democracy*, but also from the constitutional reasons given by the Court as support for the decision. For while segregation of state-supported schools such as in Topeka was declared to be a violation of the equal protection clause of the Fourteenth Amendment, segregation of federally supported schools in the District of Columbia was said to violate the due process clause of the

Fifth Amendment in the Bill of Rights (which has no equal protection clause). And in a series of later decisions, the Court struck down legal or de jure segregation in all public facilities supported by governments, whether they are golf courses, swimming pools, restaurants, or whatever. It is interesting that every one of the school desegregation decisions for the next fifteen years after *Brown* was unanimous.

The Burger Court has produced a somewhat different pattern. While upholding the use of "busing" as a "useful tool" in desegregating public schools, the Court also upheld the right of a state to return a public park to private heirs to avoid desegregation, allowed a city to sell its swimming pools when the city was under federal court order to desegregate them, and, in a major setback in the effort to eliminate de facto segregation, held that busing across district lines to eliminate such segregation was not constitutionally required.

In the First Amendment area involving free speech, press, association, and assembly the Warren Court's decisions were numerous and meaningful. While refusing to strike down the Smith and McCarran Acts, which outlawed teaching or advocating the violent overthrow of government, the Court did distinguish between discussion or academic advocacy of overthrow, and specific or concrete and intelligent, knowing advocacy of action to accomplish overthrow of government. The Court also insisted that national security was a matter for the nation, and not the states, and that sit-ins, demonstrations, and certain kinds of symbolic expression (e.g., wearing of arm bands to demonstrate opposition to government war policies) were all constitutionally protected. The use of loyalty oaths by state and local units of government was largely limited to meaningless, generalized statements, and libel was defined very narrowly, particularly as it related to "public persons." Perhaps the best example of the new freedom in expression was furnished by the subject of obscenity. While refusing (over the objections of justices Black and Douglas) to rule that obscene expression was protected, the Court moved from the position that material could be judged, taken out of context, by what offended the most susceptible member of the local community, to the rule that the material had to be taken as a whole, that to be considered obscene it must be sexually arousing to the average member of a national community (Supreme Court justices?), and that in any case it could not be censored if it contained material of "redeeming social, literary, or artistic value."

Again, the Burger Court record was mixed. The Court sustained a loyalty oath containing "uphold and defend" and "oppose and overthrow" provisions, and rejected the claim of news reporters that they could protect their sources from grand jurors asking for their testimony. The Court also refused to grant injunctions requested by civilians against surveillance by Army intelligence agencies, and denaturalized a United States citizen whose mother was a natural-born American, because he failed to live in the United States for five years prior to his eighteenth birthday. The effect of this decision was to reverse both *Afroyim* v. *Rusk*, 387 U.S. 253 (1967), and *Schneider* v. *Rusk*, 377 U.S. 163 (1964), each of which had been considered a landmark decision of the Warren Court. And in perhaps the most noticed decision in the First Amendment area, the Court moved strongly away from the Warren Court definitions of obscene expression. Contemporary *community* standards replaced the *national* community ones, and the Court stated that if the material was obscene, it could be prohibited if, taken as a whole, it lacked "*serious* literary, artistic, political, or scientific value." The Warren Court test which this replaced had stated that the material must be "utterly without" such value. But in contrast to these retreats from the Warren Court positions, the Burger Court (actually all Nixon appointees on the Court dissented, including Burger) denied the government the right to prohibit publication of the Pentagon Papers, and later extended to "private" persons the protections that "public" figures had received in libel suits.

During the Warren years, the Court's decisions in the field of religion had been almost as controversial as those in the field of racial segregation. Among other things, those decisions outlawed the saying of prayers and the reading of Bible verses in public schools, and prohibited states from legislating to prevent the teaching of evolution as a theory of human origin. Perhaps more important to a generation of young men, the Court ruled that the sincerity of a claimant's belief against war, rather than membership in an organized religious group opposed to war, created conscientious objector status and exempted the claimant from draft duty. The Burger Court does not seem to have changed much, and in fact, surprised many observers when it held, unanimously, that Muhammad Ali was exempt from military service on the basis of his religious training and beliefs. But a perhaps more significant decision affirmed the right of Amish parents to refuse to allow their children to attend public schools beyond the eighth grade, in spite of the state's compulsory attendance laws. In another schooling case, the Court declared that there was no "fundamental right protected by the Constitution" to an education.

In a society which had steadily shifted from being predominantly rural and agricultural to being urban and industrial, it may be that no decisional area was of more significance than that of voting equality. In addition to outlawing the use of the gerrymander to nullify the effect of black voters, and outlawing the poll tax as a requirement of voters in state elections, the Warren Court applied the "one man–one vote" rule to all elective offices, state and federal, where the persons elected performed essentially policy-making functions. The "substantially equal" test for apportionment resulted in one apportionment plan with a maximum maldistribution of voter strength of 3 percent being invalidated. In contrast, the Burger Court has rejected a number of voting equality cases and has upheld multiple-member districts in Indiana against a claim that the result yielded misrepresentation (or nonrepresentation) of minority groups. The Burger Court did reduce state residency requirements for voting to thirty days, but later changed its mind and increased this to at least two months. Perhaps the most serious retreat from the Warren Court position was the approval of an apportionment plan that had a 16.5-percent deviation from the "one man–one vote" principle.

One of the major and long-range controversies among justices of the Supreme Court during the past fifty years has been over the proper meaning to give the phrase "due process of law." Whatever its past meaning, by 1947 it was clear that four different views were held by members of the Court. The reason for the controversy was quite simple. The Bill of Rights (the first eight Amendments to the Constitution) guaranteed individual Americans a number of protections, but only against national government action. State and local governments were left free to interfere with those rights unless state constitutions prevented such actions. Because the states of the South had a proven record of following procedures in taking the life, liberty, or property of blacks which were different from the procedures they followed with others, the Thirty-ninth Congress of the United States submitted to the states the Fourteenth Amendment. Adopted in 1868, this amendment forbade the states to deny any "person" equal protection of the law, but it also stated that no state could deprive any person of "life, liberty, or property, without due process of law." Before long, litigants began to claim that certain areas of private behavior were part of the "liberty" that government could not take, and by 1925 the Court had admitted that there were certain liberties (in that instance, free political speech) that were so essential to a concept of ordered liberty in a free society that the framers of the Fourteenth Amendment must have meant to cover those liberties by the expression "due process of law." But from the beginning, most claimants had insisted that all those rights listed in the Bill of Rights must be "fundamental," or the framers of the Bill would not have included them. This argument came to be known as the "incorporation" position. In other words, whatever standards were demanded by the Bill of Rights when the national government was involved were also demanded by the incorporation of those standards into the meaning of due process of the Fourteenth Amendment when the states were involved.

But there were those on the Court who did not believe that all the protections of the Bill of Rights were really "fundamental," and they argued "selective" incorporation of only those rights which they saw as fundamental. A third position was that the Bill of Rights was totally irrelevant in the consideration of state action, and that the Court should only recognize those due process claims that were "essential to a concept of ordered liberty," whether they happened to coincide with the Bill of Rights or not. A fourth position, combining the first and third positions, was that due process meant the total incorporation of the Bill of Rights, *plus* anything else which seemed essential to ordered liberty, whether covered by the Bill of Rights or not. The majority of decisions in the past thirty years seem to have represented a fifth position, combining the "selective incorporation" and the "ordered liberty" positions.

The process of incorporation has been anything but uniform. Before 1948 only First Amendment claims had been treated in this manner, with freedom of religion, speech, press, and assembly deemed fundamental. But by 1948 there was a majority of seven Democrats to two non-Democrats on the Court, and that year and the next saw the very first decisions relating to fair trial processes decided by the Court in favor of the claim that those processes were fundamental. The result was that states could no longer constitutionally deny public trial, nor could they authorize unreasonable searches. But that same year saw the resignations of the affirmative-voting Rutledge and Murphy, and it was not until 1962, with the resignation of justices Frankfurter and Whittaker (both negative-voting non-Democrats) and their replacement with White and Goldberg (both affirmative-voting Democrats), that an affirmative majority was restored to the Court. The result was an immediate resumption of the process of nationalizing "due process of law." By the end of the Warren Court era, the incorporation was nearly complete, and included the Eighth Amendment (cruel and unusual punishment), the Fifth Amendment (self-incrimination and double jeopardy), and the Sixth Amendment (right to counsel, confrontation of witnesses, speedy trial, compulsory processes for obtaining witnesses, and trial by jury).

The unfavorable reactions to this series of decisions were based upon two objections. The first, and the one articulated by Justice Harlan, was that nationalizing the Bill of Rights prevented the states and local communities from handling their own law enforcement problems, and that the Court ought only to be concerned that, based upon the "totality of the circumstances," the individual got a fair trial. Development of procedures to ensure fair trial should be the concern of the states, not of the nation. The second objection was a much more practical one. Law enforcement officers were adamantly opposed, pointing out how much more difficult their job was if they were bound by the federal rules on searches and seizures, confessions, trial by jury, the admissibility of evidence, and, particularly, the furnishing of lawyers to the indigent and warning suspects of their constitutional rights. Decisions by the Warren Court in this due process area were what primarily caused President Nixon to search for "law and order" judges for appointment to the Court.

But the "ordered liberty" test was to produce even more controversial decisions than selective incorporation. For example, the majority was able to find that statutes prohibiting the transmission of birth control devices and information were a violation of the constitutional "right to privacy." Dissenters were quick to point out that no such right was listed in the Constitution, and that in fact the Court majority had been forced to combine the First, Third, Fourth, Fifth, and Ninth Amendments to create the "right." Before the end of the Warren era, the Court had decided 152 nonunanimous "right to privacy" cases.

Other Warren Court decisions in the fair procedure area included rulings that it was cruel and unusual to punish a narcotics addict for his addiction per se, and (in *In re Gault*, 387 U.S. 1 [1967]) that all the procedural protections furnished to adults must also be furnished to juveniles. Perhaps the most publicized decision of the Warren Court in this area was *Miranda* v. *Arizona*, 384 U.S. 436 (1966), in which the Court listed the rights of persons under arrest. These included a warning that the person had a right to remain silent; that if he did speak, his words could be used against him at trial; that he had a right to a lawyer at interrogation (later extended to "all important steps" of the process including lineup, appeal, etc.); that the state must furnish the lawyer if the accused was indigent; and last, that if the suspect at first decided to submit to interrogation but subsequently changed his mind, the interrogators must respect his wish and cease questioning him. Any confession which failed to meet all these standards would be inadmissible at the accused's trial.

The Burger Court's record in the fair procedure area is its most negative one. On the affirmative side, it must be pointed out that the Court found that the death penalty, as used in a discriminatory manner against minority groups and the poor, was cruel and unusual punishment. It should be noted that the decision was 5 to 4, with the five-man majority consisting of the five holdovers from the Warren Court, and the four dissenters consisting of the four Nixon appointees. For purposes of this study it is appropriate to note that four Democrats and only one non-Democrat opposed the death penalty, while three non-Democrats and only one Democrat favored it. The Burger Court also held vagrancy statutes to be unconstitutional, extended the right-to-counsel to misdemeanors, and rejected President Nixon's claim that he had a right to use electronic surveillance without warrants in domestic security cases.

On the negative side, the Burger Court upheld a life sentence given to a person who, even though he maintained his innocence, plea bargained for the life sentence because he feared a death penalty would possibly result from a jury trial. The Court also refused to apply the Warren Court rules on searches and seizures retroactively, decided (in contrast to *In re Gault*) that juveniles do not have to be furnished jury trial, and refused retroactivity for the requirement of counsel at preliminary hearings. The Court also approved the use of information gained when suspects unknowingly spoke to "wired" government agents, and even altered the traditional meaning of "entrapment" when it ruled that the conviction of a person accused of manufacturing illegal drugs was valid, even though one of the vital ingredients in the manufacture was furnished by an undercover narcotics agent. The Court extended the "stop and frisk" powers of the police, and also made it easier for law enforcement officials to search movable vehicles. The Court approved less-than-unanimous jury verdicts in state criminal convictions, and (in contrast to the *Miranda* rules) upheld the conviction of a person who had been told of all his rights except the right to counsel. In direct contradiction to Warren Court rules, the Court held a search to be valid when authorized by a co-possessor of a residence, even though the search was directed against the other co-possessor, and also stated that an inspector did not need a warrant or permission to enter the premises of a company to ascertain emission of pollutants. The Warren Court had refused to give even health and safety inspectors this right.

This recital does not mean that the Warren Court was always affirmative in dealing with civil rights, nor does it mean that the Burger Court was always negative. In fact, the Burger Court could be said to be carving new ground in areas such as women's rights and the rights of the poor. What the recital does show is that there are significant and fundamental differences in the treatment of many of the important policy issues which both Courts faced. And so a decision was made to extend this study to the Burger Court, and to see if the variables which accounted for variations in voting behavior on the Warren Court would prove of value as "predictor" variables for the Burger Court justice's voting behavior, as well as accounting for the basic policy shifts which were substantively evident.

Before proceeding, certain new hypotheses were set up, in addition to those already established for the Warren Court. New hypothesis 1 stated that all hypotheses valid for the Warren Court would prove valid for the Burger Court. A subset of this hypothesis was that the variable *"prior service as federal judge or prosecutor/no such service"* would have a positive correlation with voting in economic matters as it did on the Warren Court, even though there had been no original hypothesis stating this, and also that the two variables would be additive or cumulative in the economics area. Hypothesis 2 stated that the Burger Court decisions would be much more negative than those of the Warren Court because of personnel changes. During the Warren era, eleven Democrats served on the Court, but only six non-Democrats. During the most affirmative period of the Warren Court (the last six years) there was a constant majority of six Democrats to three non-Democrats. During that same six-year period there were five judges with *no prior service* on the Court, and only four judges *with prior service*. In sixteen years, the Court had made decisions in 762 civil rights nonunanimous cases, deciding 496, or 65 percent, in favor of the claims made. The average vote of the justices had been 59 percent affirmative. In economics claims the Court had decided 512 nonunanimous cases, ruling affirmatively in 339, or 66 percent, of the cases, with the average vote of the justices being 60 percent affirmative.

In contrast, the Burger Court began with only five Democrats and four non-Democrats, and more importantly, a six-to-three majority for judges *with prior service* to those with *no prior service*. This did not change in 1972 with the resignations of justices Black and Harlan, for they were replaced with Lewis Powell, a Virginia Democrat with *no prior service,* and William Rehnquist, an Arizona Republican *with prior service*. If the two variables were really capable of predicting behavior, the loss of one Democrat and especially the loss of two judges with *no prior service* should mean that many more litigants were now losing the kinds of cases they had been winning before the justices of the Warren Court.

And so it was necessary to read all the decisions of the five-year period of the Burger Court and code them in precisely the same manner in which Schubert had coded the Warren Court decisions. It should be stated at this time that classifying the cases into the subdivisions listed, whether done by Professor Schubert or the author of this work, is not easy or error-proof. There are ambiguities, and it is sometimes possible to classify a case into two or even three of the categories. In such instance a value judgment must be made as to which category best suits the case. For the purposes of this study the difficulty of classification was not that important, since all civil rights cases were considered together as a single group, as were the economic cases. A new table (5) had to be constructed which indicated the groups which the two variables produced. New tables (6 and 7) were then prepared, one for each of the two areas (civil rights and economics), in precisely the same manner as had been done for the Warren Court.

New hypothesis 1 states that all hypotheses proven valid for the Warren Court will also prove valid for the Burger Court. Original hypothesis 1 stated that in the field of civil rights, Democrats would demonstrate marked partiality toward the claims that a civil right had been violated, while non-Democrats on the Court would favor the claims of government rather than the individual. Table 6 shows that with the exception of Stewart, there is a perfect break between Democrats and non-Democrats in

Table 5 (Burger Court)
Groups Produced by the Two Variables

Group 1. All Democrats: William O. Douglas, Hugo Black, William J. Brennan, Thurgood Marshall, Byron White, Lewis Powell.

Group 2. All Democrats with *no* prior service as federal judge or high-level federal prosecutor: Douglas, Black, Brennan, Powell.

Group 3. All Democrats *with* prior service as federal judge or high-level federal prosecutor: Marshall, White.

Group 4. All non-Democrats: Potter Stewart, Warren Burger, Harry Blackmun, William Rehnquist, John M. Harlan.

Group 5. All non-Democrats with *no* prior service as federal judge or high-level federal prosecutor: None.

Group 6. All non-Democrats *with* prior service as federal judge or high-level federal prosecutor: Harlan, Stewart, Burger, Blackmun, Rehnquist.

Group 7. All Court members, regardless of party affiliation, with *no* prior service as federal judge or high-level federal prosecutor: Douglas, Black, Brennan, Powell.

Group 8. All Court members, regardless of party affiliation, *with* prior service as federal judge or high-level federal prosecutor: Harlan, Stewart, Burger, Blackmun, Rehnquist, White, Marshall.

Group 9. All Court members who served during the five-year period: Douglas, Black, Brennan, Marshall, White, Powell, Harlan, Stewart, Burger, Blackmun, Rehnquist.

---

civil rights, although both justices Black and White voted more negatively than they did during the Warren years. The voting of the other holdover members from the Warren Court is almost unchanged. William O. Douglas, who had voted at the 97-percent level before, voted at the 96-percent level during the Burger Court years. Thurgood Marshall slipped only one point from 83 to 82 percent, while William J. Brennan actually increased his voting from 80 to 82 percent. Interestingly, Brennan, who had achieved a reputation as a nondissenter while on the Warren Court, began to dissent with some regularity now that so many of the Court decisions were negative. And whereas John Marshall Harlan had been the most frequent dissenter while the affirmative decisions were being produced by the Warren Court, it was now Douglas who took over and who in fact became the all-time champion dissenter in one term of Court by casting an amazing 46 dissents, in 16 of which he was all alone in doing so.

All told, six of the seven most affirmative voters were Democrats, while five of the seven most negative voters were non-Democrats. Democrats as

Table 6 *(Burger Court)*
CIVIL RIGHTS—INDIVIDUAL VOTING RECORD

Name of judge	Party	Prior service	Yes votes	No votes	Percent yes
Douglas	D	No	199	8	96
Marshall	D	Yes	172	37	82
Brennan	D	No	174	38	82
Court average					46+
Black	D	No	37	43	46
Stewart	Non-D	Yes	92	120	43
White	D	Yes	69	142	33
Powell	D	No	29	88	25
Harlan	Non-D	Yes	20	59	25
Blackmun	Non-D	Yes	36	148	20
Burger	Non-D	Yes	30	181	14
Rehnquist	Non-D	Yes	0	117	0

CIVIL RIGHTS—GROUP VOTING RECORD

Party	Prior service	Yes votes	No votes	Percent yes
Democrat	No	439	177	71
All Parties	No	439	177	71
Democrat	All	680	356	66
Democrat	Yes	241	179	57
Whole Court		859	981	47
All Parties	Yes	420	804	34
Non-Democrat	No	. . .	. . .	. . .
Non-Democrat	All	179	625	20
Non-Democrat	Yes	179	625	20

CASES DECIDED

Total number of cases	Yes cases	No cases	Percent of yes cases
231	92	164	40

a whole voted 66 percent of the time to favor civil rights claims, which is only one percentage point different than aggregate Democrat voting on the Warren Court. Non-Democrats on the Court were much more negative even than they had been during the Warren years, and in fact only voted to favor the claims of civil rights litigants 20 percent of the time, in contrast to the 45 percent affirmative vote they cast earlier. This is probably explained by the fact that on the Burger Court all non-Democrats were also persons having had *prior service*. With this double negative

taken into consideration, non-Democrats were still markedly more negative than non-Democrats on the Warren Court. Hypothesis 1 of the original group is not only proven for the Burger Court, but is even more
evident.

Original hypothesis 2 stated that those with *no prior service* as federal
judge or high federal prosecutor would vote affirmatively in civil rights
cases and, conversely, that judges who had so previously served would
vote negatively. Table 6 shows that three of the four most affirmative voters on the Burger Court were persons with *no prior service*, while six of
the seven most negative voters were persons *with* such service. In all,
persons with *no prior service* voted affirmatively 71 percent of the time,
while those *with prior service* voted affirmatively only 34 percent of the
time. This 37 percent point spread is very comparable to the 42 point
spread on the Warren Court, and hypothesis 2 is proven for the Burger
Court. The holdovers from the Warren Court continued to vote about as
before, with Harlan changing only from the 23-percent level to the 25-
percent level, while Stewart moved only from the 46 percent affirmative
position to the 43-percent level. Justice Marshall changed only from 83 to
82 percent, and the only significant shift among the *with prior service*
group was made by White, who dropped from the 50-percent level to the
33-percent level.

The major change in this group's voting was caused by the addition of
Chief Justice Burger and associate justices Blackmun and Rehnquist. At
the Senate Judiciary Committee hearings on the Rehnquist nomination
several groups, including the AFL-CIO, the NAACP, The Americans for
Democratic Action, the National Lawyers Guild, and the Leadership
Conference on Civil Rights, had opposed the nomination. Mr. Rehnquist
was quoted from an earlier time as saying, "I am against all civil rights
laws," and at the time still (on questioning) appeared to favor pretrial
detention and wiretaps and to oppose busing. The NAACP charged Rehnquist with "open harassment and intimidation" of black voters in Arizona
polling places. He was said to hold a strong belief in the John Birch Society's position, and was called "the most reactionary" nominee submitted
since the nominees of President Harding more than fifty years earlier.
Questioned at great length by senators Edward Kennedy and Birch Bayh
as to his ability to put these strongly held partisan attitudes behind him
as a member of the Supreme Court, Rehnquist insisted that he would be
able to do so and to judge each case on its merits. Senators Kennedy and
Bayh voiced their doubts that he could or would do this, and the fact that
his first 117 votes on nonunanimous civil rights cases were all cast negatively appears to have justified their fears. No person in this study has
ever voted 100 percent affirmatively or negatively except Rehnquist. His
fellow non-Democrats (both former federal court judges), Burger and

Blackmun, joined him in casting 45 percent of all the negative votes cast in civil rights cases on the Burger Court.

Original hypothesis 3 stated that the effect of the two variables would be additive, and that the most affirmative voters would be Democrats with *no* prior service, while the most negative voters would be non-Democrats *with* prior service. It was also stated that this would be reflected in Democrats with such service being more negative than Democrats without, and that non-Democrats without such service would be more affirmative than non-Democrats with service. On the Burger Court all members who were non-Democrats were also persons *with* prior service, making it impossible to test all aspects of the hypothesis; however, Democrats with *no prior service* did vote at the 71-percent level, while Democrats *with prior service* voted at the 57-percent level. Non-Democrats *with prior service* (all) voted at only the 20-percent level. The spread between Democrats with *no prior service* and non-Democrats *with prior service* is 49 points, and compares almost exactly with the 52 point spread on the Warren Court. The hypothesis is fully proven.

Original hypothesis 4 stated that in economic matters Democrats would favor the claims of unions, workers, and the economic underdog, while non-Democrats would favor the claims of management and big business. Table 7 shows an almost perfect example of this. The five most affirmative voters were Democrats, and five of the six most negative voters were non-Democrats. In all, Democrats voted affirmatively at the 66-percent level, while non-Democrats voted affirmatively at only the 26-percent level. This 40 point spread is even greater than the 32 point spread found on the Warren Court and, again, is primarily the responsibility of the new appointees to the Court. In fact, justices Stewart and Harlan increased their percentage of affirmative voting from 35 and 23 percent respectively, to 49 and 43 percent, but this was not enough to overcome the voting of the Nixon appointees, who occupy the last four positions on the negative side of the table. Chief Justice Burger votes at the all-time low level of only 7 percent, while Rehnquist, who had been opposed by the AFL-CIO primarily on the basis of his own admission that he felt property rights to be more important than civil rights, showed a continued belief in this by voting for management and big business 91 percent of the time.

Original hypothesis 5 had stated that there would be no significant relationship between economic voting and *prior service,* and had proven completely false in relation to the Warren Court. New hypothesis 1 had stated that it would continue to prove false with the Burger Court, and table 7 shows that it did so. Three of the four most affirmative voters in economics on the Burger Court were judges with *no prior service,* while six of the seven most negative voters were judges *with prior service.* As a

Table 7 (*Burger Court*)
ECONOMIC ISSUES—INDIVIDUAL VOTING RECORD

Name of judge	Party	Prior service	Yes votes	No votes	Percent yes
Douglas	D	No	42	2	95
Brennan	D	No	35	9	80
Marshall	D	Yes	29	15	66
Black	D	No	7	7	50
White	D	Yes	21	22	49
Stewart	Non-D	Yes	21	22	49
Court average					48+
Harlan	Non-D	Yes	6	8	43
Blackmun	Non-D	Yes	9	26	26
Powell	D	No	4	17	19
Rehnquist	Non-D	Yes	2	21	9
Burger	Non-D	Yes	3	40	7

ECONOMIC ISSUES—GROUP VOTING RECORD

Party	Prior service	Yes votes	No votes	Percent yes
Democrat	No	88	35	72
All Parties	No	88	35	72
Democrat	All	138	72	66
Democrat	Yes	50	37	57
Whole Court		179	154	49
Non-Democrat	No	. . .	. . .	. . .
All Parties	Yes	91	154	37
Non-Democrat	All	41	117	26
Non-Democrat	Yes	41	117	26

CASES DECIDED

Total number of cases	Yes cases	No cases	Percent of yes cases
43	15	28	35

group, judges with *no prior service* voted affirmatively 72 percent of the time, while judges *with prior service* voted affirmatively only 37 percent of the time. This percentage point spread compares with the 28 percent point spread on the Warren Court very favorably. The effect of *party affiliation* and *prior service* proved to be cumulative on the Burger Court, just as it had on the Warren Court. Democrats with *no prior service* voted at the 72-percent level, while Democrats *with prior service* voted only at the 57-percent level, which is still much higher than the 26-percent level of non-Democrats *with prior service*. The spread, using both variables, is 46 points, compared to 43 points on the Warren Court. This final step completes the examination of new hypothesis 1, which is fully substantiated in every respect.

New hypothesis 2 was based on changes in membership of the Court, and stated that the Burger Court would decide significantly larger numbers of cases negatively than had the Warren Court. With a nine-member Court, it is possible to have anywhere from zero negative factors (with nine Democrats with *no prior service*), to eighteen negative factors (with nine non-Democrats *with prior service*). During the last years of the Warren Court only seven negative factors (38 percent) were present, with Black, Douglas, Brennan, and Fortas having none; Marshall, Warren, and White having one each; and only Stewart and Harlan having two. In contrast, the present Court collectively possesses ten negative factors (55 percent). This should allow negative factor voting to control the case outcome, just as positive factor voting controlled the outcome of most cases during the Warren years.

Table 3 showed that the Warren Court justices, as individuals, voted 59 percent of the time to favor the civil rights claims made, and this vote enabled them to win 65 percent of the cases decided. In contrast, table 6 shows that the individual Burger Court judges voted only 47 percent of the time to favor such claims and the affirmative voters were only able to win 40 percent of the time. The difference of 12 percentage points in voting by individual justices made a difference of 25 points in the actual cases won. It should be noted (although the tables are not broken down by years to show it) that during the last years of the Warren era (with the negative variables totaling only 38 percent), the Court actually decided more than 70 percent of civil rights cases affirmatively, with a high of 82 percent in one term of Court. In contrast, the present Court membership, with 55 percent negative variables present, has decided only 34 percent of the civil rights cases affirmatively. This means that while a claimant had a 70 to 82 percent chance of winning between 1962 and 1968, he had only a 34 to 40 percent chance of winning between 1969 and 1974.

This same pattern is reflected in economics. During the Warren years the Court decided 66 percent of the cases in favor of labor and the economic underdog, with a high of 85 percent in the 1965 term. Table 7 shows that these same claimants won only 35 percent of the time with the Burger Court, and only 32 percent of the time with the current membership. The fact is, that in both civil rights and economics almost the same percentages of winners persist, but it is a different group of winners. Today, management and big business have the same distinct advantage previously enjoyed by labor unions and economic underdogs, while the government is once again—just as in the pre–Warren Court years—winning when individuals and groups claim that that government has violated their civil rights. The new hypothesis 2 is fully substantiated. The only justice who does not fit the predicted patterns of voting behavior is Lewis Powell of Virginia, who votes far too negatively for a person who is both a Democrat and one with *no prior service*. Justice Powell's personal history made it quite evident that he would be a negative voter in civil rights. In addition to his Southern background, the Senate Judiciary Committee hearings had brought out his support for domestic wiretaps without judicial authorization, his insistence that civil disobedience was not a legitimate way to challenge the constitutionality of laws, and his open disagreement with the Warren Court decisions in the criminal law field, particularly the *Miranda* decision. His negative economic voting record is even more surprising when contrasted with that of other Democrats. The fact that President Nixon admittedly looked for a negative voter might possibly explain Powell's voting; but such an explanation cannot be satisfactorily applied to past examples. The presidential appointive power is a significant variable in understanding Supreme Court voting behavior only in the sense discussed earlier, that is, the fact that presidents usually appoint from their own party, and the fact that party affiliation is a significant variable. When one contrasts the voting behavior of Black and Douglas on the one hand, with that of Reed, Jackson, and Frankfurter on the other, and then realizes that all were appointed by Franklin D. Roosevelt (another president who announced an intention of packing—or unpacking, depending on one's view—the Court), it is difficult to see that Roosevelt succeeded in his purpose. There was very great contrast, particularly in the economic area, in the voting of Burton, Clark, and Minton, all Truman appointees. Even greater variety is furnished by the Eisenhower justices, with Warren and Brennan at almost opposite ends of the scale furnished by Whittaker and Harlan, and Stewart almost exactly in the middle. The two Kennedy appointees, Goldberg and White, show the same inconsistency, with White, a former U.S. assistant attorney general, voting far more negatively than Goldberg, a former labor lawyer. If any of these four presidents was attempting to put on the Court men with a consistent ideology reflecting his own, he failed to do so. Only the appointees of presidents Johnson and Nixon seem to fit a consistent mold, and while Johnson may have appointed Fortas and Marshall because of the partisan attitudes, he did not say so. Nixon, on the other hand, made it clear from the beginning that he was trying to change the Court away from its immediate past. This study makes it abundantly clear that he succeeded in doing so, and the Nixon Court revolution may not be over but the position certainly has been consolidated.

Today two clear blocks have developed on the Court. The affirmative block consists of Douglas, Brennan, and Marshall (representing three Democrats, two of whom have *no prior service*), with only one negative factor between them. The negative block consists of Burger, Blackmun, Rehnquist, and Powell, with six negative factors between them. One Democrat *with prior service* (White) and one non-Democrat *with prior service* (Stewart) represent a moderate position which will, on occasion, side with either block, although there is increasing evidence that White will almost always vote with the negative block on civil rights cases. This means that the negative block only has to capture one of these two voters to win, and in the 1973–74 term of the Court, the Nixon block of negative voters controlled 80 percent of the 5–4 decisions. In six cases they were able to attract White, and in nine cases they added Stewart. In that same term, in full-length decisions decided nonunanimously, the Nixon block failed to win only two times. The two positions are best seen by examining justices Douglas and Rehnquist, who are polar opposites. If only one person dissents from a negative decision, it will inevitably be Douglas, and if only one person dissents from an affirmative decision, it will just as certainly be Rehnquist. Justice Douglas, in his years on the Courts examined, participated in an amazing 967 nonunanimous civil rights cases and voted negatively only 30 times. In contrast, non-Democrat and previous assistant attorney general Rehnquist voted negatively in each and every one of the 117 nonunanimous cases in which he participated.

What, then, may one conclude from this study? Several things are evident, most important of which is that there has been, at least for the twenty-one judges serving on the Warren and Burger Courts in the past twenty-one years, a clear and statistically meaningful relationship between judicial voting behavior and the variables discovered in this study. It seems evident that if a president (any of the past six) had wished to find a judge for the Supreme Court with a particular view which would be reflected in his voting, the variables would have greatly increased his chances of doing so. Let us assume that a president seeking a negative-voting justice would always use at least one, and perhaps both, of the negative variables in selecting his nominee, while a president seeking an affirmative-voting judge would always make certain that any appointee would never have more than one, and preferably none, of the negative variables, and see what predictive capacity the two variables would have produced.

Assume that a president wished to appoint a negative voter, that is, one who would vote against the claims of labor and the economic little man and in favor of management and business in the economic area. Let him choose party affiliation alone, and make all his appointments from non-Democrats, without reference to any other variable. Of the nine non-

Democrats who were appointed, he would have been disappointed only in Earl Warren, for no other non-Democrat voted above the 50-percent level in favor of the claims made. The collective average voting percentage of non-Democrats was only 27 percent with Warren, and a dismal 21 percent without his high average added. The single variable would have worked for economics in eight of nine cases, for an 88 percent predictive value.

Next, assume that a president wished to appoint an affirmative voter, that is, one who would favor the claims of labor and the little man. Let him make all his appointments from Democrats, without reference to any other variable. He would have been disappointed in Minton (44 percent), Reed (42 percent), and Powell (19 percent), out of a total of twelve Democrats, which would give that variable taken alone a 75 percent predictive record. Had one taken the other variable, *prior service as high federal prosecutor or federal judge,* the picture would have produced the following. The president looking for negative justices would have appointed those *with prior service,* of which there were twelve all told. Those twelve justices voted collectively at a 36-percent affirmative level, and the president would only have been disappointed with Clark (69 percent), Marshall (69 percent), and White (65 percent). The predictive value of the variable would again have been nine of twelve, or 75 percent accuracy. The president looking for affirmative voters, and using the *prior service* variable by picking those with no such service, would have found that his appointees voted affirmatively 59 percent of the time, and he would have failed to predict the voting of Burton, Frankfurter, and Powell, and the variable would have been useful two times out of three.

But the thesis of this paper is that the variables are additive. What would have happened had presidents used both negative variables to produce negative voters, and neither of them to produce a positive voter? The answer is clear. No single justice out of twenty-one votes above the 50-percent level who possesses both negative factors, and only Lewis Powell possesses neither negative factor but still votes negatively. Using both variables, presidents would have named to the Court twenty of twenty-one justices (95 percent) who voted as expected. Those with two negative variables would have voted for big business and management 75 percent of the time, while those without any negative variables would have voted for labor and the little man 78 percent of the time. Taken singly, the party affiliation variable has greater predictive value (both in terms of collective percentages and individual voting behavior) than does the *prior service* variable.

In the civil rights field the following pattern emerges. A president looking for justices who did not support civil rights claims would have appointed non-Democrats, and he would have been disappointed only in

Earl Warren, for the nine non-Democrats voted collectively against the claims 67 percent of the time, and all but Warren voted far below the 50-percent level. The president who used only this variable alone to produce affirmative voters would, however, have been disappointed almost as often as not. While Douglas, Goldberg, Fortas, Marshall, and Brennan were all extremely affirmative voters, Jackson, Clark, Minton, and Reed joined Powell in voting at less than the 50-percent level. The collective voting average of Democrats was 73 percent affirmative, but five of twelve judges or 41 percent, would not have voted as predicted. The party variable alone would have had insignificant predictive value.

The president who used the *prior service* variable alone would have found the following pattern emerging. The president looking for negative voters would have picked those with experience as federal judges or high federal prosecutors, and he would have found a collective voting percentage of 65 percent negative, and would have been disappointed only in Thurgood Marshall. The predictive value would have been 91 percent. The president looking for affirmative civil rights justices would have found his appointees with *no prior service* voting at the collective 76-percent level as he wished them to, and would have been disappointed only in Frankfurter, Burton, and Powell, for a predictive individual value of two out of three judges. Again, the president who was wise enough to use both variables would have been disappointed only in Lewis Powell, and just as in economics, the two variables would have predicted the behavior of twenty out of twenty-one justices, or 95 percent of the time. Clearly in civil rights the *prior service* variable has more predictive value than *party affiliation,* just as in economics the reverse was true. But the real secret in both fields is the cumulative effect of the variables.

It seems clear that statistical methods can successfully be used to understand and possibly to predict behavior on the American Supreme Court, at least over the very broad-range issues considered for the past twenty-one years. If other studies on the order of this one are able to replicate its findings in other historical time periods and on other issues, it may perhaps become obvious that United States Supreme Court justices are at least as partisan in their treatment of law cases and litigants as they have been charged with being—if not more so.

These findings may dismay those observers of the Court for whom the Warren years were a sort of golden era, with the justices undaunted confronting social and political issues that the elective branches were unable or unwilling to resolve. It is one thing, however, to readily admit that the Court is a political—that is, a policy-making—institution and quite another to face the fact that partisanship and interest may operate within it possibly to the detriment of one's own causes. As we have seen, numerous myths about the Supreme Court have fallen before more sophisticated analysis in general and more rigorous quantitative methodology in particular. Perhaps it is time to add to this list the newer myth fostered by the activism of the Warren Court, the idea of the Court as catalyst of change and defender of the defenseless. Although the Court does have the capacity to assume these roles, we should perhaps bear in mind that precisely because the Court *is* a political institution, its actions inevitably will only please some of the people some of the time. The more objective our understanding of what the Court is and is not, the more accurate our expectations and predictions of its behavior will be.

BIBLIOGRAPHY

Adamany, David, "The Party Variable in Judges' Voting: Conceptual Notes and a Case Study," *American Political Science Review* 63 (1969): 57.

Bowen, Don, "The Explanation of Judicial Voting Behavior from Sociological Characteristics of Judges." Ph.D. dissertation, Yale University, 1965.

Goldman, Sheldon, "Voting Behavior on the United States Courts of Appeals, 1961–1964," *American Political Science Review* 60 (1966): 374.

Lindstrom, E. "Attributes Affecting the Voting Behavior of Supreme Court Justices: 1889–1959." Ph.D. dissertation, Stanford University, 1968.

Nagel, Stuart, *The Legal Process from a Behavioral Perspective*. Homewood, Ill.: Dorsey Press, 1969.

Schmidhauser, John, *Constitutional Law in the Political Process*. Chicago: Rand McNally, 1963.

Schubert, Glendon, *Judicial Behavior: A Reader in Theory and Research*. Chicago: Rand McNally, 1964.

Schubert, Glendon, and Danelski, David, eds. *Comparative Judicial Behavior: Cross-Cultural Studies of Political Decision-Making in the East and West*. New York: Oxford University Press, 1969.

Sprague, John, *Voting Patterns of the United States Supreme Court: Cases in Federalism, 1889–1959*. New York: Bobbs Merrill, 1968.

Ulmer, Sidney, "The Political Party Variable in the Michigan Supreme Court," *Journal of Public Law* 11 (1962):352.

————, "Dissent Behavior and the Social Background of Supreme Court Justices," *Journal of Politics* 32 (1970):580.

Anatomy of a Challenge

The Chicago Delegation to the
Democratic National Convention

William J. Crotty

Chicago's Mayor Richard J. Daley in his eternal search for "higher and higher platitudes" has left us with several notable quotations and many indelible political memories, not the least of which constituted the book-ends of one of the most remarkable eras of party reform in this nation's history. From his behavior as host and leading symbol of the reactionaries at the 1968 Democratic National Convention to the behavior of his delegation and its (and his) eventual expulsion from the 1972 Democratic National Convention, Mayor Daley has served as a negative reference for some and as a rallying point for others in the efforts to come to grips with the reforms introduced into delegate selection procedures by the McGovern-Fraser Commission, instituted by the national party to overcome the problems evidenced in 1968.

Although the perspective is oversimplified and personalized (no one is as good or bad as some in this story might lead one to believe), Daley provides a good vantage point from which to view the ramification of the changes that swept through one national party in an unprecedently short four-year period. First, a few words on the mayor's good points. Daley has a national reputation as the mayor who makes Chicago "work." The achievements of his long tenure as mayor (he was first elected in 1955) include reviving the city's economy, rebuilding huge sections of its downtown area, introducing one of the most extensive networks of interstate roads, and creating a series of municipal monuments that range from O'Hare Airport (the world's busiest) to the Picasso sculpture in the Daley-built Civic Center. Daley has also long been a power in national Democratic politics. Richard Nixon (and perhaps others) credited the mayor with winning the 1960 presidential election for John Kennedy. Since one of the new president's very first invitations for a personally conducted tour of the White House went to the Daley family, others were willing to concede him at least a major role in national party affairs. For these reasons alone, the Chicago challenge would prove interesting. Of far greater significance, however, as events would have it, the challenge of the mayor's delegation to the proposed changes was the biggest single obstacle the new party reforms had to face before being accepted. By coincidence, and in the heat of an unusually ugly credentials fight, some of the tactics employed, had they succeeded, would have unalterably changed the face of national politics as we know it and perhaps provided the death knell for any continually effective party organizations. The issues raised by the confrontation cannot be finally settled for many years to come and the outcome of some of them will remain unresolvable. All of this is in the future.

Daley's Chicago Style

Mayor Daley warns that power is dangerous unless "you have humility." The humility of the mayor and of the political machine he heads is legendary. It is reflected in the words of Alderman Claude W. B. Holman, presiding officer in the Chicago City Council until his death in the years after the 1972 convention, a black and the heir to Congressman William Dawson's Southside organization, a power in Chicago machine politics, a challenged delegate to the 1972 Convention, and, above all, a Daley loyalist. Appearing before a somewhat incredulous assembly of national party leaders convened to adjudicate the dispute over credentials challenges, Holman compared the possible unseating of Daley (and his colleagues) to the assassination of Caesar. "You can't take Caesar down!" the good alderman bellowed. (Or in Daley's own, more modest, words delivered on an earlier occasion: "They have vilified me, they have crucified me, yes, they have even criticized me.") Such "humility" resulted in a blindness to the changes in party rules, a predilection toward "business as usual," and eventually a stunned disbelief—a reaction shared as well by those who had no involvement with or even sympathy for the machine—at the final outcome. Mayor Daley, the symbol of oppression in 1968 but also unquestionably the single most powerful man in the loose coalition of state and local Democratic parties that nominate the presidential candidates, was ousted from the 1972 national convention. A recounting of what happened does much to highlight the nature of the reform movement and to illustrate its impact as well as its strengths and its potentially critical weaknesses.

Chicago's Attitude Toward National Party Reform

It is difficult for anyone outside of Chicago to appreciate its political atmosphere. There is a clubbiness, xenophobia, pervasive corruption, and official insensitivity of staggering proportions. Normal political processes have been so compromised as to render any reliance on these virtually useless. Everything of consequence is done through the machine—and for a price. Few appear to question or to care. And fewer yet challenge. The machine operates on the assumption that every person has his price—measured in economic rewards, power, or community honors—a pretty fair and quite successful operating principle. With such insularity, abuses are bound to grow. The concerns of the outside appear far off and, more significantly, irrelevant. Such an attitude leads to difficulties, and the problems the machine encountered in getting its people to the 1972 convention vividly illustrated just how much they can be victimized by their own parochialism and indirectly by their own past political success.

National party reforms came slowly to the Illinois Democratic party, an appendage of the Cook County (Chicago) Democratic organization. They came even more reluctantly to Chicago itself. As criticism of Chicago's performance (especially in applying the new rules) arose in the months immediately preceding the convention, Daley (who favors hyperbole) brushed aside any hint of trouble. The reforms, he asserted, "worked better here [in Chicago] than anywhere else in the country," a refrain to be heard often in the weeks to follow. From the mayor's vantage point, this boast was undoubtedly true. The reforms certainly had done little to inconvenience the machine or to change its mode of operation. As pressure mounted, the mayor was pressed further. Angered, he made his views clearer. He told a group of party workers that he didn't "give a damn about the rules of the McGovern Commission." He went on to state: "We'll elect our delegates as we always have. Why the hell should we let those people in Washington tell us how we should elect them?" Once the delegates got to the convention and took their seats, Daley concluded, "no one would dare throw them out." It should be noted that the smart money would have bet Daley to be right.

The extent of Daley's miscalculation bordered on the incredible, as it turned out. In the course of pursuing business as usual he became embroiled in the most far-reaching challenge to the essence of the reforms ever mounted. In fact, as his indignation later expanded, so did his attack on the national party, eventually questioning the authority of a national party convention to rule on its own membership, a power it had been exercising for the 140 years of its existence without serious judicial controversy. He and his lieutenants attempted to force the courts, right up to and including the Supreme Court (convened in an extraordinary summer session), into a repudiation of their historic posture of noninvolvement in internal party matters. The machine would have had the Supreme Court champion its cause—or alternatively coerce the national party to pay a heavy penalty in litigation costs and uncertainty over the outcome of the court cases, and hence the integrity of their nominating process, for its actions.

The machine's reaction was a blend of arrogance and, as events moved along, disbelief, and eventually vindictiveness (which the successful challengers were to live with for a long time to come). All involved, from national party leaders to the media, were quick to grasp the significance of the drama. Although a record number of challenges were lodged with the national party and undoubtedly the one from California would affect the nomination fight the most significantly, for long-run consequences to the party the Chicago challenge was critical. As one local commentator wrote, it "is the blockbuster. . . . Both sides appear to agree that the legitimacy of the party and its convention are at stake." Indisputably, this was the case by the time the challenge reached the national convention's Credentials Committee. As a consequence, many long-time party professionals (more significant than the reformers, newcomers, or disgruntled holdovers from the 1968 convention who voted against Daley for their own reasons) who would normally have been expected to sympathize with the mayor's plight and support his position felt the integrity of the national party was at issue, and they joined in opposition to defeat Daley's forces. The mood was best summed up by Matt Troy, a tough Irish boss from New York. In words the Daley delegates could understand (and curiously the Daley men in the audience paid rapt attention), Troy angrily charged the mayor with putting "the older-line political hacks into the convention so they would do what he told them to." He continued: "I broke my back trying to conform to those new party rules, and I'll be damned if I'm going to let Mayor Daley get away with ignoring the rules and doing things his way."

Quite obviously, the Chicago challenge grew to be something other than a fight to repudiate a holdover symbol from an earlier, discredited convention; more than a rejection of the "old" politics; and more than a local political squabble bucked up to the national level. It represented an attack on the entire conception of the reform effort leveled at its most vulnerable point (enforcement) by the most powerful individual within the party. For these reasons, it deserves extended attention; but before the challenge can be examined in depth, the new rules in effect and the forces that brought them about must be examined.

REFORM AND THE NATIONAL DEMOCRATIC PARTY: THE McGOVERN-FRASER COMMISSION

The Chicago Convention

In 1968, at Mayor Daley's insistence and despite a series of strikes in key service areas, President Lyndon Johnson scheduled the national convention to be held in Chicago in late August. It was the worst decision of a consistently unfortunate year for the Democratic party. By the time the convention met, the logical nominee, Johnson, had withdrawn from the race because of the fierce opposition within his own party to his Vietnam war policies. The insurgents had shown remarkable strength in the primary states. Alarmed, the party regulars attempted to preserve the nomination for the heir apparent, Vice-President Hubert Humphrey, who made every effort to avoid the primaries, even delaying the announcement of his official candidacy until the last possible minute. In state after state, the insurgents (banded behind Senator Eugene McCarthy and another latecomer to the race, Senator Robert Kennedy) met head-on with the party regulars in a nationwide series of conflicts of unprecedented hostility. As later hearings were to show, the party regulars exploited every advantage —including the party rules governing nominating practices which they controlled—to gain the upper hand. To add to the insurgents' woes, the figure who had emerged as their natural leader and who had a reasonable chance of capturing the nomination at the August convention, Robert Kennedy, was assassinated on the night of his victory in the last major primary (California).

The delegates descended on a hot, humid Chicago in an ugly mood. Threats of putting LSD into the city's drinking water (taken seriously by the police) and promises of Yippie demonstrations, "love-ins" on park land, and even running a real, live pig for president preceded the delegates, adding to the tension and the sense of impending catastrophe. Through it all, Mayor Daley promised in no uncertain terms that the law would be enforced and the convention should be able to proceed without untoward incidents.

In truth, convention week was chaotic, undoubtedly the ugliest and most violent experienced by either party. The convention sessions were barely controlled exercises in mass hysteria. The divisions within the party were clearly evident and although Humphrey easily commanded the nomination, wild antics, charges of "police state" procedures directed personally to the mayor, and Daley's frantic shouts and stage directions to the presiding officer of the convention all blurred together to form an image that did little to help the Democrats in the general election. Outside, the Chicago police engaged in a nightly series of bloody street fights with demonstrators that one quasi-official report referred to as a "police riot." Delegates, spectators, and, most significantly of all, television viewers across the nation were shocked. The ramifications of this convention would be felt for years to come.

Out of this melee, and little noticed at the time, the convention had mandated the national committee to establish two reform commissions. First—the (McGovern-Fraser) Commission on Party Structure and Delegate Selection—was authorized by a Credentials Committee resolution adopted by the convention to study the delegate selection processes in effect in the various states; to recommend improvements that could assure even broader citizen participation; to aid the state Democratic parties in working toward relevant changes in state law and party rules; and to make its recommendations available to the national committee and the next convention. In addition, a proposal of the convention's Rules Committee and one from a special task force established by the previous convention, both endorsed by the convention membership, added to the commission's charge. The first provided that all Democratic voters should have a "full and timely" opportunity to participate in delegate selection; that the unit rule (whereby a majority of a convention's delegation could cast its total vote) be banned from all stages of delegate selection; and that "all feasible effort" be made to assure that all facets of the delegate selection process are "open to public participation" and that they begin within the calendar year of the convention. The McGovern-Fraser Commission later interpreted the phrase "all feasible efforts" to mean that a state that attempted to comply with the reform guidelines but did not succeed on all counts must show that it had done everything in its power including, for example, introducing and pressing for needed changes in state law in a Republican-controlled state legislature. The interpretation of the standard, in short, was very strict.

Furthermore, the McGovern-Fraser Commission was to study the relationship between the national party and state parties "in order that full participation of all Democrats, regardless of race, color, creed, or national origin, may be facilitated by uniform standards for structure and operation" (the origin of the highly controversial "quota" idea requiring proportional representation of women, youth, and minorities "in reasonable relationship to the group's presence in the population of the State"). The mandates were overlapping and very broad.

The second of the soon-to-be-appointed reform committees, the Rules Commission (more commonly referred to as the O'Hara Commission, in deference to its chairman, Congressman James G. O'Hara of Michigan) was to explore the rules and operations of the convention and its committees. The O'Hara Commission was to review, evaluate, and codify the rules in existence and to recommend improvements. The Chicago challenge focused on the McGovern-Fraser guidelines primarily (although the state delegation's initial refusal under Daley's leadership to appoint the requisite number of women to the convention committees failed to meet one of the O'Hara Commission's standards), and it is on delegate selection problems that this case study focuses. The principal contribution of the Rules Commission to the controversy was the modified Credentials Committee structure that required a neutral hearing officer to

journey to the site of the delegate controversy in order to hear the presentations of both sides and whatever witnesses they might choose to bring
forward. The hearing officer would then present his findings in a report to
the full Credentials Committee, which would use it as the basis for the
debate on the challenge (both sides were also given a brief period to present their arguments in person to the full committee).

The McGovern-Fraser Commission in Action

Both reform committees were appointed in early February 1969. The
aggressive McGovern Commission, under the leadership of the senator
from South Dakota, got under way immediately. It had a first-rate staff
and encouraged volunteer workers. It held seventeen well-attended regional hearings throughout the United States designed to allow the public
and party members to air openly their grievances. At the Chicago hearing
a verbal altercation took place between Chairman McGovern and witness
Daley over the roots of the Chicago convention's problems and the disposition of legal charges still pending against demonstrators. By early fall, the
committee had collected a vast amount of evidence and was ready to turn
to the problem of writing "guidelines," some specific, others setting general standards against which to measure delegate selection systems. In
November it adopted its final eighteen guidelines and distributed these to
each of the state parties. The guidelines were as follows:

A-1. State parties must encourage the representation of minority groups
on national convention delegations "in reasonable relationship to
the group's presence in the population of the State."

A-2. State parties must similarly encourage the representation of youth
(aged 18–30) and women. (These two requirements constituted
the highly publicized "quotas," although the commission formally
claimed this was not their intent.)

A-3. Dealt with registration changes. Not required and therefore not
enforced.

A-4. State parties must remove any fee over ten dollars and all mandatory assessments from delegate selection. Petition signatures of
over 1 percent were also banned. (These changes often involved
state laws and were difficult to enact.)

A-5. State parties must have explicit, written party rules applying to
delegate selection. Stages of delegate selection should occur at a
uniform time and date within a state and should be easily
accessible.

B-1. Proxy voting was forbidden.

B-2. State parties must make clear to voters how they are participating in a process to select a presidential nominee and they must distinguish this process from other party business.

B-3. A quorum of 40 percent was set for all meetings concerned with delegate selection.

B-4. Alternates must be selected by a primary, convention, or party committee, and delegation vacancies must be filled by a representative party committee, a reconvening of the body that selected the original delegate, or the delegation acting as a committee.

B-5. The "unit rule" was banned in delegate selection.

B-6. The proportional representation of presidential candidate strength at all levels of delegate selection was not required and therefore not enforced.

B-7. National convention delegates must be apportioned within a state 50 percent on population and 50 percent on some measure of Democratic strength, and 75 percent of the delegates must be elected from a unit no higher than the congressional district.

C-1. The time, place, and rules for all meetings must be given adequate public notice and candidates or slates for delegate positions at each stage of delegate selection must be given the opportunity to declare on the ballot their preference (the presidential contender they support or "uncommitted" if such is the case). (Another provision requiring statutory change in many states. A-4 and C-1 accounted for 69 percent of the final violations.)

C-2. Automatic (ex officio) delegates were prohibited.

C-3. A confused standard striving to keep the party open to newcomers while restricting delegate selection meetings to Democrats was not required and therefore not enforced.

C-4. All delegate selection (including the election of party committees that chose a portion of the delegation) must take place in the calendar year of the convention.

C-5. Party committees may select no more than 10 percent of a national convention delegation.

C-6. Any body making up a slate to run (for example, on behalf of a presidential contender) for delegate positions must meet all the guarantees to "full and meaningful opportunity to participate" as other party bodies including qualifications as to adequate public notice, representativeness, and widespread participation. If a slate is put forward in a presidential contender's name, it must be done in consultation with the candidate and "adequate procedural safeguards" must ensure that the slate "places no undue burden on challengers" who oppose it (i.e., being the "official" slate backed by the party or not meeting financial or petition requirements challengers had to contend with).

Many of the guidelines are complex and thus some were not well understood by the party or the public. The last one is spelled out in more detail because it is among the less obvious, although its intent and provisions are clear enough and unusually inclusive. Mayor Daley's delegation was accused of violating guidelines A-5, C-1, C-4, C-6 and A-1 and A-2.

What made the exercise in guideline construction most astonishing was the boldness of the McGovern-Fraser Commission (with the backing of the national party) in declaring the guidelines mandatory—*they had to be adopted by the state parties in order to qualify for the next national convention.* The final arbiter of whether the states had fully complied with the guidelines would be the Credentials Committee of the 1972 convention (and, of course, the convention itself). The burden would be on any state not in compliance and challenged on this basis to prove that in effect it had met the spirit and letter of the new party laws. This approach reversed the traditional priorities of American parties, long considered a collection of decentralized local and state groupings over which the national party had little to no control. It also laid the basis for the Chicago challenge to the new regulations and to the new order.

The McGovern-Fraser Commission, first under McGovern and then for the balance of the period under the leadership of Congressman Donald M. Fraser of Minnesota (who took over when McGovern resigned the post to seek the presidency), spent its time in attempting to bring each state party into full compliance with the new standards. It succeeded admirably. Only thirteen state parties were not in accord with part or all of five guidelines, in the vast majority of instances because they could not change the relevant state law in time. The issues left unresolved were mostly minor and dealt with technical language difficulties. It is fair to say that the changes instigated by the reform committee, while controversial, were almost universally adopted. The burden of the challenges to come before the Credentials Committee primarily questioned whether the state parties had lived up to their new rules. The gravity of the issues raised in the Chicago challenge to the national party's authority to promulgate and enforce such guidelines and to demand basic rules of fair representation would, had it succeeded, have swept away some or possibly all of the accomplishments of four years of reform effort. Its effect, one way or the other, would be lasting.

The Facts of the Challenge

The incidents leading to the Chicago challenge are easily recounted. On March 21, 1972, the Illinois primary was held to elect, among other things, delegates to the national conventions. Expectedly, the machine candidates dominated. But the battle had just begun. Within ten days of the primary, ten individuals acting in concert and including aldermen William Singer,

William Cousins, and Anna Langford and the Reverend Jesse Jackson filed written notice of a challenge on behalf as they phrased it, of "Democrats in general, and, in particular, all Blacks, Latin Americans, Women, and Young People."

The machine at first ignored the challenge, letting the ten-day interval in which they were required to reply to the challenge elapse without official comment. This show of indifference lasted until April 19. At that point, a challenged delegate, Alderman Paul Wigoda, a machine stalwart and the law partner of another challenged delegate, City Council President Thomas E. Keane (second in importance in the organization only to Daley), filed a civil action in the state circuit court asking that Wigoda be declared a proper representative of the "uncommitted" fifty-nine delegates and thirty-one alternates being challenged; that all challenged delegates be declared duly elected under Illinois law and entitled to take their seats at the national convention; and that the defendants (Singer et al.) be enjoined from taking any action (i.e., pursuing their challenge before the Credentials Committee) that would interfere with Wigoda and associates acting as delegates. The local courts were chosen because the machine could expect a favorable ruling from these judges, many of whom had been placed on the bench by the machine and some of whom were former law partners of major figures in the city government. In filing his suit, Wigoda was quoted as saying, "First of all, I never read the laws of the [national] Democratic Party and [second] I am not bound by them." The war had been joined.

Previous Practice

Prior to the reform period, the practice of the machine had been to meet before the primary and select (slate) those it wanted elected. Nominations for the delegate positions in each presidential election year were rotated among the fifty ward and thirty township committee members who constituted the eighty-member Cook County Central Committee. Party chieftains who made the slating decisions looked on the nominations as a reward for faithful service and an honor for the recipient, although the party worker who had to pay the expense of attending an out-of-town convention might not always share the leaders' enthusiasm. Those nominated to seek delegate positions put themselves forward as "uncommitted" to any major candidate, thus allowing the mayor to control a large bloc of delegate votes and giving him maximum bargaining leverage at the national convention.

The mayor of Chicago doubled as Cook County Democratic chairman, and the decisions as to slating were made by the county organization in cooperation, formally at least, with an essentially moribund state committee. The nonelective delegate posts were filled by the state convention some time after the primary and went usually to party functionaries, fund-raisers, and public officeholders.

The organization—primarily the grass-roots-level precinct workers, many of whom were beholden to their ward captains for their jobs—then went out and worked for its slate of candidates in the primary. The machine published and distributed sample ballots with only its candidates' names on them, held pep rallies, conducted house-to-house canvasses, mobilized the vote on election day, and absorbed the costs of the campaign. In most states, party endorsements (much less the active support of a factional slate of candidates) are unheard of. The primary is considered an internal party mechanism for deciding upon the party's representatives in the general election. In Chicago, such all-out primary electioneering by the machine was an accepted fact of life. The basic position of the challengers was that despite the reforms mandated at the national level, things had changed little.

Reform in the Illinois Party

This is not to say that Illinois had remained outside the orbit of the reforms sponsored by the national-level party. In 1971 three changes had been enacted into law (Illinois was the first state in the nation to so act, according to Mayor Daley). These permitted a potential delegate to declare his support of a presidential contender or to have "uncommitted" appear beside his name on the ballot; apportionment of delegate seats through a formula based on population and former presidential vote, a refinement that ironically benefited the machine by increasing the Chicago-area representation; and limitation of filings for delegate positions to the year of the national convention. The state party also adopted written rules as required by the McGovern-Fraser Commission but did so *after* the primary had been held, a delay that hurt their position severely. Further, the machine aligned itself against (and thus killed) a bill drafted by an Illinois Muskie-backer that would have required potential delegates who wished to run committed to a presidential contender to receive his permission in writing. The purpose of the proposed legislation was twofold: to prevent overfiling (too many candidates running for too few delegate seats, a move that diluted a candidate's strength) and to assure that all those elected as delegates pledged to a contender were bona fide supporters. As it turned out, Illinois was the only state in the nation that failed to give a presidential contender some form of control over delegates filing in his name.

Such as they were, these changes represented the sum of the reforms. Given the background of Chicago politics and the machine's role in previous primaries, a challenge was not unexpected. In fact, Singer (a young, independent Democratic alderman, Daley's chief adversary, and the man behind the challenge) had let it be known before the primary that anyone wishing to challenge elected delegates on the basis of machine irregularities would receive a sympathetic hearing from him and the groups supporting his position. Chief among these groups was the Committee on Illinois Government, a reform-oriented independent group begun approximately two decades earlier by Governor Adlai Stevenson. More importantly, using volunteer help, Singer and his associates collected the evidence of organizational involvement and abuse during the primary campaign that laid the basis for the later challenge.

On the other side, the state party chairman, a Daley functionary, could claim that the organization's candidates would still go to Miami Beach. "We've always done it before. But it won't be easy as it used to be," he conceded—a prophetic statement, given the events that were to transpire. Daley meanwhile was his usual voluble, aggressive self, lambasting, as he was to do so often, the "so-called Democrats" (those who did not follow the machine line religiously) and labeling the "committed" primary candidates a "bunch of fakers." If those favoring presidential contenders have a right to put together their slates, he reasoned, "then we have a right to put together our slates, too." Excluding the bombast, the argument seems reasonable enough—that is, until the opposition's contention is examined in depth.

The challenge itself was directed against fifty-nine uncommitted delegates and thirty-one alternates elected to fill all but three delegate and three alternate (these went to Muskie-backers) vacancies in eight congressional districts in Chicago or overlapping the city and the suburbs. The challengers claimed violations in two regards: that blacks, Latin Americans, women, and youth were grossly and unfairly underrepresented in the delegations; and that the elected delegates were "slated, endorsed and supported by the Democratic Party organization of Chicago without open slate-making procedures, without public rules relating thereto, and by Party officials who had themselves been chosen prior to 1972." These constitute, as noted, abuses of guidelines A-1, A-2, A-5, C-1, C-4, and C-6.

The reformers claimed that the two thrusts of the challenge were closely related (unrepresentative procedures leading to unrepresentative results). On examination, the inability of the machine's delegation to meet the "quota" standards was obvious. To meet the McGovern-Fraser criteria, twenty-one delegates would have had to be black, six Latin Americans, twenty-nine women, and eighteen young people. In turn, the "Daley 59," as the press called them, included twelve blacks, one Latino, six women, and eight young people.

The machine made no apologies for its choices. They were put forward as the elected representatives of the primary voters. Clearly, though, the mayor's organization had no sympathy for the quota concept. As a former president of the League of Women Voters was later to testify, when she asked a precinct worker canvassing for her vote why the organization's slate did not contain more women, she was told: "Women don't belong in politics."

The crux of the challengers' case rested on the less glamorous set of charges, the argument that the machine had slated and then done its best in the primary to elect its own delegates. To meet the reform rules, the Daley organization would have had to ensure that the people doing the slating had been chosen for that specific purpose with adequate public notice and not prior to the calendar year of the national convention; that the meetings had been well publicized and open to all party members and that there had in fact been widespread participation; and that procedural safeguards had been extended to all participants including the means for initiating meaningful challenges to those included on the designated slate. Furthermore, the slate, once assembled, would have to demonstrate a "reasonable relationship" to the social characteristics of the district it purported to represent; in the parlance of the old politics, there would have to be a "balanced ticket." And party rules would have to exist explaining how members could participate in the process.

The challengers claimed that the Daley organization defaulted on each count, resulting in "gross and deliberate" violations of the reforms, according to Singer. To the contention of the Daley 59, and a powerful one it was, that the will of 900,000 Chicago Democratic voters (the primary turnout) would be voided if their delegates were unseated, the Singer group argued that the electors had not been given a meaningful opportunity to participate in the first, critical stage of slate making. The slates were drawn up in secret by party officials elected for other purposes well before the presidential election year. The organization then went out and employed its considerable resources to elect its designated representatives.

The slates themselves were typical machine creations, including mostly old-line politicians who, as one precinct worker informed a prospective primary voter, had been selected "on account of the fact that they were in the 'Organization' for many years." This last contention appears incontrovertible. The machine showed a decided preference for its own, slating Mayor Daley and thirty-seven of the fifty Chicago ward committeemen and such other organizational stalwarts as (according to the Credentials Committee report) "the Cook County Clerk [as well as the president of the Cook County Board and the clerk of courts], the Sheriff of Cook County, the President of the Chicago City Council [and twelve other machine aldermen], in-laws or relatives of committeemen, the son [and cousin] of Chairman Daley, other party officials, party candidates for public office and persons described as 'confederates of the Chairman or otherwise affiliated with the Democratic organization'." In each instance, moreover, the slate corresponded exactly to the number of positions available. In short, the organization had done its work as it normally did, effectively foreclosing any realistic chance that a sizable number of others would be represented at the Miami Beach convention.

The Contest Begins

National party leaders were aware of what was happening in Chicago and they were upset. In an effort to head off any misunderstanding as to the reforms or their mandatory status, national chairman Lawrence F. O'Brien, in an apparent reaction to the Wigoda suit, issued an unusually strong statement in late April:

> Those states that remain in noncompliance with the delegate selection guidelines must make the necessary changes, promptly. Any state delegation that comes to Miami Beach having been selected by procedures that violate the delegate selection rules of the 1972 Call is certain to be challenged. *The issue is clear and beyond debate.* [Italics added.]

The Mayor disagreed. An ugly and tumultuous battle had commenced.

The Hearings

The Daleyites' defense, initially, was tactical. It was bold; it was arrogant; and it almost worked. Their belief was that they could prevent the hearing officer from the Credentials Committee assigned to Chicago from even holding the meetings necessary to establish the facts of the case and thus making the report to the full committee necessary for its deliberations. Once the issue went to the full convention at Miami Beach, they expected little trouble. They persevered and they almost carried it off. The challenge was a nuisance, little more. Similar to many such incidents in the past, it would disappear, the challengers routed and in disarray. In essence, this is what helps to make the imbroglio so arresting: Daley was determined that no national party would apply its rules within his dukedom. Conversely, if the national party backed down, its reforms —and whatever limited authority it yielded—were meaningless, a point O'Brien fully appreciated.

The first hearing officer, Louis Oberdorfer, appointed by the acting chairwoman of the Credentials Committee, Patricia Roberts Harris, became the contest's first sacrifice. The hearing officers were to be persons "known by reputation to be fair and impartial in the context of the challenge and . . . experienced in the law." Thirty-six, all distinguished lawyers, had been assembled (primarily by Burke Marshall, former assistant attorney general under John Kennedy and Yale Law School professor).

They included men of legal reputation and unquestioned integrity. And they donated their time, serving without pay.

Oberdorfer, an assistant attorney general under both Kennedy and Johnson, soon found that Chicago politics could be tough. He came to the city and held an exploratory meeting of all the principals to set procedures and establish the ground rules for the full hearing into the facts that would serve as the basis for his report to the Credentials Committee. Under persistent questioning from challenged delegates Keane and Troy, it came out that the law firm with which Oberdorfer was associated represented the American Automobile Manufacturers' Association, whose member firms included General Motors, Ford, and Chrysler, all defendants in antipollution suits filed by the City of Chicago (thus, in the eyes of the challenged members of the city's power structure, causing the lawyer to be biased against them). Secondly, the Daley group's lawyers brought admission of the fact that Oberdorfer's firm and that of the two chief counsels (Wayne Whalen and John Schmitt) for the challengers were co-counsels in a law case before the courts. An angry and flustered Oberdorfer put in a call to Washington to Chairwoman Harris asking to be relieved. He was, and the first round went to Daley's men.

The organization men could not leave well enough alone. Practitioners of the overkill, they went on to demonstrate the flamboyance that endears one to Chicago politics. Troy, a challenged delegate from the Seventh Congressional District as well as an attorney for the delegation, concurrent with the Oberdorfer episode (late May) was waging a guerilla war with the national party headquarters. He wired national chairman O'Brien demanding that Harris be fired because she failed to answer satisfactorily a number of questions he had forwarded relating to the challenge. The effort generated some local publicity but little else.

Harris moved quickly to appoint Cecil Poole, fifty-seven, a black attorney from San Francisco and a Harvard Law School graduate, as the new hearing officer. An unknown quantity in Chicago, Poole at one time had served as U.S. attorney for the Northern District of California (1961–1970) and at another had had an appointment to a high court vacancy blocked by Republican opponents. With the arrival of Poole, the game began anew (despite, as it turned out, the effort by Keane to postpone the meeting until the local courts had ruled on the Wigoda suit—he expected that the decision would be favorable and that the challengers would be prohibited from doing anything to keep the elected delegates from taking their seats).

Poole was a shrewd lawyer and, despite his soft-spoken style and calm demeanor, a tough adversary. He was perhaps the brightest individual in the room (although this was challenged in an unintentionally comic scene when, in opposition to Poole's ruling against a motion, a red-faced, shout-

ing young alderman insisted that *he* was the smartest man at the hearing)
and unquestionably the best lawyer, and he soon established himself as
an unfailingly courteous but no-nonsense arbiter who had every intention
of proceeding with and *finishing* the hearing. The organization got more
than it bargained for; but, as usual, it seemed determined to find out the
hard way.

The initial encounter turned into quite a show. Liking a good thing
when they saw it, the Daley 59 lawyers began by demanding that Poole
disqualify himself. Their main argument was simplicity itself: since Oberdorfer had done so, Poole should, too. Alternately shouting, pleading, and
reasoning, they argued that Poole would undoubtedly be prejudiced
against them because of what had happened the first time around. Furthermore, he probably had read—or would read—the record of the initial
meeting with Oberdorfer. Since it was not particularly pleasant, this review would prejudice his thinking. And, by the way, did he perhaps know
any of the challengers, serve as co-counsel with their lawyers on any case,
or represent any group that was being sued by the city of Chicago?

When such attacks produced little result, they changed the arguments:
Poole was holding the hearings in violation of state law; the Credentials
Committee had no jurisdiction; Poole was chosen as hearing officer in violation of Credentials Committee procedures (i.e., the machine claimed it
had never been given a chance to submit its nominees); Poole favored the
Black Panthers (a convoluted argument involving a highly controversial
raid by the state's attorney's office on a Black Panther headquarters that
resulted in several suspicious deaths, and a legal point that even the machine did not appear to place great faith in); Poole was probably a friend
of Oberdorfer's since both had served in the Justice Department at the
same time; Poole was a big-city lawyer prejudiced against small midwest-
ern (Chicago!) lawyers; Poole would probably favor the challengers on
rules of procedure; and so on. But Poole persisted. He answered the objections, some many times over. He remained calm and he unmistakably
indicated that the hearing would be held.

But the organization's lawyers—seventeen in all—were at least as stub-
born. They next inundated Poole with motions, more than fifty in total,
ranging from demands that the challenge be dismissed to requests for information and the clarification of procedural points (the latter were general standards for the most part and since they had never been applied
before, they provided ample opportunity for digression). The motions
and verbal attacks were interspersed with veiled threats to Poole's well-
being, often in the guise of humor. The indomitable Troy, among others,
publicly asked what hotel Poole was staying at and wondered aloud if he
would be safe. It was suggested that he should watch his home mail and
"if it's ticking, throw it in the trash"—a crude joke that the organization

representatives thoroughly enjoyed. For others, anger replaced the heavy-handed bantering. Keane, the autocratic and detached leader of the City Council, in particular seemed incensed at Poole's conduct of the meeting, calling it a "kangaroo court." "All my motions are overruled by you without argument," the agitated leader of the City Council complained, not used to sitting while others made decisions. An unruffled Poole responded ("That sometimes happened") and went on with the meeting, a move that did not improve Keane's mood.

The wrangling continued throughout the four-and-a-half-hour morning session and into midafternoon. Then, with a few motions carried over for later decision, the challengers were given the opportunity to make a brief opening statement and to call their first witnesses. Their victory was short-lived. They decided to put the Reverend Jesse Jackson on first, primarily because he was leaving that day to join the McGovern campaign in California and they felt a strategic advantage might lie in having him testify. The choice was a mistake. Jackson knew little concerning the facts of the challenge or the contents of the reform guidelines. His testimony took slightly over one-half hour. The cross-examination took over three hours. Aldermen (and delegates) Holman and Vrdolyak (a tough newcomer to Chicago politics) demonstrated with painful clarity Jackson's ignorance of the specifics of the issues involved. Jubilant at what they heard, the lawyers from each congressional district's delegation insisted on and received their chance to take a crack at the witness, questioning him on all aspects of Chicago and Cook County government. Flushed with victory, they shouted across the room to Singer that he was next. When bored with their questioning, they took random shots at Poole (as they were to do each day) in an attempt to rattle or provoke him. As the session continued into the night, delay, harassment, and ridicule remained the basic response of the Daley 59. The only humor of note came at the end of the lengthy first session when Troy pleaded with Poole (who had court appearances in San Francisco upcoming) to postpone in "fairness and good conscience" a scheduled future meeting that conflicted with a convocation of delegates in Springfield. No one could recall a machine stalwart ever having made such an appeal.

The pattern continued into the second day. The first witness took fifteen minutes to give her statement. The machine cross-examination took five times as long, focusing on intimidation as much as anything. Adjournments were sought to allow members to attend City Council meetings. The battle of wits continued to rage. Keane threatened to go into the home of every person who filed an affidavit on behalf of the challengers and take sworn depositions. Other machine supporters felt such bullying tactics went too far. The organization objected to all the witnesses before they spoke (usually on the curious grounds that their testimony would be prejudicial to the machine) and they tried to have their comments struck from the record when they finished.

The hearing officer continued to sit it out. He refused to allow the ceaseless, repetitive questioning of witnesses. He requested the panoply of lawyers to consolidate their arguments and attempted to ration the time available to each interrogator. The restrictions were difficult to enforce, and halfway through the day's session Poole issued his "Order of June 1," establishing the remaining schedule of hearings, requiring written statements of testimony, limiting the time available for cross-examination, and, worst of all, setting aside the bulk of a two-day period for the Daley 59 to give their side (testimony they had no intention of delivering).

As the day wore on, Poole made it clear that if a pattern existed (i.e., the machine slated candidates at closed meetings and then campaigned for them), this would be sufficient evidence of abuse; witnesses did not have to establish specific guideline abuses *by each and every delegate* personally. In part, he hoped that this ruling (much disputed by the organization members, who felt it would be more damaging to them) would end the practice of asking each witness to go down the list of the Daley 59 and testify to violation by each delegate individually. The move met limited success. Still, and despite the delays, the hearings did move on in the late afternoon and evening sessions to some serious and eventually damaging witnesses. Persons began to appear who could testify to personal knowledge of hearing some of Daley's extravagant attacks on the reforms, his disregard of any intent to abide by them, and the machine's closed slating and continued electioneering. With these, the case began to be made, and the realization set in that the machine ploys had failed: a hearing was proceeding and there was little the organization could do to prevent the available evidence from coming out.

Two full days of hearings (including one that pushed past midnight) had produced less than three hours of direct testimony. Nonetheless, the tide had turned. These two rowdy days were possibly the most significant of all those during the long months of the controversy. The national party had established its right, inferentially, to hold hearings and to adjudicate the dispute. The machine had failed in its attempt to totally prohibit any interference from the national party in the manner in which its delegation was chosen.

Poole was more clearly in charge as the hearings progressed. When next they resumed, eight days later, the organization was not in a mood to repeat the earlier performances. It had brought in its big guns—dramatically adjourning the City Council to ensure that Keane, Holman, and the other aldermen would be there (precipitating a row in the council and also prohibiting any business to be conducted in their absence)—all to little avail. Poole had mastered the onslaught. Meanwhile, much had happened in the days between meetings. The 160 delegates had convened in Springfield on the Friday following the first hearings to elect ten at-large members. They heard Daley, who assumed control of the group, castigate the reformers, claiming they were the same forces behind the riots at the 1968 convention (an event he was never to forget). Daley again blamed the media ("the most lopsided reporting ever") and defended the police ("The police hit no one, but were attacked") before turning his oratorical and analytical skills to the substance of the challenge:

> Now the same forces of the [1968] convention are at work, yelling about how we should select delegates by quotas. There can be no quotas in an election. The people establish these quotas by voting. [This was Daley's principal defense, and a strong one.] I can only hope the people hoping for a confrontation hope as much for the party [sic]. And if they do, we'll elect the entire ticket.

Daley's outburst had the unfortunate effect of buttressing many of the arguments his opponents were making. His proclamation, again, that no one dare put them out of the convention placed his advocates—who were attempting to picture him as a man of reason who supported and fully applied the reform guarantees—in a difficult position.

On June 6, two days before the hearing resumed, McGovern had virtually won the Democratic nomination by sweeping four primaries, including the all-important California test. The significance of these victories was that Daley would be facing a convention presumably sympathetic to the reforms he had ridiculed. McGovern, with whom he had clashed on several occasions on reform questions and whom he inferentially blamed in part for the 1968 fiasco, now controlled the party convention. Finally, even if Daley won, his "uncommitted" delegates had lost their significance and his appeal at this stage could not entice other contenders (now seemingly out of the race) to come to his support. Matters did not turn out to be as simple as they appeared at this juncture—the California challenge launched by Humphrey again threw McGovern's nomination into doubt—but the atmosphere surrounding the third session had a finality not found in the others. All-out opposition by the machine stood to gain little.

The organization did revive its tactics of ridicule and veiled personal threats, and the paper blitz continued (motions, countermotions, affidavits, etc.), but its gusto was noticeably diminished. After several hours of renewed battle, these tactics had again failed to secure any material gains. Capitulating to the inevitable, the machine's lawyers sought the best deal they could. And they did not do badly. The challengers never did manage to present their full case orally for television and the press. Too much time had been lost and the organization now wanted to speed up and complete the hearing, fighting its battle in some other location. Also, after having mercilessly badgered the early witnesses, it shrank from the spectacle of seeing some of its bigger names (Daley) called upon to undergo similar treatment from the other side. The organization obtained agreement to avoid this unpleasantness by allowing the record for the case to be made and after one more lengthy day the hearings to be terminated.

The closing arguments, no less than the hearings more generally, demonstrated the inability of the combatants to agree on what precisely was at stake. Whalen, one of three lawyers for the challengers, accused the organization of showing "gross disregard," even "contempt," for the reforms. The results, he contended, ended in the "most flagrant violation of Democratic party rules in the nation." The arguments of the challenged delegates failed to address these points. One of several lawyers speaking on their behalf, Ray Simon (later to appear before the Credentials Committee in a similar role), charged the Singer group with wanting to take over power in Chicago, an allegation the challengers made repeatedly throughout the long struggle. He contended that national party rules cannot violate state law; that, consequently, if Chicago delegates were challenged successfully, *all* delegates from Illinois would have to be unseated. Others on behalf of the Daley 59 drew attention to the potential disenfranchising of Chicago voters (through voiding the primary decision), and Troy warned that if the challenge carried it would represent "the death knell of the Democratic party as we know it." All organization speakers hinted the party's presidential nominee would suffer if the challenge was sustained (a thought that must also have occurred to McGovern and his advisors). On such a note did the climactic sessions in Chicago stagger to their close.

The turn of events and the prospect of having their case decided on the national level forced the organization to develop its arguments more carefully. It chose two of its best lawyers to make the presentation before the Credentials Committee: Ray Simon, a law partner of one of Daley's sons and a former city corporation counsel, whose manner was to affect a sincerity and reasonableness that contrasted with the shrill harangues of many of the others; and Jerome Torshen, an aggressive private attorney of independent legal reputation who represented Keane on other matters besides the challenge. This defense of the Daleyites, the most serious they put forward, deserves attention. First, they argued that almost a million Chicago voters would be denied a voice in the convention if they were unseated. Second, they maintained that any implicit quota system is impossible in a true elective system. Third, they said any evidence of a machine-controlled primary was circumstantial (a not very convincing argument). Fourth, they attacked the manner in which the Singer delegates had been chosen and they questioned the representativeness of the challengers' delegation (a most vulnerable aspect of the challenge, as will be shown, but one the Daley forces stupidly undercut by their own violent acts). Fifth, they denied the sincerity of the challengers, who, they contended, were not "good Democrats" and who intended to destroy the party (i.e., oppose the Chicago organization).

If they had emphasized earlier their stronger and more relevant arguments (the first, second, and fourth) rather than taking the blindly obstructionist approach they did, they would have given many people who were seeking it (in the name of political reality) grounds for supporting them or for arranging an attractive compromise on their behalf early in the proceedings and well before Daley's personal authority could be called into question. The Daleyites had refused compromise; they had offered little to those willing to take their side and made no effort at coalition-building in support of their then murky defense; they had underestimated the strength of their opposition; they had ignored the rules in effect and had chosen to antagonize the national party, forcing it into the dispute on the side of their opponents; and they had persisted in seeing the fight as a local squabble (a type of encounter they never lost) and fought it in this manner. In truth, the organization people did not appear to understand the nature of the controversy they were engaged in, and consequently they wasted a good deal of time in developing weak or extraneous positions. Their more relevant defenses were belatedly arrived at (consolidated after the well-publicized Chicago hearing) and they were not well received by the Credentials Committee, who now saw the issue differently: as the total, arrogant, uncompromising defiance of the national party. Their tactical moves—court challenges, boasts as to the outcome, even continued defiance of more reform standards (see below) —which were of greater importance at this stage of the controversy, continued to be amateurish, initiated more from spite and anger than from any real effort to retain their convention seats. However, to understand the machine's response, it is necessary to appreciate the pressures the organization was under at this point in time. Within a broader context, the challenge to the fifty-nine delegates (which was to prove serious enough) was initially seen as one of many problems (and one of the least significant).

The Machine Has Its Problems

Unquestionably, 1972 had been a tough year for the machine. A pre-dawn raid over two years earlier (December 1969) by the state's attorney's office on a Black Panther apartment had resulted in the killing of two Panthers. The issues raised by the deaths and the police conduct in the raid had haunted the party over the intervening years, leading in due course to a special investigation by a court-appointed prosecutor and eventually to the indictment of the state's attorney, Edward V. Hanrahan, a Daley favorite and a machine "comer" (the next mayor, some believed). Hanrahan first received the machine's endorsement for renomination in the March primary. As the case grew more ominous and the normally docile blacks organized behind former machine lieutenant, Congressman Ralph Metcalf, to oppose Hanrahan and police practices more generally, the organization was rent by a dispute. Many favored dropping Hanrahan, while others such as the aging but still influential Alderman Vito Marzullo ("Eddie's too tough!") wanted him retained as the party's candidate. At the eleventh hour, Daley replaced Hanrahan as nominee with a lackluster traffic court judge, publicized for his court reform and traffic crackdowns, which later turned out to be nothing more than a bookkeeping gimmick and publicity drive intended to make the court's chief officer look good. Hanrahan won in a three-way race, an outcome that led to mutterings about Daley's continuing political judgment. (Hanrahan later lost the general election to a Republican in an even bigger upset. He was acquitted of all charges in court just prior to the November election, which, curiously, appeared to hurt his candidacy.)

The scars from the internecine warfare over Hanrahan did not heal quickly. But the machine had received another unexpected rebuff in the primary. It had endorsed a downstate Democrat, Lieutenant Governor Paul Simon, for governor. Simon lost a close race to Independent Democrat (and later governor) Dan Walker, an antimachine candidate who first gained prominence as the author of a highly unfavorable official report on the conduct of the city administration during the 1968 convention. The proposed Credentials challenge or the observance of the reform guidelines during the primary election were not priority items on the organization's agenda.

The machine had been buffeted. And more was to come. Poole's closing remarks as to how he was "deeply troubled" by what he had heard boded ill for the Chicago delegates. Possibly this would have been the logical point for the machine to retrench, soften its demands, and make the best of the situation. Certainly, McGovern was sympathetic and favored some type of compromise that would seat the powerful Daley (a view he held until the final convention vote on the issue), but he was not in a position to repudiate publicly (thus weakening his candidacy) the reforms he helped to initiate. The Daleyites appeared to demand nothing less. They were not open to compromise and they had yet to finish their assault on the new rules. In fact, what followed amounted to the most frantic days of a demanding election year.

The State Convention

The day after Poole concluded his hearing the state convention met in Springfield, ostensibly to ratify the choice of the ten at-large delegates selected a week earlier. The organization had other plans. Daley had been openly angered by the at-large vote of the 160 delegates which had rejected a number of old Chicago pros and two labor confidants of the mayor (although Daley's "uncommitted" slate had actually captured six of the ten vacant slots). In fact, Daley had insisted on counting irregularly marked ballots which permitted "counting in" one more Chicago Democrat at the expense of a downstate party member. Nonetheless, the mayor was not placated. He boldly proposed, and the state Democratic convention ratified, a proposal to double the number of at-large delegates from ten to twenty (giving each a one-half vote rather than a full vote) and the alternates from nine to eighteen. Daley then appointed the newcomers. The move was a crass violation of national party rules and the reform guidelines. It directly repudiated the national party's authority to set the size of state delegations and to authorize the division of the vote; it transgressed the reform provision against split votes; and it violated both national party and reform standards as to how delegates were to be chosen. Daley simply assumed the power to appoint the new delegates. The state convention's delegates had not conferred such power on him nor did they vote on the appointees to the illegal vacancies. Daley no longer appeared to care, and began preparations for two busy weeks. The end of the first week would again find him back in Springfield for a meeting of the national convention delegation scheduled to elect its officers.

CHICAGO CHALLENGE
Chronology of Events

February 24	Meeting of ward committeemen, during which Daley said that he didn't "give a damn about the rules of the McGovern Commission" and that "once the delegates were seated no one would dare throw them out."
March 21	Illinois primary.
March 31	"Written Notice of Intent to Challenge" filed with Credentials Committee by Singer et al.
April 19	Challenged delegate, Alderman Paul Wigoda, files suit in state circuit court on behalf of all the elected delegates, requesting an injunction to stop challenge.
April 20	Challengers (Singer et al.) file suit in U.S. district court to have case removed to federal court.

May 2   Wigoda files countersuit to have federal case remanded to state court denied.

May 3   Challengers file suit in U.S. district court to enjoin organization from getting an injunction.

May 18   Federal judge (in response to May 3 suit) rules that he does not have jurisdiction in Wigoda case, that forum for settling dispute is Credentials Committee of national convention; but does put off action for ten days, prohibiting machine from interfering with process and thus allowing Credentials Committee hearing officer to hold meeting.

May 24   Louis Oberdorfer, first Credentials Committee hearing officer, arrives in Chicago; holds stormy meeting with principals; asks to be relieved.

May 25   Challengers postpone caucuses intended to select alternate slate.

May 26   Second federal judge issues restraining order against "Daley 59" that permits a new hearing officer to conduct investigation into facts of case.

             Credentials Committee chairwoman, Patricia Roberts Harris, appoints Cecil Poole as new hearing officer.

May 31   Credentials Committee's Chicago hearings begin with Cecil
(Wednesday) Poole as new hearing officer.

June 1   Credentials Committee's Chicago hearings continue.
(Thursday)

June 2   One hundred and sixty convention delegates meet in Spring-
(Friday)   field to elect ten at-large delegates.

June 6   California "winner take all" primary won by McGovern (who also captures New Jersey, New Mexico, and South Dakota primaries on same day).

June 8   Credentials Committee's Chicago hearings resume and after long day are completed.

June 9   State Democratic convention meets in Springfield to ratify the election of at-large delegates and alternates; doubles number of at-large delegates from ten to twenty and alternates from nine to eighteen; additional delegates appointed.

June 12   Challenge to expanded at-large delegation initiated.

June 16   Full convention delegation meets in Springfield to elect delegate chairman and other officers and delegates to serve on three convention committees (six per committee); does not select proper proportion of women, leading to rejection of state representatives by convention committee and another Illinois-instituted court suit.

June 17   Watergate break-in.

June 19   Federal district judge in Washington, D.C., upholds Keane, Wigoda, et al. challenge and voids guidelines A-1, A-2, C-4, and part of C-6.

June 20   Federal appeals court overturns lower-court decision but indicates suit could be renewed pending outcome of Credentials Committee hearings.

June 21   Daley returns to Chicago (from Mayors' Conference in New Orleans) and convenes meeting of party leaders.

June 22   Chairman refuses to seat Illinois representatives (and nine other state delegations) to Rules Committee of convention (and other convention committees) because male-female ratio violates national party rules.

Challengers hold congressional district caucuses as first step in selecting their delegations; meetings disrupted by Daley forces.

June 23   Daley capitulates and restructures convention committee delegations, giving equal weight to men and women; new delegation permitted full voice in Rules Committee deliberations.

June 24   Challengers convene their county convention to make final selection for alternative delegation; meeting disrupted briefly at opening by Daley forces.

June 26   Credentials Committee's full hearings open in Washington, D.C.

June 27   Credentials Committee meeting continues; Cecil Poole report on Chicago challenge released.

June 28   Frank Mankiewicz attempts to mediate Chicago dispute.

Democratic caucus in House of Representatives initiated by, among others, Congressman Frank Annuzio of Chicago, a machine figure, denounces new reforms.

June 29   Humphrey California challenge to McGovern California victory sustained by 72–66 vote in Credentials Committee.

June 30   Chicago challenge of Singer et al. upheld in Credentials Committee by 71–61 vote; Daley and fifty-eight other machine representatives unseated.

July 1   John Mitchell quits as head of Committee to Re-elect the President; Clark MacGregor chosen to replace him.

July 3   U.S. federal district judge upholds Credentials Committee decisions in Illinois and California controversies.

July 4   Credentials Committee ends Washington deliberations.

July 5   U.S. court of appeals upholds Credentials Committee decision on Chicago but reverses its ruling on California and returns to McGovern 151 votes he lost.

July 7   U.S. Supreme Court rejects suits (thus upholding Credentials Committee's original decisions) stating that only the Democratic National Convention can determine a delegate's right to sit in its deliberations.

July 10   Democratic National Convention convened in Miami Beach. First session reverses Credentials Committee ruling on California (returning original 151 delegates to McGovern) and upholds committee's decision on Illinois (unseating Mayor Daley and his delegation) in session lasting well into Tuesday (adjournment comes at 4:52 A.M.).

July 12   McGovern wins presidential nomination.

July 13   Democratic National Convention recessed.

July 20   Jerome Torshen speaking for the Daley group seeks contempt ruling against Singer delegation for disobeying Cook County Circuit Court order not to take their seats in the convention.

September 14   Judge Daniel A. Covelli, on motion of Wigoda argued by Torshen, orders Singer group to show why they should not be held in contempt of circuit court; case to continue for years, up through Illinois court system to, eventually, U.S. Supreme Court.

The Battle Rages: Two Hectic Weeks

The week opened with an irate Muskie delegate (Muskie was the candidate who lost the most when the at-large vote had been diluted) filing a challenge with the Credentials Committee. Said the delegate: "It is utterly disgusting to see how they [the party's state convention leadership] push things through, shout people down, not even attempting to make it [the proceedings] look legitimate. I now understand—not that I condone it—how people can be incited to violence."

Under pressure, the machine often announces massive public-spirited projects: a new airport in the lake; a multistoried bandshell over a sunken public garage; a new business complex constructed with the air rights over the railroad yards; a new civic auditorium; a new interstate highway to knife through the city; and, the most persistent of all, a sports complex on the lake front with a new football stadium for the beloved Bears. Few of the projects ever come to pass, although they do divert public and press attention and they hold the promise of jobs for the faithful and contracts for the business community.

Tuesday, the mayor launches an unusual part of his counterattack. He holds a full-scale City Hall press conference to announce a "gigantic" project, a "War on Litter." Surrounded by the streets and sanitations commissioner, the Chicago park district board president, the acting general superintendent of parks, the police and fire commissioners, and the president of the Chicago Federation of Labor, Daley indignantly tells reporters that litter on the lakefront will not be tolerated. The mayor assigns 1,000 additional workers (including 600 new men) to the battle, increases fines from the $5–$50 range to $50–$100, announces that a citizens committee composed of representatives of business and labor has been formed to fight litter, and asks support of all Chicagoans in the battle. The mayor vows the cleanest Fourth of July ever!

Daley also reveals the creation of a Citizens' Landmark Commission, to be appointed by the mayor, to help preserve architectural landmarks. Chicago already has such a commission (appointed by the mayor) but the well-publicized action is taken after the demolition of the Old Stock Exchange Building, designed by Louis Sullivan, and the controversy it raised.

Lost in the excitement is the rumor that U.S. senator Adlai Stevenson will oppose Daley for the post of delegation chairman, a position Daley has held since 1956. Stevenson refuses to deny the accounts and a Daley supporter retorts: "If he [Stevenson] is taking on the mayor, he's playing squash in White Sox Park." The words, again, are prophetic.

Wednesday, the national party's legal counsel, Joseph Califano, responds to a request for a decision from an Illinois Muskie leader on the legality of the expanded delegation. Califano rules that the number of delegates and their full votes has been set by the National Committee in the 1972 Call and cannot be changed through the unilateral action of one state party. Daley's move is declared illegal.

Stevenson supporters claim ninety votes (eighty-six are needed to win) for delegation chairman "with more coming." Brazenly, they ask if the mayor would like to nominate Stevenson for the post "as a unity move." Stevenson and Daley speak and assure each other they are in the contest to the end. The mayor, continuing to emphasize his official duties, dedicates a controversial hotel built on public land at O'Hare Airport by private developers, including one city official and the owners of two local racetracks. The land has been leased with municipal financing. The mayor describes the hotel as a thirteen-year "vision."

Thursday, the Daley counteroffensive reaches a crescendo. Stevenson's office hedges, claiming a "solid but slim" lead. The mayor's supporters emphatically announce that Daley "has the votes and will win." Reports from various quarters circulate that the battle is "really bloody" and that the "screws are being turned." Supposedly, Daley is intent on being vindicated for 1968.

Daley, in turn, lets it be known that he will fight a cut in Illinois' enlarged delegation. Taking their cue from Daley, state party officials speak out. The vice-chairman of the state party and the acting chairman of the convention delegation, John P. Touhy, refers to Califano's ruling as "just another lawyer's opinion." The state chairman retorts: "So what's the value of the opinion? . . . any question about the propriety of expanding the at-large delegation . . . [is] a matter for the convention's committee to decide."

State legislators continue to report threats against their party privileges and patronage allocations if they support Stevenson. Touhy rules the expanded at-large delegates will participate in the vote for chairman. A reporter asks a huffy mayor if he wants to be chairman. "That's a ridiculous question," an irate Daley says before storming off.

Friday, the June 16 meeting of the delegates turns out to be as explosive as anticipated. Several Daley supporters let it be known that they consider the enlargement of the delegation a violation of state law as well as party rules. Noting that the fifty-nine challenged delegates partly rest their defense on the contention that they were properly elected under state law, one adds, "But you can't say state law controls in the one case and not in the other." Dorothy V. Bush, secretary to the Democratic National Committee, announces that she will not issue credentials to the extra ten delegates.

Stevenson people voice fears of being counted out in the election. They admit "some" delegates may have buckled under the political and economic pressure and abandoned Stevenson. To charges of pulling out all the stops, one Daley supporter replies, "Sure, this ain't no kid's game, you know." Television commentators call the confrontation an "alley fight," and remark on the "unbelievable pressure" and "arm-twisting" by the pro-Daley forces. One delegate reports that Daley "called in all the political notes [due] of me and my father before me." Sponsors of an equal rights amendment pending in the Illinois legislature report the bill is held up awaiting their actions on the chairmanship fight. Other legislators report that support for their pet bills hinges on their backing Daley. Some fear that the budgets for popular programs will be held up or defeated, including that for the superintendent of public instruction, if widespread support for Stevenson surfaces. One attorney is notified that his business may suffer if he votes against Daley. A representative of another Chicago ward is warned that a wrong vote will result in the firing of all the patronage workers in his ward. Bowing to the inevitable, Stevenson capitulates, stating that while he means no disrespect to Daley, "I will not subject my friends to continued recriminations, nor my supporters to reprisals." (Later postmortems indicate Stevenson had a likely eighty-seven votes—one more than needed—with five more probable at his peak. Daley and Stevenson supporters both agree that Daley had at least one hundred votes when Stevenson withdrew.)

When the meeting commenced, a female Muskie delegate was symbolically placed in nomination to oppose the mayor by a delegate who decried "the blatant arm-twisting, threats, coercion, and force used on delegates" by the pro-Daley forces. In turn, state representative Clyde Choate (later rewarded with appointment as delegation vice-chairman) yelled his brief nomination speech to the disorderly convention amid catcalls, noise, and general confusion. Choate did manage to praise Daley as a champion of free and open debate.

The uproar continued through Daley's easy victory (133½ votes to 25½ for his opponent, with 11 undecided). The losing Muskie delegate—saying "I will not do it. . . . I represented a group of people disenfranchised by the tactics used"—refused to make Daley's choice unanimous.

The convention was full of curiosities. Stevenson was absent from the room when his name was called, so the party regular presiding at the time cast the senator's half vote for Daley. Stevenson later returned and made it official. Twice Daley received standing ovations while the senator, also on the stage, remained seated and did not applaud. When the roll call reached the eleventh of the twenty at-large votes added illegally a week earlier, shouts arose and cries of "Point of Order!" were heard. They were ignored. The presiding officer (Touhy) announced that the delegates could do as they would, but he was going to finish the roll. Later, he threatened that troublemakers would be forcibly removed if they persisted.

Daley, appearing impervious to what had happened, made an acceptance speech. Two themes predominated. First, and familiarly, he rehashed the 1968 convention:

> I have no apologies for what happened at the 1968 Convention. I was not responsible for what happened in the streets outside the Conrad Hilton Hotel.
>
> The media and the press turned it around. No one wrote about what happened inside the convention. In my twenty years, it was the most disorderly convention I've seen.
>
> I hope to God that we don't have it again in 1972.

Daley also warned the delegates, rather curiously, that the eyes of millions would be on them (the preceding scenes had already been captured by television cameras). He spoke of democracy in action and reminded his listeners that those who try to bend conventions (presumably at the national, not the state, level) to their own will must meet with failure.

The delegation elected its representatives to the national convention committees, giving fair representation to each of the presidential contenders on all but the Credentials Committee, where the Daley people took five of the six seats. The delegation failed to divide seats equally among men and women, however, as prescribed in party regulations, thus precipitating another fight with the national party. Anti-Daley dissidents marshaled their forces in an attempt to control one delegation office, that of secretary, but failed and settled for cosecretaries.

The bizarre meeting ended. At the conclusion, commentators announced Daley's resurrection from the series of mishaps that had dogged the election year. They paid homage to his "clout" in critical tests but they did observe that, despite all, he had had less control of this delegation than any ever sent from Illinois while he held power.

Why indulge in such a bloodletting? The mayor's need to re-establish his primacy in the swirl of immediate events is one explanation. A second is that the machine does not like to be challenged and once it is, it shows little restraint in demolishing its adversaries. A third reason is suggested by an observer at the meeting who concluded: "It's vitally important to Daley, whose big moment was long ago when he got John Kennedy into the White House and who has been under heavy attack since the 1968 convention, that he end his career on top—vindicated, still the acknowledged leader." If so, it was a curiously old-fashioned road to vindication, and one destined to grow curiouser.

Saturday and Sunday. Media attention returned to the antilitter patrols which took to Chicago beaches in force. Daley's "clout" was continually admired and for the first time in months he appeared to have regained his former invincibility.

Monday, June 19. Another bombshell—and another machine victory. A federal district judge in Washington, D.C., ruled in favor of Keane's suit contesting the constitutionality of the guidelines. In a confused decision that further muddled a bad situation, the judge voided reform guidelines A-1, A-2, C-4, and part of C-6 and upheld the rest. Prior to this ruling, Keane and his associates had already lost two cases in the federal courts and one in the state courts on the same or related issues. The new ruling was unprecedented.

Confusion reigned twenty-one days before the convention. Forty-three percent of the elected delegates were under challenge at this point, and 80 percent of the challenges were based on A-1 or A-2. The national committee's counsel (Califano) characterized the decision as a "major tragedy" and "a tremendous setback for the party's efforts on behalf of minority groups" as well as one that had "gutted" the reforms. Challenger Singer noted that the federal judge did not issue the injunction against his group's appeal sought by Keane and his associates. Thus, said Singer, both groups could claim "victory," but the national party remained in an incredibly awkward position. Lawyer Torshen (counsel for Keane, Wigoda, et al.) did indeed claim "a tremendous victory for our side" but Keane, perhaps thinking the judge was a Chicago man, remarked, "He went much further than he needed to go for our purposes." Daley, in New Orleans for a meeting of the National Conference of Mayors, said that the "decision speaks for itself. It upholds everything that has been said in our petitions." Singer declared, "The Chicago challenge is alive and well and bound for Miami Beach," as many wondered.

Later Daley, in New Orleans to address the mayors, met with national chairman O'Brien, reportedly to talk about their "families," although presumably other things were on their minds also.

Tuesday, June 20. Daley, now back on top, met individually in New Orleans with presidential contenders Humphrey, Muskie, and McGovern.

Late in the day, a three-judge federal appeals court overruled the lower-court decision and declared the guidelines still in effect. Califano (speaking before the court) indicated how crucial the Chicago case was, declaring it "the hottest political issue facing the Democratic National Convention" outside of picking a presidential nominee. The court in its ruling stated that Keane, Wigoda, et al., did not have the grounds for a case; they had not *yet* been denied anything. There was an implicit assumption that if the Daley 59 did lose in the Credentials Committee, they could then reopen their suit. The Credentials Committee hearings, scheduled to begin the following Monday in Washington, D.C., were further clouded.

Singer announced that congressional district caucuses, *not open to those chosen on the organizational slate* (the challengers, among other things, feared a takeover of their meetings by organization people), would be held Thursday evening, June 22, to select alternative delegates. (Up to this point, the challengers had *no delegation* to substitute for Daley's should it be removed from the convention.) A county convention was scheduled for Saturday, June 24, to complete the process. Little realized at the time, these meetings were going to produce another upheaval.

The antilitter campaign receded from the headlines to be replaced by stories of an alleged "hit" (assassination) squad within the police department, composed of law officers (one of whom seven years earlier had been accused of killing two prostitutes, resulting in his transfer from one police district to another). The officers allegedly worked with dope traffickers and killed on contract (in at least one case reportedly executing the wrong man). The story continued in the headlines for days (and the case dragged on in the federal courts for over a year). Convention maneuvering was (only momentarily, as it turned out) overshadowed by the rush of normal daily events.

Wednesday, June 21. The mayor, still in New Orleans, took the floor at the conference to support President Nixon's war policies. "In the name of God," pleaded Daley, "stand behind the President." Many Democratic regulars appeared a little stunned.

Torshen announced that the appeals court decision "in no way undermines or detracts from our attack on the constitutionality of the guidelines." The Credentials Committee admitted to being in a fog. A spokesman reported:

> The lower court said the guidelines dealing with adequate, proportionate representation for various groups were improper—but the appeals court has not set that aside, so the guidelines are still in force.
>
> But if we use them, then the courts may throw them out—and we'll have to start the whole credentials business all over again.

This came with only nineteen days to go before the convention. Late in the day, a report from Washington said that the national committee and the Credentials Committee could refuse to seat the Illinois representatives to the convention committees because of their failure to divide their seats equally between males and females. Seventy-seven percent of the Illinois nominees for the committees were men. A national party leader admitted he did not know what to do about the situation. The Illinois state chairman professed confusion also: "I haven't yet figured out what to do about it." Congressman James O'Hara, chairman of the convention's Rules Committee, announced that the Illinois representatives to his committee definitely would not be seated when the group began deliberations on Thursday.

Late in the day also, Daley returned to Chicago and met immediately with his local party leaders, including the president of the county board, aldermen Marzullo, Holman, Frost, Gabinski, Vrdolyak, and Burke, the Cook County assessor, and county commissioners Stroeger and Bieszczat (among others), many names familiar in the challenge, to discuss "voter registration." The meeting drew little public notice.

Thursday, June 22, was another unexpectedly climactic day. The leader of the Illinois delegation to the Rules Committee (a state senator and the Democrat's nominee for attorney general) told O'Hara the state would not abide by the provisions of the 1972 Call requiring an equal division of convention committee seats by sex. "I herewith declare that any rules having to do with balancing and quotas violate 150 years of history, traditions, and principles of the Democratic party," he said. (Not true. The old rules also required an equal division by sex.) O'Hara refused to allow the Illinois delegation voting rights on his committee. The angered delegation leader told (as the machine repeatedly does) a television interviewer that Illinois had "the most open delegate selection system in the nation" and he also threatened still another suit. Lawyer Torshen was rushed to Washington to guide the legal proceedings. The Illinois challenge on these points was serious and coincided with that of nine other states (Alaska, Arizona, Florida, Georgia, Hawaii, Kansas, Minnesota, Washington, and West Virginia), all of which were refused voting privileges (lessening the committee membership considerably).

Thursday evening, the Singer group held eight congressional district caucuses to elect fifty-one delegates. The quota-conscious group selected thirty-one whites, sixteen blacks and four Latin Americans; twenty-six men and twenty-five women; and twenty-three people aged thirty or younger. This, however, was not the big story. The meetings were raided by Daley loyalists who proceeded systematically to disrupt them. Some unusually nasty and unnecessary encounters took place that did little to help the Daley 59's position (see below).

Friday, June 23. Illinois overnight capitulated to national party demands and evenly distributed its convention committee representatives between men and women. Five men resigned and Mayor Daley appointed five women to replace them (pending confirmation from the full delegation), thus evening the split between the sexes. The leader of the Illinois delegation to the Rules Committee was unrepentant. He told the committee that there were "insuperable obstacles" to a court challenge at that time and he admitted to a belated realization that a court case might result in Illinois having no voice in any convention committees. "The Democratic party has always deplored quotas of any kind as basically un-American," he continued. "The free election process is sacrosanct." (The sole holdout among the states, Florida, initiated a federal court suit on the matter which it promptly lost.)

A hearing officer in a challenge in the Sixth Congressional District, a suburban area contiguous to Chicago (but a group not included in the Daley 59 challenge), found that three delegates, all machine candidates (the county coroner, the assistant house minority leader and a sanitary district trustee), were improperly slated by the regular Democratic organization, which made no effort to include women. He recommended that they be replaced by women.

Saturday, June 24. The insurgents held a county convention to elect eight additional at-large delegates, thus completing their convention delegation. Daley supporters invaded the meeting and a shouting match preceded the session, but unlike Thursday night there was no violence (see below).

On Monday, June 26, the Credentials Committee hearings opened in Washington. The period roughly beginning with Louis Oberdorfer's abortive attempt to open the Chicago hearings on May 24 and terminating with the selection of the completed delegation of challengers, represented the most exciting and unpredictable month in the entire four-year reform effort. The Chicago dispute constituted only one of many—the Credentials Committee was scheduled to arbitrate a staggering seventy challenges from thirty states, involving 1,281 delegates or 41.2 percent of the total convention membership—but by any test it was easily the most significant to come before the convention. The events depicted parallel the close of the primary season, the ending generally of all delegate selection, the institution of the Humphrey challenge to McGovern's victory in California (based on the contention that "winner take all" primaries should not be allowed), the realization that McGovern had about won the nomination, and, finally, the anticipated beginnings of the Rules and Credentials Committee sessions. In contrast, the Credentials Committee hearings, while exciting by any reasonable standard, proved something of a letdown compared with the events that preceded it. Before recording the highlights of the hearings, however, let us turn to the explosive matter of the events surrounding the choosing of the membership of the insurgents' delegation.

The Challengers Select an Alternative Delegation

The weakest part of the Singer group's challenge lay in the absence of a legally elected substitute delegation with which to replace Daley's if the challenge succeeded. One of the curiosities of the contest was that it was not an attempt by defeated delegates (although there were some in the group of ten put together explicitly to institute the challenge) to unseat the victors in the primary, but was based on the alleged violation of national party rules for the conduct of the party elections. After the challenge had been brought, the insurgents then faced the problem of choosing their alternative delegates. The job was not to be easy.

The ideal answer would be to hold another primary. This, of course, was impossible. The most reasonable solution—and the one ultimately chosen—was to convene caucuses in each of the congressional districts to select the district-level representatives and then to hold a county-level convention to select the remaining at-large delegates. Twice meetings were scheduled to accomplish these ends and twice they were postponed. One reason for the indecision was the pending court cases. Another and more pressing concern, however, was the fear that the meetings would be disrupted by Daley regulars who would then proceed to select their own representatives or who would make the conduct of any business doubtful. With time running out, the insurgents gave in to necessity and finally scheduled the caucuses for the evening of June 22 and the county-level meeting two days later.

The selections were considered a formality. They were not expected to add substantially to the moral weight of the challengers' argument or to detract from the points being made by the machine delegates. The caucuses received little media attention, being lost in the drama of the more significant events unfolding.

The challengers had devised an awkward set of rules for the congressional district sessions that they hoped would allow them to proceed with the first step in electing an alternative delegation while at the same time avoiding any takeover by the machine forces. Their plan was to schedule open meetings and to permit nominations from the floor but to restrict voting to those who had sought delegate status in the primary but had lost. These "electors" would cast a weighted vote equal to their support in the primary. The only people specifically barred from the proceedings were organization members already elected as delegates.

The plan was fragile. It had been devised to meet a unique set of circumstances. Undoubtedly, it would be challenged before the Credentials Committee and it would be hard to defend, especially before people who had no reason to sympathize with the seemingly paranoid fears of the insurgents as to the machine reaction. Attention, however, quickly and unexpectedly shifted from the legitimacy of the selection process to the reaction of the organization to the meetings, behavior startling enough to nullify what might have been the last advantage of the Daley organization.

The meeting of Daley and his lieutenants the day before on "voter registration" had in reality been called to discuss and coordinate the organization's policy on the insurgents' caucuses. An overview of the fruits of their work on the night of the gatherings is provided by a local newspaper account (Chicago *Daily News*, June 23):

> Hundreds of Mayor Richard J. Daley's regular Democratic ward organization backers, shouting curses and obscenities, stormed caucuses called by rival independent Democrats to elect an "alternative delegation" to the Democratic National Convention.
>
> They disrupted seven of eight district caucuses held throughout the city and forced them into temporarily adjourning Thursday night.
>
> They beat two men, forcibly detained another for 10 minutes, pulled the hair of women challengers and overturned chairs and tables.
>
> Using battery-powered microphones, they "elected" their own chairman and seized control of the podium at one of the caucuses. Independents trying to flee the violence were shoved back and terrorized.

At the caucus in the Second Congressional District, when Wayne Whalen (a lawyer for the challengers) attempted to convene the meeting in a church, he reported being "rushed" by aldermen Vrdolyak, Aducci, and fifteen to thirty others who proceeded to punch him in the stomach and knock him to the floor. Vrdolyak, carrying a bullhorn, announced he had taken over the meeting. He harangued the crowd ("These are the kind of people who are trying to destroy the Democratic party."), who, in turn, cursed, booed, and heckled the challengers as the church's pastor shouted for order. When Whalen succeeded in adjourning the meeting, witnesses reported he and his group were forced to "run the gauntlet" through the crowd to the rear door of the church while they were "pushed, shoved, spat upon, and had their hair pulled."

In the Seventh Congressional District, when the presiding officer sought to open their caucus in the same room in which the Poole hearings had been held earlier, a city corporation counsel and a county commissioner stood across the table shouting at him through a bullhorn. Alderman Marzullo led five busloads of party regulars (brought in for the occasion) in shouting obscenities. When the Singer representative adjourned the meeting (hoping to reconvene later in a law office), Marzullo's yell of "We'll follow you to the grave!" apparently reflected the mood of the crowd, who would not let the insurgents leave. As the moderator attempted to make his way through the 400 or so hecklers, "he was accosted at the elevators and—while Marzullo shouted, 'Kill the mother———'—he was shoved back into the conference room and forcibly detained." An associate was pulled from an elevator, knocked to the floor, punched, and kicked before escaping.

The Eighth Congressional District held its meeting in the basement of a parish hall. Here yet another alderman (Gabinski) took over the proceedings and passed several resolutions praising the Daley delegates. When he adjourned his session and the challengers again tried to conduct theirs, "the regulars stormed on stage, switched off the lights, turned over the tables at which the independents were sitting, and began pulling the chairs from beneath them." When the husband of the woman who was chairing the meeting objected, he was informed that he would be "beaten to a pulp" if he resisted.

The Fifth Congressional District meeting, held in a Catholic church, found the oldest son of the mayor, Richard M. Daley, and still another alderman leading the troops (300 to 400 Daley loyalists who arrived just as the meeting began) in a fist-waving, shouting demonstration that had the intended effect of breaking up the gathering.

The insurgents in the Ninth Congressional District held out for an hour despite the yells, taunts, arguments, and threats from members of the crowd. To cries that the proceedings were "antidemocratic" and similar to ones "used in Russia," an unusually plucky (or danger-loving) woman in the audience rose to ask the protesters, "How many of you were invited by the Regular Democratic Organization to take part in the selection of their slated candidates?" The demonstrators were momentarily taken aback, although not enough to deter them from eventually shutting down the meeting.

The Daley supporters in the Third Congressional District arrived early, convened, and then adjourned their own meeting. When the insurgents' chairman arrived (Singer's administrative assistant), the crowd alternately ridiculed ("Get a haircut!" "Go home, button-shoes!") and cursed him. As he left, a Cook County deputy sheriff followed, screaming at him to show his credentials (whatever that meant).

The only meeting not disrupted was held in a private home in the predominantly black First Congressional District. Presided over by an official of Jesse Jackson's "Operation Push," it listened to the objections voiced by the city administration's representatives, Alderman Holman and County Commissioner Stroeger, but then proceeded without undue incident to the business at hand, the selection of a substitute delegate slate.

Reactions to the night's events were quick in coming. Singer termed the onslaught "barbaric." Jesse Jackson, reporting a number of personal threats against his life, wondered aloud if the Daley organization had gone "insane." A lawyer (Stephen Schwab) for the insurgents' delegation who had conducted the meeting in the Ninth Congressional District attempted to put the attacks in a perspective relevant to the challenge. "The Daley organization, every step of the way, has been digging their grave a little deeper in this delegate challenge. They did it again tonight."

The Daley group, however, was hardly defensive about their actions. Two principals in the night's actions made this clear. The mayor's son, for example, contended that the caucuses "made a mockery of the democratic process and were in flagrant disregard not only of the McGovern rules and party regulations, but also of the spirit of democracy." Young Daley concluded that the insurgents had "brought on themselves" the disruptions that occurred. Alderman Vrdolyak, hardly contrite, proudly claimed to have been elected twice to delegate status by the meeting he invaded, and to the allegations of violent behavior he responded that "any charges by Whalen [the moderator] that he was injured, or even touched, is a fraud." The alderman served notice that he had every intention of attending the upcoming Saturday meeting and of "encouraging everyone I know to be there, too."

Despite all, the challengers did manage to reconvene the seven disrupted caucuses in private homes, law offices, or church rectories and complete the business of choosing their fifty-one delegates. They also determined to proceed with Saturday's county-level session to complete the process of delegate selection. Apparently, another encounter was in the making.

Insurgents Select Their At-Large Delegates

The challengers needed to fill eight at-large vacancies in their delegation at their "county convention" held in a downtown hotel. Trouble was expected. The Daley people had let it be known they would be there in force. The Chicago police had declined a request to assign policemen to the meeting to prevent disruptions because, according to a police spokesman, it might inhibit "free speech."

As the moderator (again Whalen) attempted to open the meeting, young Daley, aldermen Vrdolyak, Frost, Holman, Burke, Commissioner Stroeger, and others crowded the podium, shouting loudly and repeatedly, "Point of Order!" "You're part of the Ogilvie [Republican governor seeking re-election] machine." "This isn't a democracy." "By what authority do you conduct this meeting?" And whatever else occurred to them. A press report of the incident (Chicago *Sun-Times,* June 25) noted that the meeting

> exploded in a wild vocal uproar . . . when ranking supporters of the mayor disrupted the gathering by chanting and yelling points of order and accusations.
>
> The uproar went unabated for 10 minutes and became so intense that Wayne Whalen, the meeting chairman, could not be heard over the public address system as he attempted to read an agenda and rules for the gathering. . . . Many of the hundreds of persons jammed into the meeting appeared stunned at the outburst.

The situation could have resulted in some unfortunate incidents. The room was overfull and hot, the Daley supporters were packed into sections of the meeting hall, and the atmosphere was charged. Still, violence was averted and only minor scuffles and verbal abuse marked the day. Tiring of the shouting, and apparently pleased with their performance, Vrdolyak yelled that the meeting was adjourned, and he, young Daley, and an estimated 300 machine regulars left. The insurgents then proceeded to complete their slate. With this done, the scene shifted to the opening of the Credentials Committee hearings in Washington, only days away.

What did the machine gain? Apparently it had hoped to demonstrate that the challengers' procedures were neither open nor representative, points that could have been made more easily in the verbal presentations to the Credentials Committee. The insurgents' selection procedures would not bear up under close scrutiny. What the machine leaders succeeded in doing, however, was to make themselves the point of contention again. They demonstrated why the challengers had to be so circumspect in their manner of choosing an alternative delegation. The machine, once more, would be called on to explain, if it could, its behavior in the matter. It had, as the challengers' lawyer had pointed out, dug its hole a little deeper.

The Credentials Committee Hearings

An overloaded Credentials Committee expeditiously went about its business. It was expected to resolve in one manner or another the record eighty-two challenges before it. Quite early, the chairwoman, Patricia Roberts Harris, whose appointment nine months earlier had been the center of a bitter controversy between party regulars (pro-Harris) and reformers (anti-Harris), demonstrated her complete command of the deliberations and her unwillingness to tolerate delay. The committee members also appreciated the gravity of their task: in effect, it was up to them to decide if the new reform guidelines would, in the last analysis, be applied and the severity with which they would be enforced. As the days progressed, it became quite clear that the group had every intention of supporting the guidelines to the extent they applied, settling once and for all their status as controlling party law.

The major controversy facing the committee prior to the Chicago dispute, and actually at this point far more crucial to the nomination race, was the challenge over California's "winner take all" primary. In actuality, the challenge did not involve the reform guidelines. The McGovern-Fraser Commission had considered the issue but had declined to make any recommendations. Humphrey, who had lost to McGovern in California, had first decided not to institute a challenge (to do so, he told Walter Cronkite, would mean being a "spoilsport") but had then in a last desperate bid to win his party's presidential nomination reversed himself.

His argument was that the "winner take all" primary (i.e., where the plurality victor receives all of the primary votes rather than only his proportional share) violated the spirit of the new reforms as well as, for example, prohibitions as to the unit rule. The politics of the situation were clear. McGovern, with 44.3 percent of the state's vote (as against Humphrey's 39.2 percent), had won all of its 271 convention votes. If the primary were declared illegal at this late date and the votes redistributed on a proportional basis, McGovern would receive 120 and Humphrey (who still would not have enough to claim the nomination himself) 106, with the rest scattered among a number of other contenders. The reduction of 151 votes in the McGovern total was believed sufficient to pull him below the majority needed to claim the nomination (although no other candidate at that point would have anything approaching a majority).

The hearing officer in the California case had declared for McGovern. The issue seemed clear enough. The significance for the organization (which controlled five of the six committee seats awarded the Illinois delegation) was in whom they would support. A pro-McGovern vote would lay the groundwork for a possible compromise on the Chicago question (the challengers had little independent political support) or even, although it would be difficult to justify in light of the rules, a rejec-

tion of the insurgents' arguments. An anti-McGovern stand (unless based
on pique) had better be sure that the "Stop McGovern" drive would succeed. Every vote in this contest was critical. Unfortunately for McGovern,
he had less strength on this committee than on any other in the convention. To compound his difficulties, ten California representatives to the
Credentials Committee (those who would be affected if the challenge
succeeded) were denied the right to vote on the matter. The situation
was critical.

A serious effort—the most intensive despite the fact that the McGovern
people were to try right up to the final convention vote—was made to
compromise the Chicago challenge. Conflicting reports emerged from the
principals. Frank Mankiewicz, a McGovern strategist, met with both
groups and emerged publicly optimistic. "No side," he reported, "has
staked out a total win position." The mayor reported he was "always willing to compromise" and the Reverend Jesse Jackson found an even split
of the delegation "reasonable" (although he was suspicious of Mankiewicz,
who he feared favored Daley). Daley, in turn, let it be known that some
type of split was conceivable ("depending on who he has to split with").
The fact that he refused to speak to or acknowledge the existence of the
Singer group made the admonition more noteworthy. Even more omi-
nously, reports from Chicago indicated that Daley, who believed he had
a strong case, intended to fight, alleging the insurgents had shown a "gross
disregard of party reforms" in the conduct of their caucuses. Singer meanwhile was truculent. He let it be known that he was in Washington to argue his group's case: any compromise would have to come from Daley
first (a concession, such as it was, to the McGovern camp's pressure to
reach an accommodation).

The effort at compromise fizzled. In a stunning blow, the Credentials
Committee voted 72 to 66 to strip McGovern of the 151 disputed California delegates (distributing this proportionately among Humphrey and the
seven other contenders in the primary), thus effectively throwing the
presidential nomination once more into doubt. McGovern reacted in
shock and anger, uncharacteristically speaking of "crooked and unethical
procedures" within the committee. The five Chicago loyalists had voted
the Humphrey position, exercising the balance of power in the dispute.

The next major test was the Chicago question. The Credentials Committee staff had released the hearing officer's findings. In it, Poole reported
"gross violations" of the national party standards and he ruled in favor of
the challengers. The report was explicit. Concerning the alleged role of
the machine in the primary, Poole wrote:

> From the mass of sharply conflicting evidence, there emerges a clear
> pattern of concerted action by the organization in the use of its in-

fluence and prestige in support of its regulars, encouraging their candidacies, agreements on numbers, cooperation in the preparation of sample ballots, their widespread distribution by party workers, their prominence at headquarters of ward officials, and the formidable array of party power in behalf of its preferred candidates.

All of this compels the irrefragable conclusion . . . that Guidelines C-1, C-4 and C-6 have been violated in the nomination and election of the challenged delegates and alternates in Chicago. [*The Chicago Credentials Challenge*, pp. 13–14]

As to the quota issue, Poole added that the

underrepresentation complained of was not the result of fortune, unaffected by the efforts of the organization, but was a continuation of the same conditions exposed in the Commission Report and came about because, although diligent in including its own regulars, the organization in Chicago expended no such resources on the segments of the population as required by Guidelines A-1 and A-2.

The Hearing Officer accordingly finds that those Guidelines have been violated both in letter and spirit. [*Ibid.*, p. 17]

Not much was left to be said. The wording of the report as well as its findings seemingly acted to undercut any lingering hopes the organization might harbor.

But the machine fought on, at times to dubious advantage. Simon, one of two lawyers in Washington to present the Daley 59's side to the Credentials Committee (the other being Torshen), acknowledged that women, for example, were underrepresented on the delegation: "Some of the delegates would not be averse to letting women on the delegation, perhaps their wives." On the day of the Chicago vote, the committee members awoke to find a full-page advertisement in the *Washington Post* pleading the case of the "uncommitted" delegates, a curiously expensive vehicle through which to reach its judges. An attorney for the regulars, in appearing before the committee, argued that the Daley 59 should retain their seats regardless of national party rules because they had been elected by the people of Chicago. He went on to question the committee's power to enforce any ouster. Holman, speaking for the organization in the general debate that followed, accused the insurgents of "dissension, disorganization, and venom," words not calculated to ease tensions. He went on to attack personally as a "big hero" a Muskie delegate who introduced a resolution to compromise the issue by dividing the seats between the contesting delegations, a proposal Holman rejected out of hand ("We will not share *our* seats with Jesse Jackson and William Singer" [Italics added]).

One committee member in addressing his colleagues summed up the matter: "This is not a question of presidential preferences. . . . It's a question of whether our guidelines and rules apply to Mayor Daley and his delegates." On the vote that followed, the committee—despite its previous stand against McGovern, despite the mayor's preeminent position within the party, and despite the effect it might have on the November election—voted 71 to 61 to unseat the Daley regulars and replace them with the Singer delegation.

When Chairwoman Harris announced the results, the room exploded: cheers, applause, and even hugging, kissing, and dancing in the aisles followed. Possibly, it was just the release of tension built up over the preceding days of committee deliberations or, for some, reaching all the way back to the March primary. Perhaps others felt it balanced out the California challenge or struck a blow at a hated symbol of the disruptive Chicago convention of 1968. Given the implications for the party, a more sober reaction might have been appropriate.

One dimension of the Daley 59's response quickly became apparent. Shocked by the committee action, the regulars threatened through their lawyer, Torshen, to return to the federal courts to press their claim (which they did and lost) and to bring legal action to prevent the name of the convention's nominee from appearing on the general election ballot in Illinois, an extreme threat (carried out by some Southern states in 1948 and 1960) that indicated the extent of the organization's displeasure. As it turned out, the Credentials Committee's actions on both the California and Chicago delegations were taken before the federal courts. In an accelerated series of hearings, the district court upheld the Credentials Committee's action, the circuit court supported the Chicago decision but overturned the California outcome, and the Supreme Court, convened in an extraordinary summer session to rule on the cases, reaffirmed its traditional noninvolvement in party affairs (unless compelling constitutional issues arise), in effect accepting the committee's and the convention's resolution of the matters.

The Convention

"We're going to get the old bastard today," one delegate reportedly told an organization supporter attempting to solicit his vote on behalf of the Daley 59. The day, of course, was the session in which the Chicago challenge would come to the floor of the convention. By the time the issue did arise, however, it was something of an anticlimax.

The opening night's session of the Miami Beach convention was incredibly long, lasting until almost 5:00 A.M., but by the time it was over all of the major issues to come before the assembly had been effectively resolved. The California dispute came up early and the McGovern forces won a decisive victory, overturning the Credentials Committee recommendation by 1,618.28 to 1,238.22. McGovern regained his delegates from the state and, more importantly, demonstrated his impregnable position within the convention. The nomination was assured and the bulk of the other presidential contenders quickly dropped out of the race.

Another effort was made to compromise the Chicago problem by a presidential candidate now looking forward to the November election, but too much had happened and too little time existed to lay the effective groundwork for such a move. An attempt to suspend the rules, despite the McGovern camp's best efforts to convince its followers—markedly unsympathetic to the mayor and his delegation—to support the move, narrowly failed, 1,411.05 in favor, as against 1,483.08 opposed. The Credentials Committee recommendation to seat the insurgents in place of the Daley regulars was upheld 1,486.05 to 1371.55. The mayor and his delegates were relegated to the role of outsiders. The regulars gathered their belongings and quickly vacated Miami Beach. The mayor, on vacation in Michigan (reportedly with his bags packed, ready to come to the convention on a moment's notice), reached another low point, possibly the worst in a long and tumultuous election year. As fate would have it, it would fall to Illinois a few nights later to cast the 119 votes required to put McGovern over the 1,508 needed for the nomination, the tally announced by the same (downstate) party regular who had placed Daley's name in contention for the delegation chairmanship a few weeks earlier at the raucous Springfield meeting.

Conclusion

As a long-time party loyalist, the mayor did go on to support McGovern in the general election despite threats to the contrary. He even invited McGovern to address on several occasions gatherings of Cook County party regulars, and he went as far as financing a one-hour telecast in Chicago of a local rally featuring the senator (although the program unfortunately conflicted with one of McGovern's few nationally televised addresses, and his most important). Not all of the machine lieutenants, ward captains, and precinct workers adjusted as quickly or forgave as readily. The aging and acerbic Vito Marzullo, ward boss and Daley confidant, to select one example, worked for Nixon (which prior to the events of the spring would have been unthinkable). The alderman still proclaimed himself a "Daley Democrat" and remained a principal organizational strategist. Marzullo failed to carry his ward for the Republicans, although he did claim McGovern's margin of victory was down from what normally could be expected. Illinois, along with forty-eight other states, went for

Nixon, but it would be difficult to blame the state's showing on a lack-luster machine performance. McGovern's troubles far exceeded anything Chicago might contribute.

The mayor was considerably less forgiving toward his opponents, the insurgents who had prevailed at the national level. A local court had ad-judged the Daley regulars the legitimate national convention delegates and, when the insurgents returned to Illinois, held them in contempt for taking their seats at the national convention. The judge, sympathetic to the machine (as quoted by a newspaper reporter, he compared Singer's actions to those of "Hitler in Germany and Mussolini in Italy"), threat-ened the former challengers with jail. The case, with appeals, was to drag on for over two years, working its way—at great cost in time, money, and psychological uncertainty to the insurgents—up through the Illinois courts and finally again to the Supreme Court. The challenge to national party rules was not to end with the decisions of the Miami Beach Convention. The lawyers for the challengers, after petitioning to be relieved of the case in order to move on to other things, were castigated by the judge and forced to remain on the case. Individuals associated with the chal-lengers found that their appointments to state positions by the newly elected Independent Democratic Governor Walker were routinely turned down by a state legislature in which the Chicago regulars held the bal-ance of power (and firmly believed in punishing their enemies whatever the cost). And, ironically, when the Illinois convention delegation was re-convened after the Miami Beach gathering to select national committee delegates within the state, it was the Daley 59 who were present and who made the choices.

In the November election not only was the Independent Democrat Walker elected governor and the state lost to the Republican presidential nominee but, and far more significant for the machine, a savvy Republican prosecutor was elected to the office of Cook County state's attorney. With these elections, combined with the appointment of an active Republican U.S. attorney by the Nixon administration in late 1971, the organization began to face a prosecutorial zeal it had never before had to tolerate. Within a three-year period, the federal prosecutor alone had managed to convict seventy-five public officials, many of them organization-related figures. Among those found guilty of various misdeeds relating to the abuse of public office for private gain were Keane and Wigoda (princi-pals in the convention drama from the beginning) as well as five other aldermen or former aldermen, the long-time press secretary to the mayor, and the county clerk. The indictment of another Daley protégé, the influ-ential clerk of the circuit court, a position known for its control of patron-age, indicated a willingness, unknown before, to go after the organization leaders as well as the lowly canvassers.

This time around Daley himself did not escape unscathed. Not only were many of his closest associates in difficulty, but it was revealed that one of Daley's sons had managed to gain a real estate license through a fixed exam and that an insurance firm associated with one of his sons had been awarded millions of dollars of public business in no-bid contracts. And the mayor and his wife were revealed to be secret part-owners of a real estate holding company that did well. These incidents were the first evidence of private gain for the mayor and his immediate family, previously believed to be removed from any taint of personal scandal.

Personally and politically, although matters quieted down, his problems continued. Singer announced early his intention to run for mayor in 1975. Death took its toll (Holman, for example) in an organization led primarily by old men. Daley himself suffered a stroke (the first major illness for the over-seventy mayor) that disabled him for a good period of time, although he did return later to his duties. The usual police scandals (accusations, indictments, convictions) continued, as did the annual school crisis (Would the teachers strike? Where would the budget funds come from?). The machine seemed bothered, maybe even threatened, by the continued unwillingness of blacks to return uncritically to the fold and by the spot opposition offered by a somewhat rejuvenated (but still largely disorganized and inept) county Republican party.

Lest, however, one think things had changed markedly, or before prematurely counting out the organization, some evidence from another mini-confrontation with the post-'72 national party may be relevant. The Democrats held a midterm national convention in December of the 1974 congressional election year. The machine, with the national party's implicit blessing, managed the delegate selection. Working through processes controlled by the regulars, they selected an almost uniformly loyalist delegation to the off-year convocation. Still as bold as ever, the regulars attempted to branch out and take control of the North Shore Cook County caucuses called by Independent Democrats in areas geographically well removed from the city. Their actions again ran afoul of national party intentions and a weak challenge was instituted. Many of the same people (Touhy and Simon, now chairman of the state party's "Affirmative Action Council") presented some familiar arguments to the national party body convened to adjudicate the disputes. Specifically, the organization was accused of not equally representing women in the 108-member delegation (10 percent were female, by a considerable margin the lowest percentage of any state delegation) to the midterm convention and, even more explicitly damaging, of nominating and electing in another of the now familiar Springfield conventions (the proceedings were rigged and were "like a scene out of *Marat-Sade*," one challenger testified) an at-large slate of seventeen, only two of whom were women. Simon contended it would have been "reprehensibly sexist" to elect a balanced delegation. He admitted the machine slated and elected its nominees (thus accepting responsibility for the outcome) but while claiming to be "loaded with good faith," he added that an honorable electoral process is more important than a balanced delegation. "The delegates [at Springfield] put their faith in veteran politicians, people they know something about." "Are you going to tell popular Democratic officeholders they don't mean anything because they aren't female?" he asked.

The national party committee, eager to avoid confrontations (the national headquarters had been very solicitous of Daley's organization since 1972), felt that the machine had used "questionable judgment" and that the "wise and prudent" course would have been to meet the standards. The committee then proceeded by an 18-to-4 vote to deny the challenge and thus the state party was not forced to reconstruct its delegations.

As for the national party more generally, a follow-up committee to the McGovern-Fraser Commission, convened in the post-'72 period, moderated (although without significantly diluting their overall effect) the guidelines in force for delegate selection to the Miami Beach convention, including, significantly, the provisions as to slate-making and quotas, the two items that had caused the Chicago organization such great difficulty. The national party actively courted the party regulars and federated labor (the AFL-CIO leadership) angered by the events of 1972. Mostly, however, it sat back and watched as the series of far more significant scandals associated with Watergate engulfed the Nixon presidency and the Republican party.

Who won? Who *should* have prevailed? What are the long-run implications for the national party system? For Chicago politics? Perhaps only future events will provide the answers. Meanwhile, it may be appropriate to recall a comment made by the legendary Irish ward politician and barkeeper, Paddy Bauer, that seems at times to serve as a city motto. The good alderman claimed, "Chicago ain't ready for reform!" Possibly. At the very least, it adapts reluctantly.

Epilogue

Paddy Bauer returned from his retirement in the southwestern United States to vote in the Chicago Democratic primary of February 25, 1975 (for all practical purposes, *the* election), to decide the party's mayoral nominee. The move was symbolic. The Daley forces had massed for a smashing victory. Daley, seeking his fifth term, was opposed by Singer, who had campaigned hard for sixteen months; Edward Hanrahan, one-time Daley favorite and former state's attorney; and Richard Newhouse, "the black candidate," a state senator with a fine record but little public visibility. The campaign was full of the hyperbole, countercharges, and vaudeville that mark all such local efforts. The mayor, of course, did not campaign, choosing to appear at civic functions to extol the virtues of his administration or before carefully recruited (by city hall administrators) mass audiences of old people, blacks, and others dependent on city largesse to tell them how good things were. The real work was done in the streets and in the precincts. Here the challengers had no hope of equaling the efforts on behalf of the mayor. Daley won a truly impressive victory, capturing 58 percent of the primary vote to Singer's 29 percent, Newhouse's 8 percent, and Hanrahan's 5 percent. Daley regulars actually increased their control of the City Council, taking over 90 percent of the seats (a few independents did survive). Adeline Keane, wife of the convicted former leader of the council, Tom Keane, won her husband's seat handily and did so with virtually no campaign appearances of any kind. This, as much as anything, tells the story of the election. The Daley forces, relying on strenuous efforts from park district employees, saturated the ward of the lone remaining Republican on the council and defeated him (although, as events would have it, a Republican newcomer did manage to survive the machine blitz). The Republican alderman had been Daley's token opposition in the April general election.

In a moment of wild exultation and complete triumph, the mayor chose to be humble: "I shall embrace charity, and love mercy, and walk humbly within God." The flurry of scandals—from Watergate-type assertions of illegal police spying on Daley opponents, to the institution of a mid-decade congressional reapportionment designed to eliminate from the Congress one of the few representatives who did not endorse Daley—suggests that the mayor's "humility" retains its characteristic Chicago flavor.

One other noteworthy occurrence took place. The U.S. Supreme Court in January 1975 sided with the Singer delegation and rejected the Daley 59's arguments. Speaking for the Court, Justice William J. Brennan wrote that national parties "serve the pervasive national interest in the selection of candidates for national office, and this national interest is greater than any interest of an individual state." The Court said that the national convention is "the proper forum for determining intraparty disputes as to which delegates should be seated," and, going even further, added that "the states themselves have no constitutional role in the great task of the selection of presidential and vice-presidential candidates." The decision could be of immense historic importance. It goes, as Alderman Keane pointed out in another context, further than it had to for the purposes at hand.

The impact in Chicago? Singer said the ruling would have little effect on the politics of the city because "it is not relevant to the issues facing Chicago." He was correct. Chicago is Chicago and the machine is the machine. Obviously, this has not changed. But the national Democratic party has. It has opened up its rules in delegate selection in particular, and on participation in party processes more generally, and the reforms have withstood every legal and political challenge that has been mustered against them. And this may be the real story of the Chicago challenge.

BIBLIOGRAPHY

Crotty, William J. *Party Reform*. New York: Basic Books, 1976. The most complete account of the reform movement which swept the Democratic party in particular and which laid the basis for the Chicago challenge.

National Commission on the Causes and Prevention of Violence. *Rights in Conflict (the Walker Report)*. Washington, D.C.: U.S. Government Printing Office, 1968. It is impossible to understand the reform movement or the emotions related to the Chicago contest without appreciating what transpired in the city during the 1968 Democratic National Convention. This report relates those incidents in detail.

Royko, Mike. *Boss*. New York: E. P. Dutton, 1971. The most entertaining and colorful account of Mayor Richard J. Daley and his politics, written by a Chicago columnist.

Commission on Party Structure and Delegate Selection. *Mandate for Reform*. Washington, D.C.: Democratic National Committee, 1970. The official report of the McGovern-Fraser Commission, listing the new party "guidelines" and explaining the rationale for their adoption.

The Energy Issue
Oil and the Emergency Energy Act of 1973–74
Harmon Zeigler and Joseph S. Olexa

I. INTRODUCTION

Beginning with the winter of 1972–73, the term "energy crisis"—unheard of a few years earlier—came to signify the most serious problem in the lifetime of many Americans. Many found their home heating bills increasing rapidly and some parts of the country suffered actual shortages of fuel oil. By the summer of 1973 these shortages and price increases had extended to gasoline as well. Prices of other goods and services dependent on petroleum climbed rapidly, reflecting the increased costs and shortages of this essential product. The stock market fell and unemployment jumped as the impact of the crisis spread throughout the economy. Given the commitment of most Americans to a standard of living dependent upon an abundant supply of relatively inexpensive petroleum, the drastic change in both price and quantity of the commodity began to have a profound effect on the "American way of life."

Charges and countercharges came quickly as the true nature and source of the crisis were sought by irate congressmen and a confused public. In the spring of 1973 the advertisements of petroleum companies turned from the promotion of products to an explanation of their sudden scarcity. The objective of these advertisements was to persuade consumers that the energy crisis was not the industry's fault, that the oil companies were doing everything possible to alleviate it, and that if blame must be placed somewhere, it belonged with environmentalists, bureaucrats, and short-sighted government policies.

In spite of extensive television and newspaper advertisements by the oil companies, charges that the gasoline shortage was contrived were so widespread that Frank N. Ikard, former Texas congressman and now president of the chief lobbying organization for the oil industry, the American Petroleum Institute, released a paper in response. Ikard claimed that "the energy shortfall is not artificial and is not a plot by the oil companies to get what they want, but is a matter of skyrocketing consumer demand for oil products at a time when efforts to increase supplies are being thwarted by forces outside the oil industry."

However, the oil companies' chief lobbyist failed to persuade key members of Congress that his clients were the victims of outside forces. Senator Henry M. Jackson (D–Wash.), widely viewed as an undeclared candidate for the 1976 Democratic presidential nomination in search of a campaign issue, seized on the energy crisis. Noting that "oil company earnings show startling increases during a period when independents are being put out of business, and when the American consumer cannot get gasoline," Jackson charged that the "current shortages have been calculated and engineered for private profit and advantage" by the big oil companies. He also claimed that "the fuel shortage is a *deliberate, conscious* contrivance of the major integrated petroleum companies to destroy the independent refiners and marketers, to capture new markets, to increase gasoline prices, and to obtain the repeal of environmental protection legislation." Thus, the battle was joined between hostile and influential legislators and the giant multinational oil companies which have been described as "quasi-governments." The confrontation was the first in a series of continuing debates about energy policy. Since no previous experience in severe shortages existed, the first round proved to be unusually dramatic. However, by 1975, both the Republican executive and the Democratic majority in Congress were preparing more systematic, long-term plans for energy conservation.

The Power of Oil

The oil industry has enjoyed a special relationship with government quite unlike that of the average interest group. Even though the Federal Trade Commission has initiated over 300 formal investigations of "uncompetitive" marketing practices in the petroleum industry in the past fifty years, it has met with only limited success in altering the structure of the industry.

Several reasons, which became clear during the energy crisis, can be cited for the special relationship enjoyed by the oil industry with regard to government. First, petroleum and products derived from petroleum (plastics and other synthetic materials) are crucial to a modern industrialized economy. Repercussions of oil shortages in the winter of 1974 were felt almost immediately throughout the economy. As the costs of petroleum supplies increased substantially, severe readjustments were required in all sectors of the economy.

Second, the complex nature of the industry and its near monopoly of critical information make it extremely difficult for elected representatives to develop alternative explanations to those provided by the industry. At the height of the energy crisis the government apparently had no clear idea of what national oil stocks were available or what the costs involved in providing these stocks were. At each step in its reaction to the crisis, the government was largely dependent on the industry itself for data on the nature and extent of the shortage and, therefore, on the most appropriate means of responding to it.

A third factor influencing the relationship between the oil industry and government is the immense profitability of oil production and marketing. Since political campaigns depend on enormous sums of private money, campaign contributions by the major oil corporations have guaranteed them a sympathetic ear. The oil industry contributed over $5 million to President Nixon's 1972 re-election campaign as well as smaller sums to almost every other influential senator and congressman, including its most vocal critic, Senator Henry Jackson.

A final factor for the special status of the oil industry may be described as the ecological one. For almost a hundred years oil has been the primary energy source for all industrialized nations. As with all fossil fuels, its supply is finite and cannot be used as the basis of an ever-increasing economic growth rate. An increasing number of scientists have recommended that policies designed to regulate and conserve oil consumption be instituted in order that sharp dislocations might be avoided. Industry spokesmen have long used the argument that oil was a declining resource to justify special tax benefits and incentives for exploration. For several years before the crisis of 1973–74 they warned of pending shortages and the need for controls on consumption. With the formation of an oil producers' cartel by the major foreign suppliers and the imposition of an oil embargo by the Arab nations in the fall of 1973, oil shortages became a present reality rather than a future possibility.

In sum, in spite of the central role played by oil in the nation's economy, no single agency of government is responsible for oil policy. Instead, several dozen different agencies, each dealing with one or another aspect of oil production, transportation, refining, and marketing, have been responsible for this vital resource. Ultimately, the president has responsibility for coordinating these diverse agencies and articulating a coherent policy. During the height of the energy crisis in the winter of 1973–74, the president was faced with two other major crises which diverted his attention from oil shortages. One was the Middle East conflict, which was seen as the immediate cause for fuel shortages, and the other was the increasing political pressures from the Watergate affair. Nixon was also facing a united industry front which had only recently donated substantial sums to his campaign for re-election.

Oil Mercantilism: Special Governmental Subsidies for the Oil Industry

Typical of the first six decades of the twentieth century was the development of a consensus between the petroleum industry and the government concerning the ends and means of public policy.

How did this consensus develop? To a considerable degree it was the result of economic or military crisis. Wartime mobilization in World Wars I and II impressed government officials with the need for a dependable supply of oil. The Depression of the 1930s demonstrated the suffering brought about by "ruinous price competition" and the need for government controls to "stabilize" production and prices. After 1945 the Cold War brought about a further rapprochement between government and business and the partial incorporation of petroleum industry goals into foreign policy between the United States and other oil-producing nations. The current crisis should, therefore, be placed in the perspective of a special relationship between the oil industry and the federal government. Taxes, leases, royalty payments, and well-spacing regulations are the major problems domestically, while international areas of concern range from import quotas to the functioning of multinational oil companies.

Since the early days of World War I the U.S. government has cooperated closely with the oil industry to keep the price of crude oil high and to maintain company profits. This interest stems from the belief that high crude oil prices spur exploratory activity and ensure oil reserves. Just as nations had previously used their power to increase their stocks of gold, the countries in the post–World War I era used it to enlarge their oil reserves. No major country was willing to rely on the market alone for its supplies of this resource.

By encouraging the oil industry through beneficial legislation and tax policy, the United States was following the lead of other industrialized nations of the time and, in particular, the British government. However, while the British government and other European powers relied on government ownership of a major oil company, and, in some instances, on direct political and military control over oil areas to increase its reserves, the U.S. government relied on an indirect control mechanism—the use of its nationals, acting as private businessmen—to accomplish the same end.

At the end of the first world war, Mark Requa, general director, Oil Division, U.S. Fuel Administration, disturbed by the prospect that the nation might not have sufficient reserves for a future emergency, advocated a policy of encouraging "in every way possible . . . the acquisition by our nationals of reserves in foreign lands." In pursuit of this policy, the State Department used its offices to help U.S. oil firms win concessions in foreign countries. In the period between the two world wars it assisted American companies in their attempts to enter Iraq, the Netherlands East Indies, Mexico, Kuwait, and Venezuela. After World War II, the government's aid programs in the early postwar years provided economic assistance to U.S. companies operating abroad. The U.S. government also played a direct role in opening up Iran, which until 1951 had been the private sanctuary of British Petroleum, to American oil companies. The State Department negotiated the agreement, which gave American companies a 40-percent share of the consortium. The department then invited five American-owned international oil companies (Exxon, Gulf, Texaco, Mobil, and SoCal) to participate in the consortium, even though they were at that time being sued by the Justice Department for antitrust violations in the international field.

In addition to direct diplomatic intervention, the U.S. government has encouraged oil investment abroad through its tax policy. It allows companies to claim a 22-percent depletion allowance (until 1969 it was 27.5 percent) on their foreign production for U.S. income tax purposes. It permits them to offset their income tax payments to the host governments —usually 50 percent against their U.S. income tax liabilities. Finally, under the Western Hemisphere Trade Corporation Act, it grants them a 14-percent reduction in income derived from their foreign operations in the Western Hemisphere.

Finally, there are two other special government subsidies to the oil industry: prorationing laws and import quotas. The net effect of these special benefits has been to stabilize the price of domestic oil by artificially controlling the supply. Prorationing was originally instituted as a means of conserving the supply of domestic petroleum reserves and avoiding "waste." However, it functions as a means of controlling supply and setting price. Supply and demand forecasts—at the prevailing price—are issued monthly by the Interior Department's Bureau of Oil and Gas. States with prorationing laws then translate these forecasts into allowable production from the wells in their states. In this fashion sufficient oil—at a given price—is produced each month to clear the market.

Mandatory import quotas were first imposed in 1959 in the name of "national security" and remained in effect until 1973. The Federal Trade Commission described the effects of the import quota system as follows:

> The impact of quotas on the price of domestic crude oil was substantial. The domestic price of crude has in recent years averaged $1.25 per barrel above the world price, and most of the difference is attrib-

utable to the import quota. The import quota clearly contributed to profits earned in producing crude oil by elevating prices, but the quota increased profits to the majors in another way. The right to import went only to existing refineries. Thus, the major companies through import tickets were able to purchase oil at the world price as an input for their refineries, which produced final products at elevated domestic prices. A further benefit occurring to the majors was that they were able frequently to obtain profits by trading at favorable terms domestic crude for the independents' allotted foreign crude because some independents located inland were not in a position to economically utilize imports.

In summary, the relationship of the oil industry to the federal government is very different from that of most other interest groups. Since the early days of World War I, the federal government has regarded oil as a vital national resource. Given the antipathy toward public ownership or even strict control of industry, the government has attempted to develop petroleum resources through the intermediary of the private corporation by means of a variety of tax benefits and special legislation designed to stimulate production by enhancing corporate profits. The federal government has also played a more active role internationally in assisting the oil industry by utilizing the resources of the State Department and the military establishment to facilitate the acquisition of oil reserves in foreign lands. This special relationship, marked more by cooperation than coercion, is one in which the industry has provided the leadership and direction in determining the nature of public policy. Throughout the century spanned by the life of the industry, the relationship between oil and government has been largely informal, with policy and legislation developed on an ad hoc basis. The channels of communication between the industry and government have been diffuse rather than specific. Unlike most interest groups, the petroleum industry has not had to rely on a single trade association to gain access to governmental decision-makers. Given its near monopoly on information regarding reserves, supplies, extraction, shipping, and refining techniques, the industry has taken the initiative for policy development through its lobbying organizations, the American Petroleum Institute and the National Petroleum Council, and through legislators who identify themselves as "friends of oil," such as Senator Russell Long of Louisiana and the late Lyndon Johnson and Sam Rayburn of Texas.

The consensus between government and the oil industry thus grew out of a mutuality of interest in oil as a vital resource. On the federal level the U.S. Geological Survey conducted advanced theoretical research on oil, while the U.S. Bureau of Mines dealt with practical problems. By World War I many states had created similar agencies, and most large integrated oil companies were establishing geological departments. Many young geologists hired by large oil companies received their first training in the U.S. Geological Survey and, over the years the interchange of personnel between government and industry came to be regarded as commonplace.

The Structure of the Industry

In spite of the vast size and bureaucratization of most companies, the oil industry maintains the mystique of the American private entrepreneur. The "wildcatter," an oilman who drills speculatively for oil, usually with makeshift equipment and a secondhand rig, personifies the rags-to-riches Horatio Alger theme. The history of the oil industry is replete with colorful characters such as "Dad" Joiner, who discovered on a farm in east Texas the largest single pool of oil ever found in the continental United States. Like most wildcatters, Dad Joiner died broke, but others, like H. L. Hunt, Sid Richardson, and Clint Murchison, made millions and gave rise to innumerable colorful stories of folksy and engaging Texas multimillionaires. There are still an estimated 7,000 wildcatters left in Texas alone, but they are a dying breed. Wildcatters found 85 percent of the oil in Texas and own 15 percent of it, while the "majors," large vertically integrated corporations, found 15 percent of it and own 85 percent.

Even though there are 10,000 to 12,000 oil producers operating in the United States, the industry is dominated by relatively few companies. The top four, eight, and twenty oil-producing companies in 1969 accounted respectively for 31, 51, and 70 percent of the average daily barrels of crude oil produced domestically. It has further been estimated that in 1970 the four, eight, and twenty firms controlled approximately 37, 64, and 94 percent, respectively, of domestic proven reserves.

To understand the Byzantine structure of the oil industry a distinction must be made among the types of companies. The term "major" includes all those firms which are "vertically integrated," that is, which operate on all four levels of oil production: crude oil extraction, transportation, refining, and marketing of finished product. The Federal Trade Commission has identified eighteen such companies, but for the most part the phrase "majors" is reserved for eight giant multinational firms which dominate the industry and which tend to function cooperatively rather than competitively. These are Exxon (until 1972, Exxon was Standard Oil of New Jersey, the original Rockefeller "Trust"), Gulf, Standard of Indiana, Texaco, Shell, ARCO, Mobil, and Standard of California. Since company operation and ownership records are not open to public scrutiny, it is not completely known to what extent joint ventures, exclusive buying-selling contracts, interlocking directors, and outright ownership are represented in rankings and statistics. For example, Getty Oil owns 72 percent of Skelly Oil, but most of the present statistical sources represent them as separate companies.

The term "independent" usually refers to companies which operate at one or more, but not all, levels of oil production, transportation, refining, and marketing. The independents make up the vast majority of the roughly 12,000 oil companies in the United States. If nonmajor affiliated distributors and dealers of gasoline and fuel oil are included in the definition of "independent" oil companies, the number exceeds 200,000.

The Oil Lobby

The American Petroleum Institute (API) is the major trade association for the oil industry. Seven of the twenty largest corporations in the United States are oil companies and all are API members.

The API was founded in 1919 by oil executives who had coordinated petroleum supplies during World War I. It was the first trade association to encompass all branches of the oil industry—refiners, producers, distributors, transporters, geologists, economists, and so forth. The API's membership—350 oil and gas companies and associations plus 7,000 individual members—accounts for about 85 percent of the total business volume in the industry. While the API is considered the major spokesman for the oil and gas interests, many large companies maintain their own staffs in Washington, and other national associations represent specialized segments of the industry. Some companies and oil officials belong to three or four specialized associations in addition to the API; at the same time, other trade organizations, among them the Oil Jobbers Council and the Independent Petroleum Association, are represented on the API's governing board. Although the API has a large membership and represents all phases of the industry, it is generally regarded as representing the interests of the major oil companies. The API's management committees, for example, are dominated by the top officials of the largest oil firms.

The API's operating budget in 1974 was estimated to amount to $15.7 million with about $15 million in cash reserves. Institute operations are financed by membership dues that are scaled to company size: six corporations contributed from $1 million to $1.3 million each in 1973, while two others were assessed $1 million each. The institute is a nonprofit, tax-exempt corporation. Under Internal Revenue Service regulations, funds used by the API in lobbying for and against proposed legislation are considered ordinary and necessary business expenses, which allows API members to deduct their dues from taxable income.

Policies of the institute are determined and guided by a board of directors composed of oil company executives and independent producers elected at annual API meetings. The principal API officers—elected by the board—are the chairman (always an industry executive) and the president, who serves the institute full-time. In 1974 the posts were held by Charles E. Spahr, chairman and chief executive officer of Standard Oil (Ohio), and Frank Ikard, a former member of the House (D–Tex., 1951–61) who left his elected office in December 1961 to become executive vice-president and chief Washington lobbyist of API. He became president of the institute in 1963. For seven of his ten years in Congress, Ikard was a member of the Ways and Means Committee, which has jurisdiction over tax matters, and was a close associate of two other "friends of oil" in Congress: Lyndon Johnson and former House speaker Sam Rayburn.

Reorganized in 1973 following a $270,000 consultants' study of its operations, the institute's staff structure consists of three major committees: industry affairs, policy development, and public affairs. Policy development, set up as a result of the reorganization, is intended to improve the institute's information on bills and policy proposals pending in Congress. The API's statistics division, from which the federal government obtains much of its data on oil supplies, falls under the policy development committee.

In addition to Ikard, the API maintains nine other lobbyists in Washington, and in 1973 spent about $2.5 million to promote its positions on the energy crisis and other matters. Because of differing views on the lobby law's disclosure requirements, the API reported only $121,000 in 1973 lobby expenses.

Whenever there is substantial agreement among its members on matters affecting the petroleum industry, the API will take a clear position. On issues where division exists, however, the institute makes no statement. For example, API has consistently supported the depletion allowance but remained neutral on the question of import quotas (which were supported by domestic producers but opposed by major companies which produce much of their crude abroad).

The API generally supports broad issues related to energy matters such as government-sponsored energy research and development programs, particularly the use of federal funds for developing energy sources. Much of this research, such as solar energy research, is expensive and promises little return for private capital. The API's lobbying efforts in this area have been very successful, with the Department of Interior substantially increasing moneys allocated to research and development.

The API takes a negative view of environmental concerns and has supported enactment of proposals dealing with the immediate expansion of offshore oil development, authorization of deepwater port facilities, construction of supertankers, continuation of oil depletion allowances, relaxation of air quality standards, and elimination of delays on environmental grounds in the construction of new refineries and nuclear generating facilities.

When there is general agreement within the industry regarding a particular measure, the API serves as a rallying point for other industry associations and individual companies. The Alaska pipeline controversy that confronted Congress in 1973 provided a clear picture of the amount of force the industry could generate in Washington. Lobbying by the API was very aggressive. A member of the House Interior and Insular Affairs Committee described the behind-the-scenes lobbying on the issue: "Lobbyists were here every day for weeks combing the halls. They are talented people who are very well paid and have nothing to do but lobby. They seemed to know everything that happened right after a conference session. Then the phone would ring the next morning and they would say this or that is unacceptable. They had a tremendous input into the process."

The API does not rely entirely on direct lobbying. In 1973 it launched a massive advertising campaign. Focusing on "opinion-forming groups," which they identified as the readers of *Time, Newsweek, Harper's, Atlantic, U.S. News & World Report* and other specialized publications, the API spent $2.5 million on magazine advertising. For 1974 the API budgeted $1.4 million for advertising in major newspapers and the more prominent general circulation magazines. The ads were designed to be less general than in previous years and were tied to issues facing congressional action.

Besides initiating a newspaper ad campaign, increasing its staff of registered lobbyists, and setting up a new policy development committee, the API has taken other steps to make its lobbying more effective and to influence public opinion. Early in 1974 the API launched a series of news conferences by institute officials to counter what they called "misinformation" about energy shortages, denying vigorously that oil companies were "withholding products, gouging the public on prices, and reaping windfall profits." In addition, API has increased its use of news releases with industry critics singled out by name. The institute is also strengthening its ties to state and regional petroleum associations and dispatching speakers to discuss energy matters before local groups and on radio and television talk shows.

In addition to API, seven other major gas and oil trade associations are active in Washington and cooperate with API. These groups represent various subdivisions of the industry, such as the independent oil and gas producers, interstate natural gas and oil pipeline companies, independent petroleum wholesalers, public and corporate distributors of natural and mixed gas, and manufacturers of gas appliances.

Also the National Petroleum Council (NPC), an organization not usually thought of as performing lobbying functions, is quite active. An industry organization consisting of oil company executives and technicians, NPC functions in a quasi-official advisory capacity with regard to the Department of the Interior. It is responsible for developing statistics used to project U.S. energy needs and resources and advises Interior and other government officials on energy policy.

II. THE ENERGY CRISIS

1969–72: Early Warnings

Nineteen sixty-nine was a very bad year for the oil industry. First, Union Oil's Platform A blew open in the Santa Barbara Channel, spilling hundreds of thousands of gallons of oil on coastal beaches and causing an estimated $10–20 million in damage to property and wildlife. The public outcry was intense, and came from so many sources that Secretary of the Interior Walter Hickel (formerly Republican governor of Alaska and subsequently forced by Nixon to resign from the Cabinet) placed a ban on future drilling and, for a time, seemed to be considering the removal of existing offshore drilling platforms. Environmentalists, aroused by the Santa Barbara oil spill, launched a series of massive suits in federal courts to halt construction of the 800-mile Trans-Alaska Pipeline until oil companies could guarantee there would be no more ecological disasters.

Next, a presidential committee studying oil import quotas recommended their removal; and Congress ended forty years of debate by cutting the oil depletion allowance from 27½ percent to 22 percent, effective January 1, 1970. Oil industry spokesmen indicated that it would cost the industry some $600 million a year and warned that it would reduce the incentive to expand crude oil production.

Finally, the "major" oil companies reported a decline in year-end earnings for 1969 to $6,092 billion from $6,125 billion in 1968. The explanation for the decline in profits was that the prices of crude oil and petroleum products had not kept pace with the costs of doing business. The oil industry as a whole was also troubled by excessive gasoline stocks, and oilmen were hoping for an early spring season to reduce inventories. In mid-1970 it was reported that nearly all of the ten largest majors lost ground to the independents during the prior year. The rate of sales increase for the independents was three times that of the majors.

In 1970 the seeds of the energy crisis sprouted. Even though the reduction of inventories was judged to be a serious problem, the following year saw the expression of concern about the growing *shortages* of supplies. The rumblings appeared first at the state level. In February of that year, the Texas Independent Producers and Royalty Owners Association

(TIPOC) announced that the United States had no more surplus-producing capacity and urged industry to admit that the surplus capacity had been exhausted. A report issued by the Department of Conservation of the State of Louisiana found that the state was rapidly approaching the time when oil production would peak. Finally, the position of possible shortages became official when the American Petroleum Institute also announced that estimated American crude oil reserves had suffered their largest decline in history during 1969. An editorial of May 25, 1970, in the *Oil and Gas Journal* (the official publication of API) stated, "A shortage of energy is a stark possibility if present trends continue." Almost simultaneously, the National Petroleum Council warned of a probable shortage of 250,000 barrels of residual oil a day for the winter of 1970–71.

The profit picture for the major oil companies in 1970 promised to be almost as bad as in 1969. The retail price rise on the part of the majors set off a series of gasoline price wars, making it difficult to realize much profit improvement. Environmental lobbying became so aggressive that, in mid-June, President Nixon asked Congress to cancel twenty offshore leases in the Santa Barbara Channel.

Coupled with these adverse circumstances, the twin developments of growing shortages and deteriorating prices posed major problems. Foreign crude oil became more expensive and was in shorter supply. A dispute between the new government of Libya and the oil companies led to a reduction of 400,000 barrels per day of low-sulphur crude oil. The Trans-Arabian Pipeline was out of action, cutting off its usual flow of 500,000 barrels per day to the Mediterranean. Tankers were required to move more oil from the Persian Gulf around Africa to Europe and tanker rates soared. Oil Producing and Exporting Countries (OPEC) was increasing its demands for higher taxes and royalties on their oil, and also demanding and receiving ownership in the petroleum operations taking place in its member countries. The higher rates made imported crude oil as expensive as domestic crude.

Uncertainty led to a reluctance to take risks, as indicated by an unwillingness to engage in refinery construction. On March 22, 1971, the *Oil and Gas Journal* reported that the United States might be on the brink of a shortage of refining capacity. Refinery starts and expansions were down and no new capacity was scheduled for 1973. The API noted that refineries are built in about three years, and concluded that a shortage of refinery capacity was inevitable before 1975. Uncertainty over oil import policy was cited as a factor in the industry's reluctance to build new refineries. Refiners were reportedly waiting for government action on long-range policies concerning distillate and heavy fuel oils before making commitments to expand their domestic refinery capacity.

As an article in the *Oil and Gas Journal* (Nov. 16, 1971) pointed out:

Refiners at this point aren't sure which way to jump. A plant built in the U.S. to supply a product which can be freely imported would be bankrupt.

On the other hand, a plant built offshore to supply the U.S. could be a white elephant if U.S. regulations are changed to emphasize crude imports and discourage further increases of products. The longer a decision is delayed by Government, the more certain is a refining capacity crunch.

Then, on August 15, 1971, President Nixon imposed a wage-price freeze on many industries, including oil. The action froze gasoline prices at seasonal highs and fuel oil at off-season lows. The freeze had the effect of discouraging the production of distillate fuel oil just as the peak fall season was coming on.

1973: The Crisis in Full Swing

During the winter of 1972–73 shortages of heating oil developed as predicted. Nevertheless, the quota system (restricting imports) was still maintained. On January 10, 1973, Office of Energy Policy director George A. Lincoln told the Senate Interim and Insular Affairs Committee that the administration was not actively considering a change from the quota system. Nevertheless, quotas were increased, if not abandoned. One week later, Lincoln announced that crude oil imports would be increased by 915,000 barrels per day over 1972 and all import controls on heating oil would be suspended for the first four months of 1973.

The seriousness of the shortage was indicated by President Nixon's move to reverse his previous decision and bring to an end the fourteen-year-old oil import program, which "is of virtually no benefit any longer . . . [and] has the very real potential of aggravating our supply problems." William E. Simon, the deputy secretary of the treasury and now the nation's top oil official, praised the move and was critical of past import policy. Simon told the press:

> Probably the greatest shortcoming in this present program [of oil imports] is its uncertainty. As you know, industry cannot plan in an uncertain climate. Our import allocations were subject to annual realignment. We were making the guesstimate. In recent years, the program has been altered frequently, and now it is a patchwork of exceptions.

Frank N. Ikard, president of API, also praised the move and said, "All the elements of the petroleum industry agree that there is a definite need to increase imports substantially over the next decade if we are to meet the energy requirements of the American people." The ending of the import program, while not attracting much publicity (and criticized by some as coming too late), was a major shift in policy. It would not have occurred without the concurrence of API. The concurrence of API—which a few months earlier had urged the retention of quotas—may be taken as an indication that the industry and the president were not anticipating an increase in domestic production.

Who's to Blame: The Debate Expands

The lifting of import quotas temporarily halted the direct participation of the executive office in the energy controversy. The debate expanded and shifted to the Senate Committee on Interior and Insular Affairs, chaired by Henry Jackson. An aspirant for the Democratic party presidential nomination in 1976, Jackson had long attempted to establish a reputation as an authority on environmental matters, and he quickly became the leading spokesman in Congress on energy legislation. The issue before his committee, therefore, became not so much the increasing of available supplies of oil; rather, Jackson's committee was more concerned with the economic structure of the oil industry as a possible underlying reason for the shortage. Jackson was interested in pursuing a line of inquiry suggesting that the oil shortage was deliberate.

His committee was given a report from the Federal Trade Commission on June 6 which indicated that the major oil companies' structure and performance were far from competitive. It charged that eighteen major companies, often with the cooperation of the federal government, controlled every aspect of the petroleum business, including foreign crude oil production, and were collectively using their power to squeeze independent refiners and marketers out of business. The major firms, the FTC study asserted, "have behaved in a similar fashion as would a classic monopolist: they have attempted to increase profits by restricting output."

In his response to the FTC's complaint, Senator Jackson said:

> While I am not yet ready to definitely conclude that the current crisis can be fully explained in terms of "conspiracies" between or "excessive market power" exercised by a relatively few oil companies . . . the shortages [do] threaten to extinguish the independent refining and marketing sectors as a viable competitive force in the petroleum industry. It is furthermore a fact that retail gasoline and fuel prices . . . have risen drastically and will continue to rise. At the same time, the earnings of the five biggest oil companies jumped by an amazing 43 percent. The earnings for 27 smaller oil companies jumped by 32.1 percent during the same period.

Jackson went on to cite what he called "disturbing signs that the present shortages are being accompanied and perhaps caused by major structural

changes in petroleum marketing which could seriously limit competition."
He asserted that "it is a classical first step of any small group of companies who wish to restrain trade and raise prices to first centralize their
marketing areas so as to reduce competition." He listed a number of examples of major oil companies selling hundreds of retail stations as they
shifted their marketing areas, and went on to conclude:

> There are instances of other oil companies which are abandoning
> certain "uneconomical" areas. Moreover, many of these and other
> major oil companies are apparently terminating existing dealer
> franchises and, *at the same time,* establishing new chains of dealer-
> ships under new second- and third-name "fighting brands."
> It is highly suggestive to those who have studied the dynamics
> and structure of the national and international oil corporations
> which dominate the industry and the patterns of marketing that all
> of these factors are not the result of happenstance. In major respects,
> they may represent conscious, knowing decisions to shift traditional
> profit centers from "production" in historically low-cost, profitable
> Mid-East sources to the downstream sources of "refining" and "mar-
> keting" both in the United States and Europe. This shift in profit
> taking sources was compelled by the nationalistic attitude of Mid-
> East nations to control their own resources and to maximize . . .
> revenues.

The oil companies responded to such charges by intensifying their advertising claims that it was the American consumer who was responsible
for the gasoline shortage. A Standard Oil (Indiana) advertisement, published in *Business Week*, expressed the industry's position:

> America has a tremendous appetite. Not just for food, but for the
> natural resources that produce energy—gas and petroleum.
> And we're running short of them, because the country is growing
> so fast, and using up its currently available resources even faster.

The "energy crisis," as the gasoline shortage was soon named, became
an international issue and rapidly came to equal the Watergate affair in
terms of public awareness, and in terms of public doubt as to who was to
blame. A question of fact was involved. Was it true that the world was
running out of oil as the major companies and key government officials
such as the president and the secretary of the interior claimed? Or was
the oil shortage a "created crisis" as an increasing number of critics
claimed?

The public was soon subjected to a huge amount of publicity on the
issue. The oil industry spoke through its lobbying organization, the American Petroleum Institute, but primarily it spoke as individual companies,

each giving its views of various issues involved. The "big eight" (Exxon, Texaco, Gulf, Shell, Standard [California], ARCO, Standard [Indiana], and Mobil), led the fight for the industry with a steady stream of company statements on television and in selected newspapers and magazines. They argued the oil industry's case aggressively and provocatively. The oil companies maintained that demand for petroleum products had outstripped supply and that inconveniences and even hardships could be expected until new sources could be developed.

President Nixon largely agreed with the oil companies' assessment and lamented the nation's gluttonous, wasteful ways in energy consumption. There was a great deal of public discussion about ways of conserving energy, and an atmosphere of crisis prevailed as people prepared to meet the hardships promised by oil shortages.

But dissenters increasingly came to be heard and doubt was cast on the reality of the crisis. In a series of widely quoted articles, the *Philadelphia Inquirer* called the oil shortages a "created crisis." The paper said:

> Periodic "crises" in the oil industry have begun to remind Americans of the boy who cried "Wolf!" once too often. So much so that necessary conservation controls may be difficult to impose should a genuine oil shortage ever materialize.
>
> This summer, independent gasoline dealers were forced to close their stations, while major refining companies in many cases limited the amount of gasoline a motorist could buy.

The newspaper wanted to know why, and assigned two outstanding investigative reporters—Donald Bartlett and James B. Steele—to uncover the answers. Their story, "Oil—The Created Crisis," appeared as a three-part series beginning Sunday, July 22, 1973. The facts developed in their investigation were in direct conflict with the claims of the oil companies and administration spokesmen. They claimed that some years ago, the five largest, multinational American oil companies made deliberate, long-term policy decisions to sharply expand operations in foreign countries. They invested billions of dollars in facilities for producing, refining, and marketing petroleum products overseas to meet spiraling demand for oil products in Europe and Asia. *The Inquirer* claimed that expansion came at the expense of the United States and that the Nixon administration made one blunder after another in dealing with oil policy matters, beginning with the president's failure to lift oil import restrictions after taking office in 1969 and "climaxing with soothing assurances last winter that there were no oil supply problems."

"At the same time American oil companies with world-wide operations are telling their customers in the United States to cut back on their consumption of oil products," said the paper, "the companies are urging their customers in Europe and Asia to buy more oil products."

III. THE EMERGENCY ENERGY ACT OF 1973:
THE FRUSTRATION OF CONGRESS

It was in this atmosphere of crisis and doubt—both exacerbated by the Watergate affair—that the Emergency Energy Act of 1973 was debated.

On November 7, 1973, in a televised address to the nation, President Nixon proposed the act, setting up a wide-ranging energy conservation program to curb the nation's fuel consumption in the face of growing shortages. The program would give the executive sweeping authority to ration gasoline and fuel oil, reduce auto speed limits, exempt industries from environmental controls, and impose taxes on excessive use of energy. The president warned that the Arab embargo on oil shipments to the United States "sharply altered" earlier expectations of "temporary shortages" that winter and advised Americans to consume less energy by lowering thermostats, washing clothes in colder water, reducing highway speeds, tuning autos more frequently, and forming car pools.

"We must . . . face up to a very stark fact," Nixon declared. "We are heading toward the most acute shortages of energy since World War II." He attacked environmental standards that prevent the use of certain fuels, saying, "Those who particularly and exclusively . . . concentrate on the need for cleaner air and a better environment must recognize the truth that if one freezes to death, it doesn't make any difference whether the air is clean or dirty."

The president announced a "Project Independence" designed to free the United States from "foreign energy sources" by 1980. He said the only answer to present shortages was "self-sufficiency, the capacity to meet our energy needs with our own resources." He compared his program to the Manhattan Project, which developed the atomic bomb in World War II, and to Project Apollo, which placed an American on the moon in 1969. He also declared that it was "imperative" that the emergency legislation "be on my desk for signature before Congress recesses in December."

The oil industry was generally supportive of President Nixon's proposed legislation, particularly rationing. The National Petroleum Council recommended that "mandatory rationing of all petroleum fuels—gasoline, distillates, and heavy fuels—should be undertaken in the U.S. on a national scale immediately." It said, "The nation must establish priorities and determine where cuts in demand should be made," adding that the choice lay between the individual consumer and industry, and that "mandatory rationing of gasoline for private transportation and of home heating oils offers the opportunity for significant reductions in petroleum use with minimal impact on the economy." Support for rationing may at first glance seem contrary to the self-interest of the oil industry and to the traditional antipathy toward governmental regulations. However, the reason for industry support for rationing was readily apparent. The *Oil and Gas Journal* editorialized that "rationing is the answer only if experts operate it."

> [Rationing involves] a complex producing, processing, and distribution system demanding immediate and accurate decisions by knowledgeable experts. . . .
> Legislation is needed to give emergency antitrust and conflict of interest clearances to free the pool of talent in the petroleum industry for public service. Congress and the Nixon Administration should clear these obstacles quickly.

Thus, the intention of the industry was to—in effect—administer any potential rationing program.

The Senate Debate Begins

The administration, however, was considerably less enthusiastic about rationing than was the industry or Henry Jackson, chairman of the Senate Interior and Insular Affairs Committee. Jackson's committee, prior to the president's November 7 message, had already begun drafting similar legislation. John A. Love, director of the Energy Policy Office, announced that the administration, instead of sending its own legislation to Congress, would support the committee version. In announcing administration support for Jackson's legislation, Love said rationing probably would not be necessary. Jackson disagreed, arguing that rationing was inevitable and predicting that energy shortages ultimately would force some industries to close. "I see no way to avoid rationing," he warned. "They ought to be planning for it, they ought to go ahead and print the [rationing books]." He announced that his committee would complete action soon on a bill to give the president authority to ration gasoline and reduce highway speed limits to fifty miles per hour.

Acting with uncharacteristic speed, Jackson's committee hastened to prepare a series of bills that included most of the president's recommendations for meeting the energy crisis. Jackson took personal responsibility for quick passage of energy legislation. He kept his committee in session for a full day—without a lunch break—and into the evening to hear witnesses on his energy bill. John Love gave strong administrative support by indicating that the Jackson bill encompassed most of the president's legislative requests, and urged bipartisan support. Jackson cooperated by taking the unusual step of agreeing to draft the final version of the bill in open session, the day after it was first introduced, with the help of administration experts. He vowed that the final bill would be ready for full Senate vote within a week. On the House side, Chairman Harley O. Staggers (D–W.Va.) of the Interstate and Foreign Commerce Committee introduced a similar bill on November 10, and said hearings would begin immediately. "We are going to proceed in a bipartisan manner," Jackson said. "The best politics now is no politics."

To a remarkable degree, Jackson was true to his word. However, beneath the spirit of bipartisan cooperation there lurked a difference in philosophy which was soon to prove destructive to the bipartisan coalition and which became the focus of the first round of opposition to the energy act.

John Love indicated that Jackson's bill was "too restrictive" in its provisions allowing for waivers of clear-air laws. A committee print of an earlier administration proposal for dealing with energy shortages indicated that the White House at one point wanted to go further in putting aside laws to protect the environment. The White House wanted to exempt oil refineries from the clean-water laws as well as clean-air requirements.

A provision that all actions by the executive would be exempt from the National Environmental Policy Act caused dismay among environmentalists. In the administration version, upon declaration of an emergency by the president, all regulatory agencies would consider energy conservation as one of their chief purposes. The Federal Power Commission could suspend regulation of natural gas and the Atomic Energy Commission could grant licenses without public hearings. API president Frank N. Ikard strongly endorsed the draft and indicated that it would be helpful if the government granted resumption of oil production in the Santa Barbara Channel. Jackson himself entertained no serious concern that energy legislation was a threat to environmental standards. In terms of his priorities, energy conservation and development was more important than the preservation of the spirit of the Environmental Protection Act. Jackson's vigorous support of the proposed legislation represented somewhat of a reordering of priorities. In his urgency to achieve prompt passage he apparently disregarded his previous concern with oil company profiteering and also modified his long-term commitment to environmental protection.

Jackson, the *Washington Post* observed, "conducted his committee like a symphony orchestra, forged compromises on some amendments, passed by others until a compromise could be worked out, and allowed votes on still others." Consequently, an energy bill was cleared by Jackson's committee on November 13, scarcely a week after President Nixon's address to the nation on the energy crisis. Jackson's Democratic colleague from Washington, Warren Magnuson, confidently predicted that the legislation would pass both houses of Congress within a week.

As approved by the committee, the act declared a national emergency and directed the president to set up plans to ration and conserve fuel. The act contained an amendment to the clean-air act to allow power plants variances from antipollution regulations. It gave the president unprecedented peacetime powers under the guise of coping with critical fuel shortages. The powers granted to the president would affect private citizens, businesses, and public services. The legislation reserved for Congress the right to disapprove all or part of the contingency plan it directed the president to implement and to terminate the plan after six months by concurrent resolution.

The president would have very broad authority to "reduce energy consumption" through a series of "conservation measures" which, if applied fully, could bring about substantial changes in American society through the mechanism of central energy planning.

Under the Senate bill (S. 2589), the president could—

1. implement transportation control plans, which could include reduced speed limits;
2. restrict the use of fuels for lighted outdoor advertising, recreational activities, and decorative lighting;
3. ban all advertising that encouraged increased energy consumption;
4. limit fuel consumption in commercial establishments and public services such as schools;
5. order industries and utilities that use oil and natural gas to convert to coal and prevent industries and utilities now using coal from reconverting to oil or natural gas;
6. require oil fields on nonfederal lands to produce at their maximum efficient rate and fields on federal lands to exceed their maximum efficient rate (maximum efficient rate is the level of production at which it is estimated the production can be sustained at optimal levels);
7. require domestic oil refineries to adjust their product mix in accordance with national priorities as defined by the president (refineries are able to adjust the amounts of various refined products they recover from crude oil);
8. allocate materials and fuels to ensure the continued or new production of fuel supplies (the president would also be able to make fuel allocations to economically depressed areas or regions with special problems, such as New England and the upper Midwest, which

experience extreme cold and lack adequate facilities to transport fuels);

9. order temporary suspensions of clean air standards for stationary sources (such as power plants as opposed to vehicles);
10. revise state plans for clean-air standards to take into account projected fuel shortages;
11. approve requests from power plants for suspensions of emission requirements if the owners had a long-term contract for a supply of low-sulphur coal or a system to clean up coal emissions;
12. redistribute low-sulphur fuels to avoid pollution problems.

The Response of the Environmentalists

The portions of the legislation which generated the most controversy were those allowing a relaxation of the standards established by the National Environmental Protection Act of 1969. Environmental groups had lobbied long and hard for legislation to achieve federal air and water quality standards, and were afraid that in the rush to cope with the immediate problem of oil shortages, permanent damage to the environment might occur. Certainly, the oil industry did little to allay their fears.

Clifton Garvin, Jr., president of Exxon, asserted it was unlikely that voluntary energy conservation measures would be sufficient to compensate for the loss of oil shipments from the Middle East. He suggested that the United States speed up development of offshore oil reserves, stimulate coal mining, and open up federal land for oil-shale development. Frank N. Ikard of API agreed, arguing that environmental protection actions had "certainly influenced our ability to meet consumer demand" and that secondary environmental standards restricting the burning of higher sulphur coal and residual oil should be reconsidered. Edward M. Cole, president of General Motors, contributed the idea that five billion gallons of gasoline annually, 5 percent of the gasoline used by passenger cars, could be saved if clean-air devices were removed from automobiles.

Environmentalists began expressing fear of wholesale assaults on environmental standards as Congress started rushing through emergency legislation to deal with the energy crisis. "There's definitely a panic situation up there [in Congress]," said Jim Conroy, legislative coordinator for Environmental Action, Inc. "They're ramming things through committees and they'll be law. . . . It's very alarming. If all these proposals pass, we're in for some bad times." Brock Evans of the Sierra Club and Barbara Keller of the Environmental Policy Center both characterized proposals for dealing with fuel shortages as "assaults on the Clean Air Act." "It really isn't necessary to forfeit clean air to have energy," said Keller. "It's possible to have both. But," she added, "people have become so frightened, so governed by their fear of shortages, that Congress is moving at a frantic pace. Even the dedicated environmentalists [in Congress] are scared." These traditionally active organizations were joined by a more multipurposed organization, Congress Watch, a lobby group sponsored by Ralph Nader, in urging a cessation in the assaults upon the Environmental Protection Act under the guise of a temporary emergency.

As environmentalists saw it, there were two separate energy crises—the one in the winter of 1973–74 and the long-term one. Concern over the first should not be a reason for panic legislation affecting the second, they felt. "We're likely to take the wrong steps at the wrong time," warned Mack Messing of the Environmental Policy Center. "What is needed for the immediate crisis are stringent conservation measures, including allocation and possibly rationing of fuel." He concluded, "Longer-range proposals should be thoroughly studied, not rushed through in a crisis situation, perhaps unnecessarily and perhaps to be regretted later."

Criticism of "Big Oil" Escalates

The objections of environmental groups did not, in themselves, generate much enthusiasm. Americans shivering in gasoline lines on dark winter mornings did not care very much about protecting the environment.

However, even as the Senate began the debate on Jackson's legislation, traditionally powerful economic groups began a new line of criticism. The question of oil company profits, at record levels in spite of supposed shortages, was raised by AFL-CIO president George Meany in a letter to Senator Jackson. Meany called for an excise tax on "windfall profits" that the industry made from the fuel shortage and asked for increased benefits for workers laid off because of the shortages.

The industry defended its profits in what was to become a familiar litany. "Profit gains such as those being shown this year must become commonplace," said the *Oil and Gas Journal.* "Oil companies can make higher profits palatable to the public and government only as they translate them into investments that will produce more fuel."

Rationing?

The main thrust of the oil industry's lobbying efforts continued to focus on the establishment of petroleum rationing or some form of mandatory allocation and the positioning of oil people in governmental positions relating to petroleum policy.

The oil industry received both support and opposition for its program within the administration. John Love, the president's energy advisor, announced that "rationing is coming," and that the government should call on the "expertise and manpower of the nation's oil companies" to manage the rationing program. He urged that antitrust restrictions on oil companies be lifted to eliminate charges of collusion and conflict of interest in managing rationing. Rogers Morton, secretary of the interior, also supported rationing and the inclusion of oil people into petroleum policy-making positions in government. On the other hand, Melvin Laird, Nixon's chief domestic advisor, treasury secretary George Shultz, Economic Council chairman Herbert Stein, budget director Roy Ash, and commerce secretary Frederick Dent all favored a tax or a rise in price (which would have the same effect as a tax) of petroleum products instead of rationing as a means of restricting consumption.

President Nixon, increasingly embroiled in staving off impeachment pressures from the Watergate affair, refused to take a stand on the issue. Washington columnists Rowland Evans and Robert Novak noted that "the Nixon Administration still has not made basic policy decisions on conserving energy [to tax or ration]. What's worse, it has not yet even perfected decision-making machinery. Nobody is in charge of managing the energy crisis and the president remains characteristically aloof."

Passed without serious debate in the Senate Interior and Insular Affairs Committee, the legislation now encountered intense efforts at modification. The bill did not require rationing; it merely authorized it. Jackson, however, believed that stronger language was required because of the ambivalence of the administration. Consequently, while serving as floor manager, he introduced on November 15 an amendment to require rationing by January 15. Mike Mansfield (D–Mont.), majority leader of the Senate, served as cosponsor. The oil industry was in close agreement. The National Petroleum Council, urging approval of the amendment, anticipated that fuel shortages would cause an 8 percent unemployment rate and an annual loss of $48 billion from the gross national product unless rationing was imposed. Joining the National Petroleum Council in its plea were numerous majors, notably Atlantic Richfield, Texaco, and Gulf.

In addition to the amendment's sponsors, and the oil companies, support came from some sources conspicuous in the past as critics of the oil industry, such as Senator William Proxmire (D–Wis.), an aggressively liberal critic of big business. The coalition of Senate liberals and oil companies was made all the more unusual by the support of David Rockefeller, chairman of the board of Chase Manhattan Bank (a major stockholder in a number of large oil companies), who urged rationing in "the very near future," even though the choice was "unappetizing and inefficient."

The administration, however, did not agree with the oil companies. Although there was obviously some administration sympathy for rationing, the powerful voices of Secretary of the Treasury Shultz and budget director Ash were raised in opposition. Although both Shultz and Ash were known to favor a heavy tax on gasoline purchases to curtail use (in keeping with their conservative economic philosophy), the administration's position, as expressed by Senator Paul Fannin (D–Ariz.), was that the mandatory rationing amendment destroyed the necessary flexibility needed by the president in dealing with shortages.

The amendment, after minimal debate, was defeated on its day of introduction by a 48–40 vote. Voting against it were thirty-six of thirty-eight Republicans; they were joined by twelve Democrats (eight Northern Democrats and four Southern Democrats). The president himself, apparently absorbed in nonenergy matters such as Watergate, did not take a position. Jackson, obviously expecting a more positive administration response, remarked, "We simply did not expect, in all candor, a division in the administration on the question of rationing."

The Jackson amendment represented the only serious challenge to the original legislation. After a number of minor amendments during the days of debate on November 19, and only twelve days after the president's energy message, the Senate voted 78 to 6 in support of S. 2589 The Senate thus approved unprecedented peacetime power to the president. A single Democrat, J. William Fulbright (Ark.), and six Republicans, led by Mark Hatfield (Ore.), opposed the grant of new powers to the president. The fact that the act itself was passed after only three days of debate is testimony to the sense of urgency felt by most senators. Hatfield's comment that the act handed vast new powers to the president, while Congress was trying to "reassert ourselves in the budgetary process, in confirmation powers, and as initiators of—not just reactors to—policy and programs," fell on deaf ears.

The Creation of the Federal Energy Office

Even as the Senate was rushing to pass energy legislation and hearings on similar legislation were beginning in the House, the executive department moved ahead with its plans to integrate oil company personnel into government decision-making posts. Interior Secretary Rogers Morton (a former Republican congressman who replaced Walter Hickel) said that about 250 oil industry executives would be brought into the federal government to help run new fuel allocation programs being implemented. An Interior Department spokesman claimed that "there is no antitrust or conflict of interest involved," but it was learned that the president had informally asked the Senate to exempt the oil companies from antitrust laws and other conflict-of-interest regulations, but was turned down.

On December 4, President Nixon signed an executive order which created a Federal Energy Office within the White House pending congressional action on the proposed Federal Energy Administration with ex-stockbroker William E. Simon as head. The new agency would acquire from the Department of the Interior the offices of Petroleum Allocation, Energy Conservation, Energy Data and Analysis, and Oil and Gas; the Energy Division of the Cost of Living Council also would be included. The net result of this bureaucratic transformation would be to centralize energy policy making and application within the White House.

In a press conference December 4, new energy czar Simon said that the administration wanted to reduce gasoline consumption by 30 percent in the first three months of 1974. He asserted that higher fuel prices and possibly rationing would be needed to achieve national self-sufficiency in energy supplies. The Federal Energy Administration, he said, would focus on saving energy and finding new sources. He declared that Americans had been "energy wastrels" and would have to change their life styles and "be more thoughtful." The oil industry greeted the Simon appointment as "a plus," noting in the *Oil and Gas Journal:* "The national psychology has shifted dramatically in favor of domestic development and appointment of a new energy czar has improved confidence for the short run."

In effect, the creation of the Federal Energy Office accomplished by executive order what Congress had not yet agreed to sanction. In fact, the president had authority to impose rationing under the Defense Production Act of 1950. Indeed, the question now seemed less a matter of what to do about gasoline shortages than one of what to do about the oil industry. The initiative seemed to have shifted.

Panic Subsides, Doubts Increase: The Debate in the House

While the Senate was rushing to approve the Jackson legislation, the House Interstate and Foreign Commerce Committee was holding hearings on energy legislation introduced by its chairman, Harley Staggers. Staggers' legislation, while similar to that passed by the Senate, was more restrictive of the power of the president. Also, unlike the situation in the Senate committee, Staggers' legislation was not endorsed by the administration (indeed, it appeared to surprise the administration when hearings began).

From the beginning, it was clear that a different atmosphere prevailed in the House of Representatives. An intensive investigation by the various mass media, in addition to publicity given to an investigation by Senator Frank Church's Subcommittee on Multinational Corporations dealing with the structure of the industry, raised again the issue of responsibility. While the House committee was preparing legislation, Senator Church's subcommittee (of the parent Interior committee) attracted more attention and generated a plethora of bad publicity for oil companies.

On December 6, Senator Lee Metcalf (D–Mont.), appearing before the

Church subcommittee hearings, charged that oil companies and a few banks dominate federal energy policy through an "interlocked apparatus" that virtually excludes other concerned segments. Metcalf displayed a table of organization of this "shadow government agency" listing 476 positions, most of them filled. In key positions were twenty-four officials from ARCO, twelve from Sun Oil, eleven from Northern Natural Gas, and nineteen from Gulf.

The assault continued with the testimony of the National Congress of Petroleum Retailers. This organization accused the major oil companies of using the energy crisis—for which they were "most responsible"—to gain total control of retail marketing of gasoline.

Congressman Les Aspin (D–Wis.) echoed the charge of a "false crisis." Using production figures published by the American Petroleum Institute, he accused the oil industry of contributing to the energy crisis by holding back on production. He used the API's figures to show American oil wells producing at 16 percent less than their maximum rate.

As the testimony became more acrimonious, Church, in essence urging the House to slow down, called for a "great national debate." Church's concern was directed toward the apparently powerful position of big oil in economic and political decision making. Others—including those who had supported the Jackson legislation—voiced anew concern for environmental protection.

A further brake on House action was the revelation that major oil companies had made massive, illegal contributions to President Nixon's 1972 re-election campaign. On December 5 it was announced that Phillips Petroleum Company and its board chairman pleaded guilty to making a $100,000 illegal contribution to Nixon's campaign. Several congressmen promised an investigation of the campaign contributions of other oil companies. Senator Edward Kennedy (D–Mass.) accused the oil industry of steering the White House into the energy crisis after giving more than $4 million to the re-election campaign.

House Speaker Carl Albert joined the increasingly partisan debate on the energy crisis with a twenty-two-page "white paper" charging that "the American people are now being asked to pay with their patriotism the price exacted by the misguided policies and negligence of the Nixon administration." Albert said the administration had "failed to foresee the fuel problem and is now trying to rewrite history to shift the blame to Congress." He charged President Nixon with being "intent on deceiving the American people with regard to both the severity and causes of the energy shortage." Thus, the Democrats moved farther away from the administration's chief legislative supporter in the energy crisis, Democratic Senator Henry Jackson, who said he was disappointed that Congress did not vote mandatory gas rationing immediately.

Lobbying groups with a position opposed to that of the oil industry were also heard from. The AFL-CIO position on the energy crisis was outlined in a letter from its lobbyist to committee chairman Staggers. The AFL-CIO said it wanted "equality of sacrifice" in dealing with energy shortages and that it did not believe "Nixon would use emergency power to adopt fair and equitable" measures. The letter asked Staggers to "make it clear to your colleagues in Congress that the Congress and the American people will not tolerate industry making huge windfall profits from an emergency and urge immediate consideration of an excess profits tax." The union called for "no rationing by taxation," "elimination of tax credits and depletion allowances in all foreign operations of U.S. oil companies," "establishment of export controls," "insistence that those put in charge of administrative machinery have no connection, direct or indirect, with gas, oil, coal, or utility industries," and a provision to "aid workers unemployed by the energy crisis."

The appearance of the AFL-CIO's lobbyist at the House committee hearing was significant in that the organization appeared as concerned with the influence of the oil industry as it was with shortages. Labor's proposal to end depletion allowances and tax credits, and its opposition to the participation of oil executives in the fuel allocation program, signified the beginning of a dispute which would move beyond the limits of the Senate debate.

Representative Staggers' committee now became the focus of three distinct sets of pressure: (1) efforts by the AFL-CIO to persuade the committee to recommend an excess profits tax; (2) efforts on the part of the oil industry (supported by the administration) to further relax environmental standards; and (3) fears that the Senate version of the legislation would create an executive dictatorship. As the shape of the bill became obvious, each set of pressures was responded to.

In the process, seventy-five amendments were adopted in committee. The result was legislation substantially different from that which had cleared the Senate. The president was authorized to establish priorities for fuel allocation, impose gas rationing, and require maximum rates of oil production. A Federal Energy Administration was established with a director required to submit energy plans to Congress for approval. Auto emission standards were to be abandoned after 1977, and clean-air standards were suspended for industrial and power plants. Coal burning was also allowed by such plants. Finally, the legislation would restrict windfall profits by oil and coal industries.

The bill, lamented Brock Adams (D–Wash.), became a "Christmas tree" as special interests lobbied to "protect themselves." Because of the complexity of the amended legislation, Chairman Staggers introduced the final amended product as a substitute for the original bill.

The House Vote

On December 12, three weeks after the Senate had passed its National Energy Emergency Act (S. 2589), the House opened debate on its own version of the bill. There were a hundred different views presented and almost as many amendments proposed on how to deal with the energy crisis, including an antibusing amendment. Several efforts to kill the bill or limit debate failed as members sought to pass a bill before the Christmas recess to show constituents they had acted to meet the energy crisis. Several speakers suggested that any bill would do, that a House-Senate conference committee would, in effect, write the bill. Staggers, floor manager for the bill, objected to this line of reasoning, saying Congress should have "enough courage" to write laws itself instead of delegating that right to executive agencies.

The House version contained substantial changes from the legislation approved by the Senate. The two most offensive changes from the point of view of the administration and the oil industry were the requirement that energy plans be submitted to Congress, and provisions for dealing with excess profits by oil companies during the shortage. However, organized labor strongly supported both changes. Neither received an effective challenge during the debate.

However, a variety of amendments were quickly approved which again altered the shape of the legislation. Principal floor amendments adopted in the first days of debate included the following:

—A ban on busing of students to a school farther than the one nearest their homes was adopted, 221–192. (Aye: 105 Dems., 116 Reps.; nay: 127 Dems., 65 Reps.) John D. Dingell (D–Mich.) said his antibusing amendment would save more than 78 million gallons of fuel a year. The amendment was denounced by black and liberal members of the House.

—The coal industry was exempted from provisions restricting windfall profits on a 256–155 vote. (Aye: 120 Dems., 136 Reps.; nay: 110 Dems., 45 Reps.) An effort to eliminate the restrictions on the oil industry failed, 188–213. (Aye: 51 Dems., 137 Reps.; nay: 172 Dems., 41 Reps.)

—The deadline for compliance with auto emission standards was advanced one year in an amendment which passed, 199–180. (Aye: 69 Dems., 130 Reps.; nay: 142 Dems., 38 Reps.)

The House also approved an amendment that gave oil companies limited exemptions from antitrust laws in order to "help government solve the oil shortage." The issue threatened to stall the bill until Congressman

Peter W. Rodino, Jr. (D–N.J.), chairman of the Judiciary Committee with jurisdiction over antitrust legislation, compromised. Rodino had fought an amendment offered by Congressman Clarence J. Brown (R–Ohio) which would have provided broad antitrust exemptions for the oil industry. The Rodino compromise would ensure that the antitrust division of the Justice Department and the FTC were involved in the very beginning of any agreements within the oil industry. Moreover, the burden of proof would be on the industry to show that its actions were not designed to restrain competition. Once these modifications were agreed upon, debate subsided and Staggers' legislation was approved on December 14. The vote was substantial, 265–112, with strong majorities in both parties voting yes. (Aye: 151 Dems., 114 Reps.; nay: 59 Dems., 53 Reps.)

A Frustrated Congress Adjourns for the Holidays

As there were now two quite different versions of the legislation, both were sent to a Conference Committee—made up of members of both houses—to work out an acceptable compromise. Now looming as an important consideration was the rush to reach a decision before adjournment. President Nixon was in the fortunate position of castigating Congress for its inaction, and the appearance of decisiveness became crucial.

The labors of the Conference Committee dealt primarily with the most controversial modifications initiated by the House: windfall profits and congressional approval of energy plans. During a week of bargaining, the House conferees resisted intense White House and oil industry lobbying and, while compromising slightly, refused to drop these provisions entirely. As the administration became aware of the probability that the Conference Committee would retain some form of congressional approval of energy plans and some form of windfall profits tax, the threat of presidential veto was raised.

Clearly, the main stumbling block was windfall profits. According to the version approved by the House, an elaborate, detailed definition of excess profits was contained in the actual body of the legislation. If, under the statutory definition, price gouging was found to exist, the guilty company would have to either repay the overcharged consumers or institute a general price reduction. During the House debate, the administration had sought unsuccessfully to have the bill modified to allow the president to define excess profits. Now, during the hearing of the Conference Committee, energy czar Simon was more successful. Although he also argued for a free hand for the administration in planning every policy, Simon suggested an exchange. If the Conference Committee would abandon the House requirement for congressional approval, the administration would accept at least a symbolically satisfying excess profits tax. The approval provisions were retained under the Conference Committee version, but the president was given the authority to set petroleum prices to allow for "fair" but not excessive profits.

Thus, the oil industry had, in actuality, gained more than it lost. Among the major gains were the relaxation of environmental standards. The windfall profits provision could barely be regarded as a loss, since—at least for the immediate future—a friendly president could define fair profits. However, the Conference Committee did provide a potentially troublesome addendum. Companies were required to disclose their reserves, thus providing heretofore private information to energy planners and, potentially, reducing the information monopoly enjoyed by the oil companies.

Sent immediately to the Senate and House December 21, the Emergency Energy Act came up for final consideration by both houses. The report had been finished only that morning, and it was immediately brought before the Senate. Forty of the 100 Senators had already gone home for Christmas. Many of the remaining ones did not have a copy of the report, and many more had not read it.

The final compromises had presumably been made, and Congress was expected to send the legislation to the president's desk. So a murmur of surprises went through the Senate gallery when Clifford Hansen of Wyoming, one of the most loquacious oil senators, took the floor to denounce the bill as a "diabolical, three-tiered pagoda of confusion and delay." The administration and he would not tolerate the windfall profits section or the reporting requirement, Hansen declared, because these were "attempts to paint the oil industry as the black pot of the energy crisis."

A filibuster was on. Russell Long (D–La.) said he did not like the windfall profits section either, because it seemed to involve an explicit tax on the oil people. Tax matters, he said, should come out of the Finance Committee (of which he was chairman). The filibuster would not be broken as long as he supported it.

Henry Jackson, the floor manager of the energy bill, became extremely agitated when the filibuster emerged. His reputation as one of the most powerful men in the Senate was under serious attack; he faced the humiliation of having his prize bill killed by a coalition of oil lobbyists and the administration.

Mike Mansfield, the Senate majority leader, also became agitated late in the afternoon. He asked for a gentlemen's time-out on the filibuster, and urged that the Senate act promptly. "This is a pretty sour performance," he began. Mansfield's anger was directed at the administration's efforts—led by Simon and Shultz—to convince the Senate on the eve of adjournment to substitute a separate White House bill for the one approved by the Conference Committee. The filibuster against the Conference Committee recommendations—specifically, the excess profits tax and disclosure of reserves—was being organized by Russell Long and Paul Fannin (R–Ariz.). Later, two conservative Republican senators representing states with strong interest in petroleum, Clifford Hansen (R–Wyo.) and Henry Bellman (R–Okla.), joined in.

While the filibuster was being conducted, White House congressional lobbyists met with Republican senators in the vice-president's office to propose the administration's substitute legislation, which contained neither of the controversial sections objected to by the president and the oil companies. Close at hand were lobbyists for the American Petroleum Institute and Continental Oil, both of whom were actively engaged in last-minute negotiations.

Thus it appeared, correctly, to Mansfield that the filibuster was being staged while the oil companies and White House lobbyists hammered out legislation more beneficial to their interests. Indeed, as Senator Hansen was participating in the filibuster, an aide handed him the substitute legislation and he announced that "new criteria have just been developed that will help us move on from here." He referred to the White House bill, which he then revealed to Jackson. Jackson retired to confer with Long. From this conference an end to the filibuster was achieved in exchange for Jackson's agreement to drop windfall profits and reserve reporting. The new bill passed by voice vote and the Senate adjourned.

Thus the Senate had, in effect, rejected the Conference Committee report and—by accepting the version supported by the oil industry and the administration—returned to the legislation it had originally approved. However, the action was taken more because of the urgency of adjournment than because of any expectation that this session would actually approve energy legislation. Unless the House accepted the Senate bill without modification—a remote possibility—there would be no legislation. Jackson assumed that this would be the case and began preparations for beginning again when the next session of Congress convened after the Christmas holidays.

As the House, facing the same adjournment pressures as the Senate, began the deliberation, Senator Jackson (prior to the adjournment of the House) expressed disappointment that Congress was not able to deliver an energy bill. He was bitter that the White House had not supported the bill he had rushed through the Senate. "I can't distinguish the White House position from the oil industry's position," Jackson told reporters. "I'm not born yesterday. I know who's behind all this. It's the White House and the oil industry." Jackson warned them both, saying, "Unless we make rational moves now we are going to see in 1974 the most punitive legislation ever adopted by the Congress affecting any one industry. If they don't face up to this, there's not going to be an excess profits tax but there's going to be punitive legislation. That's what's going to face the oil industry and senators from those states." By punitive legislation, Jackson said, he meant stricter regulations of oil companies, making them a public utility and perhaps placing them under federal charters as banks are.

Jackson's warning came on December 21, the day of Senate adjournment. The same day, the speaker of the House called the representatives back into session. Under the rules, the House could not take up the energy bill until the Senate had finished. The representatives were tired, and several of them were in black ties for farewell parties they would probably miss. As they scurried around trying to find out what had happened in the Senate, Carl Albert gaveled the House to order and quickly recognized Harley Staggers, the floor manager for the legislation. He called up H.R. 760, a measure to suspend the rules and pass, with a two-thirds majority required, an amendment in the nature of a substitute for the conference report on the original bill, S. 2589.

No one knew what H.R. 760 or the new amendment was—understandably, since Staggers had given them to the House clerk about five minutes earlier. Prior to the introduction of his legislation, Staggers had been under heavy pressure from oil company and White House lobbyists to accept the Senate bill without modification. Staggers did not yield, however, and H.R. 760 and the included amendment contained, once again, the excess profits tax and the requirement for reporting of reserves. In effect, then, H.R. 760 was comparable to the legislation agreed upon by the Conference Committee. Staggers tried to explain the legislative complications to his colleagues. His bill, he explained, was different in some detail from both the conference report and the last-minute Senate substitute. Congressmen interrupted him at random to exclaim that they did not know what was in either of the bills.

The Republicans, upon learning of the outlines of Staggers' bill, made a point of order that a quorum was not present; and when Speaker Albert began counting heads, many Republicans ran for the exits. They returned when Albert maneuvered through several parliamentary thickets to bring the Staggers motion to a vote. As the vote dragged on, several representatives managed to be heard over the general din. "Mr. Speaker, we don't have the slightest idea what is going on," shouted Congressman Fernand St. Germain of Rhode Island, "so how can we vote?" Congressman Robin Beard of Tennessee grabbed a microphone: "Mr. Speaker, when we first considered this bill last week I voted 'present' on all the amendments because I didn't know what was in them. I voted 'yea' on the final passage of the bill because I thought the Conference Committee would clear it up. Now I don't know what has come out or what we are voting on."

H.R. 760 was nevertheless favored, 169–95 (Aye: 135 Dems., 34 Reps.;

nay: 21 Dems., 74 Reps.). But it failed for lack of a two-thirds majority necessary to suspend the rules (a parliamentary device normally used to pass noncontroversial legislation). Staggers then took the floor and shouted, "Mr. Speaker, I'm very sorry that the House has taken this action tonight, because I think many men did not know what they were doing." Someone seized the opportunity to cry out in response, "Mr. Speaker, the reason the gentleman's bill was voted down was precisely because he could not tell us what was in it." Staggers tried to explain what had occurred in the Senate. His denunciations of the "other body" won some favor on general principles, but the appeal was doomed as Staggers conceded, "Mr. Speaker, I don't know what's in the Senate bill, either, and I'm asking the members to support their House conferees."

Staggers then brought up a compromise that omitted the windfall profits section but kept the reserve reporting requirement. Led by John Dingell of Michigan, liberals deserted the bill. Dingell, ironically, was also the author of the antibusing amendment. He began circulating among his conservative allies, urging them to vote against the bill altogether. "We'll get busing back in there next year," he promised. The substitute bill also failed by a 240–22 vote. (Aye: 19 Dems., 3 Reps.; nay: 138 Dems., 102 Reps.)

The next day—the day of adjournment—found the only remaining business the inevitable defeat of the Senate bill.

Staggers introduced the Senate version while urging its defeat. "The Senate bill does not even allow us to find out how much energy we have," he said. "How can we vote for a bill that will leave us in the dark? How can we legislate without information?" With little more than half its members present and voting, the House rejected by a 228–36 vote the Senate (and White House) substitute for the Conference Committee report. (Aye: 8 Dems., 28 Reps.; nay: 149 Dems., 79 Reps.) Both Democrats and Republicans expressed their displeasure at the substitute, and the House clearly expressed its support for windfall profits legislation. Thus, Congress adjourned without clearing the energy legislation that President Nixon wanted on his desk by the end of the year.

IV. ANOTHER ATTEMPT AT LEGISLATION

Even though no legislation emerged, there was obviously strong sentiment for some sort of excess profits tax. Jackson's stern warning, and the subsequent refusal of the House to abandon the idea, were messages not lost on either the president or the oil industry. It was apparent, as the attempt to legislate unfolded, that the main thrust had shifted from rationing gasoline sales to regulating oil company profits.

The Oil Companies on the Defensive

After the windfall profits tax was defeated along with the rest of the Emergency Energy Act, the administration prepared its own tax program which it said was designed to raise oil prices, thus encouraging oil companies to explore and produce while at the same time depriving them of windfall profits. The tax program, which was supposed to phase itself out in five years, assumed that $7 per barrel is the long-run price necessary (up from the November 1973 price of $4.50) to call forth new production.

The president called his plan an "emergency windfall profits tax," a title critics claimed was not so much an accurate description of the program as an attempt to deflate substantial congressional pressure for an excess profits tax. The administration intended to propose the plan to Congress when the holiday recess ended in January. It involved a graduated tax on crude oil prices with a "plowback" measure under which producers could receive tax credits for putting their profits into "some energy-producing investment." When critics said that such a measure could give producers back money for undertaking something they would have done anyway because of the higher oil prices, Secretary of the Treasury Shultz agreed. Some congressmen felt the tax plan would be counterproductive in that the plowback measure would amount to a new tax deduction.

The oil lobby made it clear that it preferred the administration tax plan over any other, noting in its journal, "If Congress is dead set on a tax bill, the plowback option appears the best way for politicians to have their tax and oil producers to have their cash flow for expansion capital."

Even though many retail gasoline stations were closing down completely or operating on restricted hours, public doubt regarding the energy crisis continued to grow. A Gallup survey taken December 7–10 reported that 25 percent of the public blamed the oil companies for shortages, 23 percent blamed the federal government, 19 percent blamed Nixon, but only 6 percent blamed the Arab nations and only 2 percent blamed ecologists. Six percent said there was no shortage at all.

Although the administration and the oil industry blamed the Arab embargo for the shortages, increasingly reports questioned the extent to which the embargo actually restricted oil shipments to the United States. It was reported that all of the OPEC countries except Saudi Arabia and Kuwait were "leaking" large amounts of oil through the embargo, and most of the leaked oil was said to come directly to the United States through three large refineries in the Caribbean, the largest of which is in the Bahamas and is owned partly by Chevron Oil, Texaco, and Ameranda-Hess.

As the year drew to a close, a number of reports indicated that the major oil companies had made record high profits in the year before. This led to increasing criticism of the industry and further demands for a "windfall profits" tax from various political activists and consumer groups. For instance, the Reverend Jesse Jackson, civil rights leader and head of PUSH (People United to Save Humanity), called the energy crisis "a hoax, a contrived crisis." "There is no energy crisis, there is enough of everything. The question is, who is controlling the storehouse?" said Jackson.

Four congressional panels on January 11 announced the opening of hearings. Joint Economic Subcommittee chairman, Senator William Proxmire (D–Wis.) asserted, "We are holding these hearings because of widespread concern about the validity of energy statistics." There was also congressional reaction to oil industry lobbying. In particular, some congressmen reacted negatively to oil company statements in newspapers and to television advertisements. Such ads sought to explain the energy situation and to defend high company profits and product prices. For example, a Mobil ad argued:

> We're a big company. We sell thousands of products ranging from natural gas and asphalt to gasoline and gear oil. In 1972 we made $574 million. But our average profit was slightly more than a cent and a half a gallon [on petroleum products sold]. Even though we don't have all the 1973 figures as this goes to press, we know that last year we sold more and we made more. But our average profit still was only about two cents a gallon. That's not much when you consider how much we invest, the risks we take, and the products and services we provide.

Congressman Les Aspin, chairman of the House Interior Committee, was particularly critical of industry lobbying efforts on television and in newspapers. "Many of the major oil companies and utilities are engaged in an unprecedented and unsubstantiated propaganda blitz concerning their role in the current energy crisis. Although the companies are trying to convince the American people they are innocent of responsibility for the current energy crisis, the facts are that the energy industries must share major responsibility for the current crunch and must be prohibited from making false and misleading claims about their activities," he charged.

The administration appeared to be cognizant of the public doubt regarding oil company statements. Energy chief Simon set up a task force on January 10 to check the price profit and supply records of selected U.S. oil refineries. Simon claimed the move was to help relieve the government of its heavy reliance on oil industry data and to ensure that price increases "reflect only increased costs to refineries for petroleum supplies and not increased profits." Simon also started to back away from his earlier support of the industry's call for mandatory gas rationing by saying, "If present conservation measures continue, there is a better than fifty-fifty chance rationing can be avoided." He did say, however, that he expected the price of gasoline, diesel oil, and home heating oil all to go up by at least ten cents a gallon by March.

Joining in the growing broadside against the oil industry, 600 presidents of United Steelworkers locals issued a statement charging that data released by the American Petroleum Institute and the American Gas Institute were unreliable. "There are indications that the so-called crisis may be one-third less than the daily shortage predicted in the president's message of November 25, 1973," the steelworkers charged. They were supported in this charge by the Conference Board, an independent economic research institute in New York and one of the nation's leading research organizations. The Conference Board said it felt the Nixon administration was overstating the oil shortage in the United States, by as much as 1.3 million barrels a day.

Other revelations in early January added to public doubt regarding the energy crisis. Columnist Jack Anderson charged that at least eight senators had received large contributions from the oil companies. All the senators involved were strong supporters of the oil industry. It was also learned that Henry Jackson, a vocal critic of the oil companies, had received an illegal contribution of $10,000 from Gulf Oil. Congressman Wilbur Mills (D–Ark.), whose House Ways and Means Committee was writing oil company tax legislation, was also the recipient of an illegal donation of $15,000. Gulf pleaded guilty to both charges in a federal court and an embarrassed Mills and Jackson promised to give back the money. In addition, Congressman Aspin accused the National Petroleum Council, whose function it is to advise the Interior Department on petroleum policy and to develop statistics on energy needs and resources, of making large contributions to President Nixon's 1972 re-election campaign. Of the 125 persons who are current members of the NPC, seventy, or 56.8 percent, contributed a total of $1,202,248 to the Committee to Re-elect the President, Aspin said.

The oil company defense was led by William Simon. In a speech in Houston, he sought to allay what he called "the pervasive public skepticism" as to the oil shortage. Although "today's inventories are higher than our initial projections," he said, "this does not mean that the oil companies are perpetrating a hoax. It means that all the variables have been running in our favor."

Simon, however, was increasingly criticized for his continuous reliance on data supplied by the oil companies and for his failure to press for more reliable information. Testifying before the Joint Economic Subcommittee on January 14, Simon announced that he was drafting legislation that would require oil, coal, and uranium companies to provide industry data to the government in order to strengthen the authority of his task force. "An adequate energy data system was never needed or even desired until recently," Simon said. He added that companies must be allowed to retain proprietary information or trade secrets "for national security reasons." Consumer advocate Ralph Nader called this a "cruel joke" because companies collude to disclose the information to each other in trade associations and joint ventures. Perhaps most bluntly of all, Congressman Fernand St. Germain charged Simon with "representing the oil industry."

The New Legislation Takes Shape

It was apparent, given the uproar which occurred between sessions, that neither the original excess profits tax nor President Nixon's proposed "emergency windfall profits tax" would be adequate to satisfy the extreme critics. These critics—notably Congressman Henry S. Reuss (D–Wis.)—developed an alternative device: legislation to "roll back" the price of oil to that existing prior to a certain date, usually May 15, 1973.

The notion of a rollback gained a powerful ally when Senator Jackson, on January 22, released figures indicating that oil company profits had increased radically, sometimes actually doubling over the previous year. Once again, Jackson's committee became the focal point for legislation, this time of a substantially more threatening nature to oil companies. Not only was Jackson sympathetic to rolling prices back, as an alternative to excess profits; he now began to think in terms of a fundamental overhaul of taxing policy with regard to the oil industry. Most notably, he questioned the necessity of the two foundations of the government's tax policy: the oil depletion allowance and credits for overseas tax payments. Jackson warned that the government must write "a whole new tax code" to curb the "unconscionable profits" of the international oil companies.

In response, oil industry executives strongly implied that Jackson's presidential ambitions were clouding his judgment. Z. D. Bonner, president of Gulf Oil, charged in Houston that Congress has "got politics mixed in with the oil shortage and it shouldn't be there. The hearings were run like a criminal trial. We didn't have a chance. Some of those people have great political ambitions. Some are running for the highest office in the land. Jackson's committee is not the way to get at the truth."

The oil industry commented on the unusual treatment the industry was receiving at the hands of the investigating committees in Washington and outlined its strategy in remarkably clear language.

> A revolution is taking place in the relationship between oil companies and the U.S. government.

As government forges this new structure, it may place the greatest internal strains on industry in years. The incipient major-independent conflict over percentage depletion is an example.

The trick is to give up something before more is taken away. It is a delicate balancing act.

Nixon's Proposal

On January 23, President Nixon delivered a sweeping message to Congress asking for a battery of legislation that included proposals to reduce some tax breaks for oil companies and to relax present clean-air standards. The president said the urgency of the energy crisis compelled him to "break tradition, outlining to Congress my legislative requests on energy before delivering my State of the Union address." Among the new legislative proposals were the following:

—elimination of the 22 percent foreign oil depletion allowance that parent American companies can use as a deduction against their taxable income;

—reducing the amount of foreign income taxes that American oil firms can credit directly against their U.S. taxes;

—requiring energy efficiency labels on all major appliances and automobiles sold in the United States;

—accelerating licensing and construction of nuclear facilities "without compromising safety and environmental standards";

—eliminating the requirement for a 90 percent reduction in nitrogen oxide emissions in 1976 model automobiles sold in the United States while extending for two more years the emission standards that now apply to 1975 model cars;

—establishing machinery for faster and more coordinated siting of energy facilities such as electric power plants.

In addition to these legislative requests, the president directed Interior Secretary Morton to increase the area leased for oil and gas exploration on the outer continental shelf to 10 million acres—a move that tripled previous leasing acreage. The president also directed William Simon to evaluate possible steps to stimulate domestic production of synthetic fuel by nearly doubling—to $1.8 billion—his 1975 budget for "direct energy research and development."

Nixon repeated his earlier call for what he called a "windfall profits tax"—a proposal which would tax 85 percent of the receipts of crude oil sold above the ceiling price set by the Cost of Living Council. He said he was "deeply committed" to preventing "private profiteering" at the expense of public sacrifice. Nixon also called for legislation to require the "major energy producers" to report vital information on production, inventories, and reserves to the government. However, he said that where required for "national security" or "competitive purposes," his legislation would give the industry information a "blanket of confidentiality."

Neither the oil industry lobbyists nor congressional critics had anything good to say about the president's tax plan. Tax lawyers both in and out of the Treasury Department concluded that the new oil tax provisions would cost the oil industry little, because the industry makes little use of the depletion allowance abroad, since it has other means of reducing its U.S. taxes on foreign earnings—chiefly, the credit that oil companies get for taxes paid to foreign governments. Nixon proposed reducing that credit, but a Treasury analyst claimed the proposed reduction would be relatively small. "I wouldn't expect, on the basis of these proposals, that any large new sum of money would start flowing into the Treasury in oil taxes," he said.

The president argued that he was proposing the two tax changes partly to make foreign oil drilling less attractive and domestic drilling more so and to increase the country's self-sufficiency. API president Frank Ikard criticized the proposals, however, saying that "foreign tax credits are absolutely essential to the petroleum industry and to American business generally. The only way we can compete in world trade is to have a valid recognition given us in domestic taxes to our foreign tax burden." Ikard claimed that withdrawal of the depletion allowance, even limited to only foreign drilling, would have "a tremendous psychological impact and might discourage increased production."

A major fissure soon appeared within the administration. William Simon criticized any attempt—whatever its source—to place additional taxes on the oil industry. He testified that the House-backed excess profits provision would be unworkable and would take away from the U.S. oil companies the incentive to seek out new oil and expand production. Simon said that there was no doubt that "some windfall profits have been made in recent months" but that "oil company profits have not been exorbitant in relation to the rest of industry in this country." He flatly declared that "the administration does not contemplate elimination of the depletion allowance."

Jackson Tries Again

By late January, Jackson was ready to try again to push the conference report of the previous session through the Senate. His hope was that it would be approved without being recommitted to the Conference Committee, even though it contained excess profit limitations. His hope was based largely upon President Nixon's January 23 statement which endorsed the principle of limitations on profits. Presumably, with presidential acquiescence (in spite of Simon's dissent), the alliance of oil-state

senators, oil lobbyists, and administration spokesmen which had successfully filibustered the last session's legislation, could be defeated.

However, Nixon's public statements were not supported by his behavior. Rather than encouraging passage, in a letter to minority leader Hugh
Scott (R–Pa.) on January 29, President Nixon wrote, "I strongly support
. . . a motion to recommit the Conference Report." The administration
had been able to make do without the legislation so far, the president asserted, adding that more time should be taken to develop "a truly responsible product." The letter requested deletion of provisions to
(1) limit windfall profits, (2) expand unemployment compensation, and
(3) create a Federal Energy Administration. These measures were already before Congress, the president observed, and should be passed
separately.

The motion to recommit to Conference Committee passed by a 57–37
vote on January 29. (Aye: 25 Dems., 32 Reps.; nay: 30 Dems., 7 Reps.)
Offered by Gaylord Nelson (D–Wis.), the recommitted motion brought
together some conservation-minded senators—mostly Northern Democrats
—who wanted less stringent modifications in the 1970 Clean Air Act's
standards, oil state senators who wanted the windfall profits limitations
expunged, and backers of President Nixon, who wanted everything
dropped from the bill except the basic authority to impose rationing and
conservation programs and provisions easing the federal clean-air regulations. Nixon's position, then, had not changed in spite of his January 23
message.

Henry Jackson, floor manager of the conference report, declared that
the vote was "a victory for the oil industry." He said the effort to recommit the bill had brought together "the most unusual coalition I have ever
seen." He accused the administration of joining with big oil to defeat the
windfall profits provision. He had thus, by this time, returned to his
original position of suspicion of oil companies.

A Victory for Rollback Advocates

Having failed again to break the coalition, Jackson directed his attention to the deliberations of the Conference Committee.

In early February, he urged the House-Senate conferees to include a
rollback provision as a partial substitute for the controversial "windfall
tax" proposal which had stalled consideration of the bill. Jackson's proposal would require the president to set ceilings on all crude oil produced
in the United States and on all refined oil products sold here. His "intention and expectation" was that the president would set a ceiling no higher
than $7 a barrel; "new" domestic crude oil was then selling for about $10
a barrel. Jackson claimed prices ought not exceed the total of actual costs

of production plus sufficient profit to induce new exploration and development.

Lee C. White, former Federal Power Commission chairman, supported Jackson and testified in favor of a rollback. White, head of an energy task force of the Consumer Federation of America, said, "The only approach that makes any sense is to control prices . . . that means only one thing: a rollback of prices."

The oil lobby was bitterly opposed to both a price rollback or price controls. Collis P. Chandler, Jr., a member of the API's executive board, warned that a price freeze or rollback "would strike down much of the enthusiasm for and acceleration of domestic exploration."

On February 4, the House-Senate Energy Conference Committee voted the rollback with only three dissenting votes (Senator Fannin, R–Ariz.; Senator Hansen, R–Wyo.; and Congressman Clarence Brown, R–Ohio). The Jackson amendment would roll back the price of all crude oil produced in the United States to $5.25 a barrel, effective thirty days after enactment of legislation. The president could let prices of certain kinds of crude oil go higher if he deemed it necessary, but no higher than $7 a barrel.

While the Conference Committee continued its deliberations, Nixon administration witnesses took differing and sometimes conflicting positions on a rollback or other types of controls on oil prices.

Given such contradictory administration positions, the Conference Committee had no difficulty, on February 6, in sending to both houses a revised bill containing Jackson's rollback provision, as an alternative to windfall profits. However, dissenters Fannin, Hansen, and Brown refused to sign the report.

The Final Act: Passage and Presidential Veto

On February 10, in spite of the threat of a presidential veto and intensive oil industry lobbying, the Senate approved the Conference Committee Report by a 60–38 vote. (Aye: 10 Dems., 28 Reps.; nay: 47 Dems., 13 Reps.) The vote was taken on a motion by Fannin to recommit to conference, a move which would kill the legislation. The coalitions of oil-state senators and liberals who sought more stringent measures evaporated as Fannin's motion was defeated. The liberal Democrats, who objected to relaxation of environmental protection, offered no objections as they had during earlier votes. Without their participation, no coalition was possible. Debate, however, was intense until the end. Senators Bartlett and Fannin argued that the price rollback would result in a $50 billion loss in gross national product and that the 1973 increase in prices had resulted in significant increases in drilling activity, with exploratory drilling up 33 percent. During the debate, Simon revealed that Nixon had decided to veto the legislation because of the rollback provision. The earlier threat was now made explicit. Senator Jackson, however, was jubilant, and predicted that the Senate would override a presidential veto.

Before any action could be taken on a veto, however, there was still the problem of a decision in the House. Having failed to present approval of the Conference Committee report, administration and oil-company lobbyists concentrated their attention on the House Rules Committee. Congressman Staggers, supporter of the Conference Committee bill, sought unsuccessfully to persuade the Rules Committee to grant a rule waiving all points of order against the conference report. It was not until February 27 that Staggers was able to pry the Conference Committee bill out of the Rules Committee.

On that date, however, the legislation was brought to the floor of the House for final action. Debate focused on the price-reduction clause. Speaking for the administration, minority leader John Rhodes (R–Ariz.) urged the deletion of the Jackson rollback provision from the legislation. However, his urgings fell on deaf ears as the House rejected by a vote of 258 to 173 the motion to delete, thus dealing a major defeat to the oil industry (and the administration), which had lobbied intensively against any sort of price reduction. Sixty-five Republicans joined 193 Democrats to defeat the motion. Republican defections were also apparent in a motion to delete the rationing provision from the legislation, as 42 voted with the Democrats. On final passage, 79 Republicans joined 179 Democrats in sending S. 2589 to the president on February 27. Without Republican support, the legislation would not have been approved by the House. Even Southern Democrats, those most sympathetic to the president's position, were evenly divided.

The veto-bound legislation—

1. authorized a rationing plan to be put into effect only after all other conservation measures failed;
2. provided that energy plans proposed after September 1, 1974, be enacted by Congress (proposals prior to that date could be disapproved by Congress);
3. authorized the Federal Energy Administrator to require industrial and power plants to burn coal instead of oil or gas;
4. postponed until 1977 implementation of automobile emission standards mandated by the Clean Air Act, and allowed another year's delay if requested by Automobile manufacturers;
5. waived fuel emission regulations through 1978 for facilities converting to coal;

6. required the president to report to Congress every sixty days on the administration of the act;
7. directed the president to reduce to $5.25 per barrel the price of domestic crude oil.

Although the legislation represented a severe congressional defeat for the oil industry, a presidential veto was a certainty. On March 6, the president vetoed. A few hours later the Senate voted 58–40 to override the veto, eight votes short of the two-thirds required to override a president. It will be recalled that the vote two weeks earlier, to approve the Conference Committee report, was 67–32, one vote more than required to override. On the earlier vote, fifty-one Democrats and sixteen Republicans supported the Conference Committee report. On the March 6 vote to override the veto, forty-six Democrats and twelve Republicans voted together. On the override vote four Southern Democrats (McClellan of Arkansas, Sparkman of Alabama, and Johnson and Long of Louisiana) switched from support of the legislation to support of the president, thus ensuring the administration victory.

CONCLUSIONS

A jubilant oil industry, speaking through the *Oil and Gas Journal*, applauded the Senate's failure to override the president's veto of "this odious legislation." According to the industry, the rollback "would only have aggravated the energy shortage by reducing the domestic oil supply and would have eventually resulted in higher prices. . . . Any temporary gain enjoyed by a price rollback soon would be wiped out. . . . Congress should join the president in junking price concepts . . . and write [a bill] that lets free markets work to increase the energy supply."

Although Jackson vowed the battle of the price rollback was far from over, and various rollback provisions cropped up periodically, the momentum against the oil industry was ended. Several attempts at modifying the depletion allowance also received temporary attention. Clearly, there would be no energy legislation during this new session of Congress.

On March 18, the Arab oil embargo was ended. Gasoline once again became plentiful, and demands to "do something" diminished rapidly. Oil company advertising became much less strident, Senator Jackson found other tasks with which to occupy himself, and American motorists began making plans for summer vacations.

However, the off-year elections produced a new Congress with a strong reform mood. Democrats, especially those supported by liberal and labor groups, were unusually successful, defeating forty-three Republicans (many of whom were supporters of Nixon's every policy). Democrats also enjoyed an increase in their Senate strength.

Encouraged by these developments, Senator Jackson redirected his efforts toward his earlier goals of a rollback in domestic prices and the provision of authority for presidential rationing, both of which President Ford opposed. Frank Ikard expressed well the oil industry's fear that its influence might be diminished: "I don't know how this new Congress will be. The greatest change in the House is lack of strong leadership."

Ikard's fears proved well grounded. Wilbur Mills, long regarded as one of the most influential members of the House, resigned his chairmanship of the Ways and Means Committee because of a series of personal misfortunes and was replaced by Al Ullman (D–Ore.). Ullman did not attempt to duplicate Mills's influence. His Ways and Means Committee was considering, as part of a general tax reform package, the repeal of the 22 percent tax depletion allowance. Ullman's preference was to consider the depletion allowance separately from individual tax relief. However, the enlarged Democratic caucus ordered the depletion allowance included in the general reform package, which passed both houses of Congress. President Ford, although he agreed with Ullman, had little alternative but to sign the legislation, as it provided rebates to individual taxpayers. Thus ended, with startling suddenness, one of the most substantial benefits to the oil industry.

This incident illustrated the determination of the new Congress to develop its own energy policy. President Ford's January State of the Union message contained relatively modest energy proposals. His goals were to reduce U.S. dependence on foreign oil by raising import fees. He also proposed substantial modification of previously enacted environmental legislation, especially those laws dealing with clean-air standards. In an attempt to encourage Democratic support, he proposed a windfall profits tax similar to the one which had generated such controversy in the previous Congress. However, he avoided any mention of rationing.

In response, the Senate Democrats began working on an alternative. An ad hoc subcommittee of the Democratic Policy Committee (which schedules legislation for floor action) assumed primary responsibility. Ford's program was intended to raise the cost of oil, thus reducing the demand. The Democrats, however, leaned more toward rationing, and were especially opposed to the relaxation of clean-air standards.

Although Ford indicated he would veto any mandatory rationing scheme, leading Democrats (e.g., majority leader Mansfield, Jackson, and Ullman) indicated a growing prorationing sentiment in Congress and announced their personal support.

By Spring of 1975, the nature of the Democratic alternative was apparent. In general, the Democrats' proposed legislation was similar to that vetoed by Nixon. Energy rationing powers were authorized for the president, with the provision of congressional review, and veto, of the use of these powers. This legislation was approved by the Senate on April 10 by a 60–25 vote (Democrats voted 51–3 in support of the legislation; Republicans opposed it 22–9). However, in spite of the victory in eliminating the depletion allowance and in spite of the reform mood following the 1974 Congressional elections, Congress ultimately proved unable to agree on a comprehensive energy program. After months of maneuvering it became apparent that no single measure had strong support and that the much-touted "congressional alternative" had failed to materialize in opposition to the administration's energy program.

What conclusions can be drawn from the sequence of events associated with the Emergency Energy Act of 1973? On the face of it, the oil companies suffered a serious defeat. What started out in the Senate as a more or less routine bill giving the executive emergency powers to respond to fuel shortages had turned into legislation which threatened not only the profits of the oil companies but the relatively free hand with which they conducted their affairs. The fact that the House, led by labor, consumer, and liberal groups, was able to alter the original Senate legislation to include a price rollback provision was a significant setback for the oil lobby and a diminution of its "special relationship" with the government.

However, on closer examination, a somewhat different picture emerges. While it is true that the oil lobby was unable to prevent the House from attaching a price rollback provision to the energy bill, the president did veto the bill and Congress was unable to override the veto. The failure to override ensured that oil company profits would remain unchanged and that existing tax advantages would be untouched in the immediate future. The oil companies were battered by bad publicity but unhurt by any form of new taxes or restrictive controls.

In the broader context, the events surrounding the energy crisis of 1973–74 resulted not only in the oil lobby's staving off the attacks of a hostile Congress, but also in its making significant gains in its relations with the government. With the establishment of the Federal Energy Administration, with authority to impose conservation measures and to develop export and import policies for energy resources, the government took its first tentative steps toward developing a comprehensive energy policy. The new agency and its regional branches were liberally sprinkled with former oil company officials who could be in positions to influence agency policy in dealing with energy issues. This development changes the "special relationship" between the oil industry and government from one in which the companies worked to influence government policy in the same manner as other lobbying groups, to one in which the companies are able to place their own executives in policy-making positions.

Additionally, the energy issue illustrates the influence of technological elites. In spite of efforts on the part of some congressmen, at the height of the energy crisis the government was not able to accurately ascertain such critically important information as available supplies of petroleum products and reserves in the ground. Such information was the exclusive property of the American Petroleum Institute. The problem became even more complicated when the questions of a "fair price" and "adequate profit" were introduced. Clearly, the political decision-makers were at a severe disadvantage when confronted by problems answerable only by technological elites with a virtual monopoly on information. Although some political elites were antagonized by what appeared to be a manipulation of the energy crisis by the major oil companies and by their enormous surge in profits, they were unable to propose any acceptable alternative to supplying energy.

A final problem posed by the governmental response to the energy crisis is the relation between economic and political power. Clearly, the oil industry differs from "normal" lobbying groups in that it controls a crucial economic resource. At least for the foreseeable future, oil will be both a scarce and an essential commodity. How Congress, the president, and the Federal Energy Administration can match resources with the oil industry will be a question worthy of continued investigation.

BIBLIOGRAPHY

Adelman, M. A. *The World Petroleum Market*. Baltimore: Johns Hopkins University Press, 1972.

Allvine, Fred, and Patterson, James. *Competition, Ltd.: The Marketing of Gasoline*. Bloomington: Indiana University Press, 1973.

Bartlett, Donald, and Steele, James B. "Oil: The Created Crisis." *Philadelphia Inquirer*. A three-part series beginning July 22, 1973. A well written and documented discussion of the national and international politics and economics leading up to the energy crisis of 1973–74. Available as a reprint from the paper.

Engler, Robert. *The Politics of Oil: A Study of Private Power and Democratic Directions*. New York: Macmillan, 1961.

Medvin, Normin. *The Energy Cartel: Who Runs the American Oil Industry?* New York: Vintage Books, 1974. Examines the anticompetitive structure and practices of the oil industry. Argues that the industry's cobweb of joint ventures, interlocking officials, and ownership of competing energy sources have converted the free enterprise system into a private cartel.

Miller, Roger LeRoy. *The Economics of Energy: What Went Wrong.* New York: William Morrow, 1974. Sees the culprit as not so much a scheming industry as an inept government. Not that the two can be easily separated, however, since government policy and the oil industry have traditionally been locked together in mutual self-interest. Focuses on government programs that ultimately proved not to be in the public interest.

Rand, Christopher T. "The Arabian Fantasy." *Harper's* 248 (January 1974): 42–54. An excellent description of the politics and economics of oil production in the Middle East by an ex–oil company executive.

Ridgeway, James. *The Last Play.* New York: Dutton, 1973.

Ruttenberg, Stanley H., & Assoc. *The American Oil Industry: A Failure of Anti-Trust Policy.* Marine Engineers' Beneficial Assoc., 1973. A description of the myriad relationships which exist among the oil companies and especially among the seven integrated oil companies, all of which can be built into a structured pattern based on concentration of control, interlocking directorates, financial services, joint ventures, professional conformity, reciprocal favors, and commonality of interest, none of which are illegal under existing anti-trust law but which serve to make the oil lobby one of the best organized and most effective in the world.

U.S., Congress, Senate, Permanent Subcommittee on Investigations of the Committee on Government Operations. *Investigation of the Petroleum Industry.* July 12, 1973, 93d Cong., 1st sess., 98–209 0. Preliminary Federal Trade Commission staff report on its continuing investigation of the petroleum industry. Represents fifty years of continuing investigation and is perhaps the best introduction and description of the structure and economics of the oil industry from production, transportation, and refining to marketing.

The Authors

ROBERT L. PEABODY, Professor of Political Science at The Johns Hopkins University, is a close observer of American politics, especially Congress, and author of numerous articles and several books, the most recent being *Leadership in Congress: Stability, Succession, and Change* (1976).

RICHARD P. NATHAN is a Senior Fellow at the Brookings Institution and directs the Institution's revenue-sharing studies. His most recent book, *The Plot That Failed: Nixon and the Administrative Presidency* (1975), examines Nixon's domestic policies and the New Federalism.

SUSANNAH E. CALKINS has been a staff member of the Advisory Committee for Intergovernmental Relations. She is a co-author with Richard P. Nathan and Allen D. Manvel of *Monitoring Revenue Sharing*, the first book in the Brookings Institution series on this subject.

LOUIS FISHER is a Specialist in the Government Division of the Congressional Research Service of the Library of Congress. His most recent book was the well-received *Presidential Spending Power* (1975). He is also author of *The President and Congress* (1972).

RICHARD E. JOHNSTON is Professor of Political Science at North Texas State University. He is the author of several articles on the courts and civil rights and a book, *The Effect of Judicial Review on Federal-State Relations in Australia, Canada, and the United States* (1970).

WILLIAM J. CROTTY is Professor of Political Science at Northwestern University. The author of *Party Reform,* he served as a consultant to the McGovern-Fraser and O'Hara commissions as well as Co-Director of the Task Force on Political Assassinations of the National Commission on the Causes and Prevention of Violence.

HARMON ZEIGLER is Professor of Political Science at the University of Oregon and Program Director of the Center for Educational Policy and Management there. He is the author of *Governing American Schools* (1974), and coeditor of *The Irony of Democracy,* 3d ed. (1975).

JOSEPH S. OLEXA, who received his doctorate from the University of Oregon, is Field Research Coordinator for the Oregon Research Institute.